"A fantastic piece of work, and a guide you must hold at hand when traveling in Innovation-Land. Use it as a reference in outlining your plan to future growth and profits. The business world has to be different, just start to build it ... with this Master Plan."
   Léopold Demiddeleer
   Solvay

"Authentic Leadership among the companies of the 21st century is naturally a commitment to sustainable growth, profit, and image. And this can only be achieved with a complete dedication to sustainable innovation at the core of the organization. Langdon Morris' intelligent, passionate and inspiring messages in his master plan make sustainable innovation possible. This dynamic, focused and simple process takes us from concepts and ideas to reality. It is hugely important and productive to guide us in creating valuable innovations for our organizations. Langdon is a true innovation leader, and wherever you are in your innovation journey it is wise to follow these best principles."
   Signe Gammeltoft
   L'Oréal

"*The Agile Innovation Master Plan* is another revolutionary innovation masterpiece by Langdon Morris, a framework which brings practicality to the concept of innovation. This book will compel and inspire any executive reader to adopt an innovation culture and framework for their organization in order to survive and succeed in the 21st century."
   Genevieve Bonin
   PwC

"*The Agile Innovation Master Plan* is one of those books that captures your imagination and keeps you grounded in reality at the same time. Langdon Morris describes the driving forces impacting our businesses and the worlds we live in everyday. He exposes how the 'great ones' have innovated, and provides one of the most simple and powerful models to transform your business and empower people to be more innovative; altering the innovation landscape. A powerful call to action!"

Jacqueline Byrd, Ph.D.
Creatrix, Inc.

"For anyone who is wrestling with the challenges of innovation in their organization *The Agile Innovation Master Plan* is a must read. Langdon offers a comprehensive handbook that maps this uncertain territory by asking (and helping you answer) five key innovation questions; Why? What? How? Who? Where? Having taught "Needfinding" and design research methods at Stanford for the last 2 decades, it's clear to me that this book is a significant contribution to the field that will benefit students and experienced practitioners alike."

Michael Barry
Stanford University and Quotient Design Research

"I love this book a lot.
I can be an innovation leader, because I keep providing my own industrial and educational visions to the related parties.
I can be an innovation champion, because I support all kinds of innovation activities in the industrial and academic societies.
I can be an innovation genius, because I learn, think and practice all sorts of innovation methodologies.
Most of all, I can be a master of innovation."

Justin Lin, Ph.D.
Chaoyung University of Technology

"Thought-provoking, enjoyable, and indeed inspirational! The key messages here are incisive and convincing. A very worthwhile achievement that deserves the widest readership."

John Holmes
RathBeau Technologies Limited

the
agile
innovation
master
plan

how to align innovation with strategy
the CEO's guide

langdon morris
with moses ma

this is a revised version – the original book was titled simply
The Innovation Master Plan

FUTURELAB PRESS

For more information please contact:

FUTURELAB PRESS
WWW.FUTURELABCONSULTING.COM

About this Book

During the six years since the first edition of this book was completed we've continued to refine our understanding of the innovation process through our work with many organizations, and we've found that senior managers have a continuing interest in receiving sound guidance in the design and management of their innovation initiatives and processes.

To this edition Moses Ma and I have added the principles of Agile, and hence *The Agile Innovation Master Plan* extends the concepts expressed in the original book, called simply *The Innovation Master Plan*. This revised version builds, naturally enough, on our recent book *Agile Innovation,* also authored by myself and Moses Ma, with Po Chi Wu as well. It describes the fusion of agile with innovation to yield a powerful new set of innovation management tools, and happily, readers have told us that it's a pioneering work. We hope they will say the same about this one.

Also by Langdon Morris

Foresight and Extreme Creativity
Strategy for the 21st Century

The Innovation Formula
The Guidebook to Innovation for Small Business Leaders & Entrepreneurs

Soulful Branding
Co-authored with Jerome Conlon and Moses Ma

Agile Innovation
The Revolutionary Approach to Accelerate Success,
Inspire Engagement, and Ignite Creativity
Co-authored with Moses Ma and Po Chi Wu

The Chief Innovation Officer

Permanent Innovation
The Definitive Guide to the Principles, Strategies
and Methods of Successful Innovators

Fourth Generation R&D
Managing Knowledge, Technology, and Innovation
Co-authored with William L. Miller

The Knowledge Channel
Corporate Strategies for the Internet

Managing the Evolving Corporation

As Series Editor & Contributor
The Aerospace Technology Working Group Innovation Series

Space for the 21st Century
Discovery, Innovation, Sustainability

International Cooperation for the Development of Space
Cultural and Social Dynamics, Opportunities, and Challenges
in Permanent Space Habitats

Space Commerce
The Inside Story by the People Who Are Making it Happen

Living in Space
Cultural and Social Dynamics, Opportunities, and Challenges
in Permanent Space Habitats

Beyond Earth
The Future of Humans in Space

Langdon Morris

Langdon Morris is co-founder and senior partner of InnovationLabs LLC, one of the world's leading innovation consultancies, and also president of FutureLab Consulting, a leading strategy and innovation incubator. He works with organizations around the world to help them improve their proficiency in innovation.

He is an external partner of the University of Wisconsin Center for Corporate Innovation, Editor of the Aerospace Technology Working Group Innovation Series, Associate Editor of the *International Journal of Innovation Science*, and a board member of the International Association of Innovation Professionals. He is formerly Senior Practice Scholar of the Ackoff Center of the University of Pennsylvania and Contributing Editor of *Knowledge Management* magazine.

He is author, co-author, or editor of ten books on innovation and strategy, various of which have been translated into six languages, author of many articles and white papers, and a frequent speaker at workshops and conferences worldwide.

He has taught or lectured at universities in Argentina, China, France, Kenya, Portugal, Taiwan, and the USA, among them Stanford University, the Ecole Nationale des Ponts et Chaussées and the Conservatoire National des Arts et Métiers, Paris, the University of Belgrano, Buenos Aires, and Chaoyang University of Technology, Taiwan.

contents

the
agile
innovation
master
plan

introduction

Is there any doubt in your mind about the importance of innovation?

Do you recognize that innovation is vital to the future of your company? And perhaps to your own future as a business leader?

Since you're reading this book, it's reasonable to assume that you do.

And of course I agree with you.

As you've been thinking about innovation it's likely that you've already discovered that the process of innovation is difficult to manage. It's risky, expensive, and unpredictable.

This explains why Einstein supposedly said, "It's called 'research' because we don't know what we're doing." If we did know what we were doing we'd call it something else, like "engineering," or "product design," or "marketing."

And even when we think we *do* know what we're doing, the results from the innovation process frequently fail to live up to our expectations.

Further, our innovation efforts must improve not only to our products and services, but also the very processes we use to run the business. Louis Gerstner puts it this way: "In almost every industry, globalization is leading to overcapacity, which is leading to commoditization and/or price deflation. Success, therefore, will go to the fittest – not necessarily to the biggest. Innovation in process – how things get done in an enterprise – will be as important as innovation in the products a company sells."[1]

Yes, innovation is important, necessary, and difficult; this much is obvious.

magic or methodology?

Yet some executives look at the innovations that come from companies like Apple or P&G, and they think to themselves, "Well, we don't have people or the resources like theirs. We can't do that kind of magic."

But the truth is that Apple's success, or P&G's, or Toyota's, or the innovation successes of any company that you admire, isn't due to their proficiency with magic; it's because they follow a disciplined innovation process.

So if you want to compete with companies like that, and you want to be admired as their peer, then the best way to get better at innovation is by developing and applying methods that will improve the results by improving the process: adopt a systematic approach that makes use of the best tools, and also goes beyond tools to address the bigger patterns and issues to help you manage the large scale risks and opportunities that your organization faces. This system elevates innovation to what it really should be, a strategic asset to your organization.

Defining that system is the intent behind *The Agile Innovation Master Plan*.

When you have a good plan and you implement it well, the results will be evident and powerful: dramatic improvement to your innovation practice, all the way from the strategic perspective at the beginning, to the heart of the innovation process in the creative endeavor, and then to the marketing and sales processes at the end when you reap the rewards for your efforts in the form of

---

[1]   Louis V. Gerstner. *Who Says Elephants Can't Dance*. HarperBusiness, 2002. P. 270.

competitive advantage, brand enhancement, revenue, and profits.

Results will also show up as a culture of innovative thinking and innovative results that pervade your entire organization, leading to a virtuous cycle in which you get better at innovation, and your results in the market improve, which then gives you more resources to get better still.

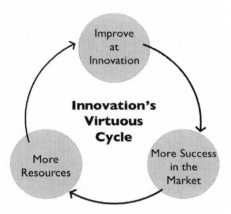

Figure 1
Innovation's Virtuous Cycle
The reverse also applies – lagging at innovation creates cascading problems.

This is what a well crafted and well executed master plan ought to do. So let's get started.

mindset
the hidden problem of innovation

A plan, even a master plan, will only be as good as your ability to execute it, and your ability to execute depends to a great extent on your mindset.

Most executives, however, lack both experience with innovation and they also lack the innovation mindset, so it's no surprise that their companies aren't very good at producing innovations. This partly explains why the ones that are good stand out so prominently. For every Google, Starbucks, or Nike there are 1,000 or 10,000 companies that innovate poorly, or not at all.

This raises 2 questions that are very much worth examining:

Why are the good ones so good, and what do they do that the others don't do?

That's the main subject of this book.

Why are the others not so good?

This is the topic we'll explore in this section.

In our experience, there are two enormous problems that hinder the companies that lag at innovation. The first is the nature of today's change, the brutal pace that has put so many organizations on the defensive as they struggle to adapt to everything that's coming at them.

And the second is the mindset that their top managers bring to the problems of innovation.

Let me explain.

The first issue, about change, is that it's occurring differently today than in the past. Twenty or thirty years ago most large companies were buffered from outside impacts by their size, and they could withstand many strategic challenges just by using their sheer bulk to block new entrants from accessing the market. They outspent newcomers on marketing, followed their competitors' successful innovations with their own copies, tied up distributors with exclusivity agreements, slashed prices below cost, and used economies of scale to out-muscle their competitors.

But many of these tactics don't work as well as they used to, and consequently the strategic vulnerabilities of all firms, large and small, is increasing.

Why don't they work? Because the nature of marketplace competition is different today than it was in the past. An example, and one of the big lessons from the meltdown of the financial sector in the fall of 2008, was the fact that the changes devastated well established organizations and institutions just like it did to small ones. Huge banks and brokerages failed, which triggered a chain reaction that immediately affected automakers, airlines, consumer goods makers, and retailers. Within a month the consequences spread across the entire economy, leading to the worst recession in 75 years. This tells us that not only is competition different, but so is the marketplace itself. The scale of and interconnections between the institutions that compose the economy are unprecedented, and as a result its complexity is also unprecedented.

The challenges of increasing complexity and accelerating change bring us to the second issue, the problem of mindset. When the role of management is understood to be "managing the business," then 99% (or more) of the effort goes to the here and now, to sustaining market share. This is not a trivial job, and to keep a large organization functioning smoothly and continuing to crank out the profits that lubricate the entire system of business growth (and of executive compensation), is enormously difficult. This is not only because of the sheer enormity and complexity of today's organizations, but also because the markets in which they compete today are, as I noted, changing so fast, and they're so brutally competitive.

However, while the sense of urgency and the feeling of time compression caused by accelerating change is certainly real, the underlying dynamics of the competitive marketplace are not new. In the mid twentieth century economist Joseph Schumpeter described the overall capitalist process as "creative destruction," and he pointed out that the natural behavior of capitalist systems brings revolution not as the result of undefined external factors, but from within, due to the very nature of competition.[2]

Change, Schumpeter observed, is the common condition, not stability.

The significance of this is impossible to overstate, and it's true

---

2   Joseph Schumpeter, *Capitalism, Socialism, and Democracy*, Harper & Brothers, 1942, 1947, 1950. p. 84.

all the more so today as the process of competition-driven change is happening much faster than when Schumpeter made his observation in the midst of the previous century. But unfortunately the day to day mindset of managers still causes them to look backwards to the past to guide a course into the future. In this era of accelerating change, it is an approach that cannot succeed. Hence, the mindset problem is largely a matter of focusing on the wrong thing.

Military leaders are familiar with this problem. They refer to it as "preparing to fight the last war." Such preparations, even fully implemented with rigor and discipline, consistently fail. Whether it's armored knights slaughtered by the longbow, France's Maginot Line (a 20th century monument to 19th century thinking), the Polish horse cavalry that rode out to face Panzer divisions, or civilian aircraft hijacked and turned into guided missiles, the histories of warfare and of business are histories of innovations that render past strategies ineffective.

However, the misplaced focus is often evident only in hindsight, when nations, wars, lives, fortunes, market share, jobs, or stock value have already been lost. For managers as for generals, hindsight is not sufficient. It's therefore essential to have an effective way not only to look toward the future, but to create it. This is the goal of innovation, and the intent towards which *your* Innovation Master Plan must be focused.

The term "creative destruction" gives us a warning, a name, and a general explanation for the waves of change that move continually through the marketplace, and reminds us to direct our attention toward understanding the forces of change rather than wasting our time reinforcing the illusion of stability.

"Creative destruction" also helps us to recognize that change is created, either intentionally or unintentionally, not by mysterious and unknown forces, but as a result of purposeful innovation in the competitive arena of the market. Innovation makes change, which means that your firm needs to make innovation in order to both make change and adapt to it.

However, by their very nature organizations tend to seek some sort of status quo, which often reinforces an illusion of stability. This is not because of shortcomings on the part of the people working inside the organization, but simply because short term success is usually enhanced in environments that are predictable and repetitive. Profit depends on efficiency, and to achieve efficiency managers seek, logically enough, to stabilize their operations.

Consequently, these are the characteristics that managers are trained to strive for. In the title of his recent book, Larry Bossidy, CEO of Honeywell, characterized this as "execution," perfecting the art of getting the job done well. And the "job," as usually visualized, is in reference to the day to day.

Trapped by these intense short term pressures in the form of the need to grow revenue and generate market-rate returns on their organizations' capital, leaders frequently choose growth opportunities that look like "sure things," safe options that usually seem predictable, and also look a lot like incremental adjustments. They are considerably less risky than bold innovation bets.

Given the unpredictable nature of technology-driven competition and the acceleration of change that technology has brought, the focus on the profitability of existing operations inevitably leads to a dangerous trap: focusing too much on the day to day leaves organizations vulnerable to fundamental change introduced from the outside by competitors who risk big, and who occasionally do win big.

Compounding the difficulty is the fact that managers know perfectly well that it's a mistake to focus so intently on the day to day, even as they repeatedly surrender to the pressure to do so. They consequently endure enormous anxiety and stress that results from the tension between short and long term issues.

The organizational risks due to this behavior are large. A study by Richard Foster and Sarah Kaplan calculated the historical death rate for S&P 500 companies and found that at the currently prevailing rate of mortality, a full 75% of 2010's S&P 500 companies will disappear by 2020. That's 375 out of 500 companies, which will disappear through merger, bankruptcy, acquisition, or being broken up and sold in pieces. Stated succinctly, if you happen to work for a company that is currently listed in the S&P 500, the chances are about 3 in 4 that your company will disappear before 2020.

This statistic should concern you.

The vast majority will fail because they don't adapt to change, to accelerating change that is, which will render their products or services obsolete. In other words, they'll be displaced by more innovative firms.

Managers know this as well. In a recent McKinsey survey more than 70% of the senior executives responding said that innovation will be one of the top three growth drivers for their companies in the coming three to five years, as well as – and this is important – a key means of adapting to the rapid pace of change.[3]

The companies that endure are often described in terms that we see on magazine covers, and that we'd all love to be able to apply our own organizations - flexible, adaptable, foresighted, courageous, and yes, innovative. They produce more than just short term, incremental, market-share-preserving innovations; they also develop and introduce long term, bigger-bet breakthroughs.

And what funds the innovation-seeking work that leads to the breakthroughs? Profit from efficient, ongoing operations. And what leads to the next generation of profit-generating efficiencies? Innovation.

So in the optimal situation, the two, operational efficiency and fundamental innovation, are inextricably linked.

However, while many executives tell us that they're working on incremental innovations and big breakthroughs, if you observe what their companies actually do, and the products and services they bring to market, you'll see a heavy bias toward the incremental, and a painful shortage of breakthroughs.

---

3   Joanna Barsh, Marla Capozzi and Jonathan Davidson. "Leadership and Innovation." *McKinsey Quarterly*, 2008, no 1.

If you ask them about it, and I've asked a great many, they'll readily admit that they're short on potential breakthroughs, and overloaded with incremental ideas. They're hoping, sometimes desperately, that change doesn't catch up with them, that it doesn't expose their innovation deficit. But three-quarters of S&P 500 executives will come out on the wrong side of that one, their hopes dashed.

Thus, driven by day to day pressures to "run the business," and by the need to sustain the momentum of the status quo, and by incentives that practically force them to optimize for the short term rather than for the long term, the dysfunctional mindset develops insidiously, and takes root almost of its own accord.

When Louis Gerstner was CEO of IBM and was charged with turning the company around from its near-death experience of 1991-1992, he was confronted with a collapsing market and a company that had been so tremendously successful in the past that it suffered from a mindset of entitlement. In discussing the enormous strategic decisions that needed to be made to transform IBM's business model and return the company to profitability he remarked, "The hardest part of these decisions was neither the technological nor economic transformations required. It was changing the culture – the mindset and instincts of hundreds of thousands of people."[4] Yes, that mindset thing.

The history of science illustrates the aggregated nature of these problems, as seen through the lens of Thomas S. Kuhn's study of scientific revolutions.[5] Kuhn has shown quite convincingly how the field of physics, in this example, gradually shifts from one organizing "paradigm," such as Newtonian physics, to the much different model proposed by Einstein. Such a paradigm shift is often a prolonged and traumatic episode through which generations of specialists gradually come to understand that the flaws in their

---

[4] Louis V. Gerstner. *Who Says Elephants Can't Dance*. HarperBusiness, 2002. P. 177.

[5] Thomas S. Kuhn. *The Structure of Scientific Revolutions*. University of Chicago Press, 1996.

organizing model are better addressed with a new and much different model. Typically, younger scientists adopt the new models with enthusiasm, while older practitioners remain attached to the old models. In the extreme, older scientists become defensively fixated on their preferred models, and they feel personally and intellectually threatened.

The situation with managers and executives is not so different. So that's the issue with mindset; when one's viewpoint is innately anti-change or anti-innovation, it becomes a tremendous obstacle to nearly everything you need and want to do to build a successfully innovative company. When you are fixated on the ways of the past, change is a threat that you are largely incapable of facing effectively.

In summary, these are the four most devious mindset traps:

1. Fixating on the way things are now, on the status quo;
2. Short term thinking at the expense of the long term;
3. Too many incremental innovations and not enough breakthroughs;
4. Ignorance of the meaning of change, the rate of change, and the impact of change.

Do any of these characteristics describe yourself, your colleagues, or your organization? If so, the purpose of your innovation master plan will be to overcome them, and any others across the wide range of issues that obstruct success at innovation. In the process you will enable managers to overcome the mindset trap that modern business practice has placed them in.

The frameworks, principles, and tools presented here will show you how to engage in the search for innovation without compromising your day to day responsibilities, and by doing so you'll significantly enhance both your short and long term prospects for success.

overview of the agile innovation master plan framework

Progress in any field requires the development of a framework, a structure that organizes the accumulating knowledge, enables people to master it, and unifies the key discoveries into a set of principles that makes them understandable and actionable. Law, government, science, technology, business, and medicine have all evolved such frameworks, and each field progresses as new insights emerge that enhance the depth and effectiveness of the principles, and which are then translated into improvements in practice.

From a broad perspective it seems reasonable to say that humanity's understanding of innovation hasn't progressed as much as our understanding of law, to take just one from that list, because while the intuitively-driven practice of innovation is as old as humanity (and by some accounts it's much older than humanity, inasmuch as nature itself is the innovator extraordinaire), the pursuit of innovation as a systematic, manageable discipline has been part of human culture for only the last couple of hundred years, since systematic research and development began in the chemical industry in the 1850s, a mere 160 years ago. We're still separating the myths and magical notions from the hard realities of reliable methodology.

The ideal innovation framework, our goal here, should be useful to all types of organizations, large and small, public and private, and must necessarily address and organize a very broad range of issues, from the 30,000 foot perspective of innovation strategy to the inner secrets of creative thought, and everything in between.

We need to know how to create and manage a rigorous innovation process, and how to nurture the innovation culture and bring forth the creative and innovative spirit from the people in our organization. And we also need tools.

And while these are complex topics, it's best that the framework itself remains simple and accessible.

After exploring a great many options and issues, we've found that a powerful framework for thinking about and effectively managing innovation, and for defining a very useful Innovation Master Plan to support this, can be developed by asking five simple questions:

Why?
What?
How?
Who?
Where?

This is the overall structure for the innovation framework, and while the questions are simple, the answers, of course, are not. In fact, they're quite detailed; hence a book.

To give you an overview of what's coming in the following chapters, here's a summary the Innovation Master Plan framework.

the agile innovation master plan framework: 5 key questions

We ask, "**Why innovate**?" and this quite simple question leads us to examine the strategic nature of innovation. We know that innovation is a strategic necessity because the purpose of innovation is to assure that our organization survives, and the evidence shows overwhelmingly that any organization that doesn't innovate probably won't stay in business. Hence, your innovation process must be aligned with your organization's strategy, and innovation will be a key actor that defines how your strategy will be realized. This is the subject of Chapters 1 and 2.

We ask, "**What to innovate**?" and we recognize that the unpredictable nature of change requires us to prepare many innovation options for a wide range of possible futures. These options constitute an investment portfolio. As with any portfolio, some projects will do well, while others will not. In the case of the innovation portfolio, the disparity between success and failure will be very wide because this portfolio is created and managed as a tool for disciplined exploration, and it is necessarily geared toward higher risk in order to successfully meet the onrush of change. Designing your portfolio is the topic of Chapters 3 and 4.

We ask, "**How to innovate?**" and we grasp that a rigorous innovation process is essential. The process must be driven by strategic intent, the "why" of innovation, so in fact the innovation process itself begins with strategy, as noted above. The second step is the "what" of innovation, the design of the ideal innovation portfolio. And while many people tell us that "coming up with ideas" is where innovation begins, we see that to the contrary, ideation actually occurs in the middle, fifth step of the rigorous innovation process. Read the details in Chapter 5. (Chapter 6 then explores how to measure the effectiveness of the innovation process.)

When we think about "**Who innovates?**" we see that while everyone participates in a robust innovation culture, there are three distinct roles to be played in achieving broad and consistent innovation results. These roles are Innovation Leaders, who set policies, expectations, goals, and the tone for the innovation culture; Innovation Geniuses, who come up with great ideas and insights; and Innovation Champions, who organize the pursuit of innovation and support those who develop great ideas and turn them into business value. All three roles must be well played for innovation to flourish, and they must be aligned together in a system. This is the subject of Chapter 7.

The "**Where?**" of innovation constitutes the tools and infrastructure that support the innovation process and the innovating people. The four principal elements of this infrastructure are open innovation approaches that engage a broader community in the innovation process; the virtual infrastructure that supports effective remote communication and collaboration; the physical infrastructure, the work place where people engage together face to face; and the collaborative methods that bring forth the best ideas from all participants, inside and outside the organization, in the most efficient manner possible. These are the subjects of Chapter 9.

Together these five key elements constitute the Innovation Master Plan. This book explains the concepts, and also walks you through the key steps to begin applying the concepts to your organization.

And a last point before we continue is the sixth question, the one I didn't mention: "**When**?" But it's really not worth a detailed discussion because you already know the answer: if you understand that change is accelerating, and if you know how important it is to develop the innovation mindset and your innovation practice, then the "when" of innovation is obviously *now*. The market, which ruthlessly demands innovation, and your competitors, who are relentlessly creating innovations of their own, wait for no one. You'd better not wait either.

agile and the master plan

In preparing your innovation master plan, it's essential to address each of these five key questions, and naturally you're going to end up with quite a lot of very useful detailed structure and guidance to enable, empower, and optimize our innovation efforts. This may require you to engage in a pretty large scope of planning work, and if you do it in the traditional, linear fashion you're likely to get bogged down in a massive analytical effort long before you see much if anything in the way of useful results.

And this is where the benefits of agile come in.

You may know that "agile" not only means quick, but that it's also a quite significant movement in the software development world. "Agile" in software refers to the very innovative process model that is now used for developing complex software systems with a clever iterative approach that breaks down giant jobs into bite-sized chunks. By working in this way to create the innovation master plan you can avoid the black hole of endless planning and start creating usable value almost immediately.

The agile process applies a process called an "innovation sprint," which fuses the design thinking approach that was developed at Stanford University's d school with the idea of a speedy working sprint as agile software developers have defined it.

the agile innovation sprint

As shown in Figure 2 (next page), the agile innovation sprint breaks complex thinking, design, and creative tasks into a logical sequence of six stages that support our ongoing quest for optimal solutions.

The initial stage is *Understanding,* where we seek a profound appreciation for the nature of the issues or problems being addressed. In designing new products and services, the focus might be on understanding the needs and experiences of users and customers to set a foundation for thinking about how innovation could better meet their needs and improve their experiences. To accomplish this we might apply techniques such as "painstorming" (identifying what's not working), persona design (creating archetypical user models), and ethnographic research to expose the critical tacit dimensions of customer and user experience.

In preparing the innovation master plan, some efforts will be directed outwardly, toward gaining an understanding of those outside of your organization, but some also will be directed inwardly, at designing and planning to meet your own future needs. Hence, an agile innovation sprint that addresses the *why* of innovation will necessarily engage you in a study of your own strategy, and you'll study the forces that are driving change in your markets, and how these forces may unfold in the coming years.

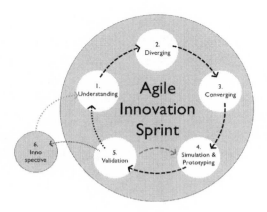

Figure 2
The Agile Innovation Sprint

We begin by seeking to *Understand*, based on which we *Diverge* in our thinking to explore a wide range of possibilities. We then *Converge* on the best options, and *Simulate* or *Prototype* our design to test and *Validate* our thinking. We conclude with an *Innospective*, a review of our work process and products which we undertake to express and systematize our commitment to improvement.

To do this you may therefore apply techniques such as scenario planning, forecasting and backcasting, and most likely a great deal of trend tracking and perhaps detailed research on new technologies.

Next you will engage in *divergent thinking* to assure that your views and expectations are not narrow and simple extrapolations of current events, but that you really are considering how different the future may be for your customers, and for your own organization. One of the techniques to apply here is multivisioning, the art of examining questions from many viewpoints.

In the divergent thinking stage you'll examine a very wide variety of perspectives and come up with tens or hundreds of ideas and possibilities, following the tenets of brainstorming to build progressively to create more and more ideas that fully exercise your imagination.

Rigorous divergent thinking will help to prevent you from falling into the trap of "groupthink," the tendency of working groups to favor collegiality and harmony over the messy and sometimes difficult process of digging deeply.

The complement of divergence is *convergence*, and so in stage 3 you will converge on the key themes that provide the essential structure to the story of your work product, whether that's a new design for a breakthrough product or the innovation portfolio for future innovation investments.

Of course by diverging first, by thinking as broadly as possible, you create a rich pool of ideas and insights from which to draw when you then converge on a set of essential core elements.

The fourth stage is *simulation & prototyping*, the process of transforming ideas into real, usable elements and artifacts that can be seen, held, used, and thus tested. It's easy to imagine the prototype of a car or a phone and to understand how important it is to make such a prototype in the process of designing such complex technologies. Creating such a prototype enables us to see if all the pieces really do fit together as intended. Architects also make prototypes, although they generally call them "models," and of course the model of a house or skyscraper is usually smaller than the eventual house or skyscraper, a simplified version that helps us assess the essence. Many products and services can't be modeled in tangible forms, and so through simulations rather than prototypes we gain a deeper knowledge about their potential to add value.

Planning projects also produce prototypes, although we're more likely to call them "schedules" or "Gantt Charts," and these are in fact simulations (and intended predictions) about how complex projects will unfold over time in complex execution environments. Normally we'll prepare a first draft and circulate it among our team to get everyone's inputs and corrections before moving on to a more defined "second draft," and even perhaps a third draft before finalizing.

Hence, chances are that every form of prototype will become part of a family, as you'll create not just a single prototype, but a series of them, each more refined than the previous, as you converge toward a final design.

Engaging in cycles of prototyping refinement means that you are actually alternating between the stages of *prototyping* and *validation* to progressively refine your work in very fast cycle iterations, which is what we do when we test our prototype, or edit the draft of our document, or build a second and third model. Each subsequent version reveals to us additional details and nuances that enable to us move progressively toward a final version that meets all of the requirements that we identified in the understanding stage.

It's important to note that full validation requires real-world testing to assure that the prototype is as robust as it needs to be. Thus, you should test not only in a highly controlled lab environment, but also in the field, with real users or customers, in possibly dirty, chaotic, and messy real world environments.

Did you notice the loop between prototyping and validation? Think of it as a way to create and then ask progressively better questions, and then to find satisfying answers to them on the road to optimizing your design.

Often the validation phase includes interviews with users who are given hands on experiences with prototypes or simulations, following which we talk with them to learn what they experienced. It's important that they express their feelings in their own words, as it is often the subtle nuances of their experiences that will enable us to improve our results and create something that is truly outstanding.

Once the rounds of prototyping and validation are complete, then our product – if it's a product – will likely be turned over to development or to manufacturing. If it's a service, we'll roll it out through our delivery channels. And if it's a document like a master plan, then we'll start implementing it.

And this bring us to the sixth and final stage of the agile design sprint, which we term *"innospective."* This is where we turn our attention inward to consider how well we did through the previous five stages of the innovation process, and seek to learn how we can do better next time.

As you see in the diagram on page 16, the innospective stage lies outside of the core sprint loop. That's because it addresses not the subject of the sprint, the innovation you're working on, but the process of creating the innovation. Hence, the innospective is an essential element of "the process to improve the process."

Military organizations often undertake a comparable process called the "after action review," wherein the participants in a war game or an actual military engagement will discuss the process and the outcomes and seek to identify what's gone well and what must be improved for next time. This is essential to successful training and to attaining high performance.

If we compare this with what sports teams to the parallels are obvious. A typical NFL football team practices 30 – 40 hours per week, all to prepare for a 1 hour game. (And during that game the actual playing time amounts to less than 30 minutes.) In business, however, most people don't practice at all – they just play full time. No wonder it's so difficult to improve; if you don't step back and consider what's gone well and poorly, you're often just improvising all the time, and systematic improvement is nearly impossible. The innospective builds process improvement into the process, and this is how the good get great, and how the great sustain greatness.

An entire sprint cycle may last a day, or a week, or a few weeks, but no matter the duration, by rigorously following the six stages you'll increase the likelihood of producing outstanding results while simultaneously building your capacity to do even better next time, because you're intentionally learning how to do it better through a focused effort of reflection and discussion.

As this discussion has hopefully made clear, the innovation sprint process is applicable to an infinite variety of design and creative activities, and in fact one could also say that it's the codification of the natural creative process that artists, scientists, designers, and innovators do quite spontaneously and naturally.

It's also pretty easy to see how we can apply this process to the creation of your innovation master plan. With five major themes to address, we can conceive of an agile design sprint lasting a few days to a week in which the entire master plan is created whole in a concise working version, and we can also apply this process by thinking of it as five consecutive design sprints of multiple days each, one for each major element of the plan.

The choice of which approach is best for your organization will likely depend on the size and scope of your innovation effort. Smaller firms and startups will naturally choose the shorter version, as it will likely provide all the necessary detail, while large and multi-unit corporations will almost always prefer a more detailed version, as the number of people engaged in innovation is so high, the amount of innovation investment is so much, and the number of projects so many that a detailed planning effort is essential to master the many nuances and specifics.

As I noted above, in the chapters that follow I'll introduce the five elements (why, what, how, who, and where) in detail. At the end of each discussion I'll then give a quick overview of what an innovation sprint pertaining to that element would look like. In addition, in Chapter 5, How to Innovate, you'll find a much more detailed description of the Agile Innovation Sprint process, with more diagrams and explanation of the six steps.

defining "innovation"

Now that I've introduced the book and given you an overview of what we're going to cover, the last bit of context I need to provide is a definition of the central concept of this book, "innovation." And the first point to be clear on is that the word "innovation" refers to *three* different things:

Innovation is a *process*,
And it is a *result*,
And it is an *attribute*.

No wonder people get confused...

process

Innovation the *process* happens mostly through the work of developing ideas and turning them into valuable realities.

But wait a minute – where do the *ideas* come from?

That's the part we call "creativity," and it's something that people do, by thinking, questioning, exploring, and wondering .... Creativity produces ideas, which are the raw materials of the innovation process, but which are not the same as innovations. This is important because many people get "ideas" and "innovations" mixed up, and when they want to improve their innovation system they sometimes start by setting up an elaborate process to gather ideas, not realizing that a randomly gathered set of ideas rarely leads to success. I've seen this in dozens of organizations, and I'll discuss it in more detail in Chapters 5 and 8, where we explore the design of the ideal innovation process in detail, and the nature of creativity itself.

results

The innovation process is intended to lead to innovative *results* in the form of new products, new ways of working, new strategies, new business models and new ventures.

We often say, "Innovation," meaning the innovation process produced the new thing, but the word "innovation" also refers specifically to the new thing itself; we say, "*That* is an innovation."

attribute

And one of the qualities that distinguishes the new thing is its "innovativeness." The *attribute* of innovativeness can refer to its distinctiveness, its originality, its usefulness, and most importantly, the value it provides.

Not that you'd actually want to do so, but if you put all three meanings into one sentence you could say, "Innovation produced an innovative innovation." What you meant is that, "The innovation process resulted in an innovation artifact that has innovative qualities."

But there's more. To be worthy of being called an "innovation" in a business context, the "thing" must yield value in the form of new or improved functionality or quality, reduced cost, better or more widespread availability (i.e., bringing a new tool or capability to a location where it had not been available before), a price increase (good for the seller), a price decrease (good for the buyer), better margin for the seller, or some combination of these.

According to this definition, then, not every new or different idea qualifies as an innovation. In fact, only a very small percentage qualify, and they will probably not be raw ideas in their early form.

Innovations will certainly start as ideas, but innovations are *only* those ideas that are transformed into something that creates or provides value for their users (buyer and/or seller) and which may yield valuable competitive advantage for their owners, and thus produce economic rewards.

"Innovation" describes the finished results, not the initial ideas. Ideas may therefore be "creative," but only finished, value-adding things may be "innovative."

In the case of organizations whose goals are not commercial, such as governments, social services groups, and non-profits, innovation still plays a vital role. In government, in education and health care and social services and many other fields, innovation may not necessarily be measured by financial profit, but it can certainly result in cost savings as well as an equally important benefit we might call "social value." In a world of limited resources, doing more with less is as important for governments as for companies, and innovation has a critical role to play in increasing the productivity of all kinds of efforts.

innovation and economics

Innovation is also a significant factor in macroeconomics at the level of nations and the economy as a whole. Economists know that it is only through effective innovation that real economic growth occurs, because the underlying economic impact of innovation makes resources more productive, which is literally how wealth is created. Hence, innovation is crucial to the economic viability of nations, while the lack of innovation is likewise an indicator of imminent or eventual decline.

And in this larger context of nations and entire economies the concept of productivity is also essential if we are to fully appreciate the importance of innovation. It is *only* by improving productivity that we improve the standard of living for people in a city, a nation, or on a planet, and it is through innovation, and *only* through innovation, that the productivity of our efforts is improved.

Increased productivity in agriculture enabled humans to develop civilization; increased productivity throughout civilization led to the successive economic revolutions of industry, transportation, communications, and now knowledge, upon which our astonishingly high standard of living is based. Without innovation, none of that would have happened, and without further innovation our own future would loom pretty darn depressing. But given the economic incentive that companies have to propel the pursuit of innovation forward, we need not fear that the pace of innovation will slacken, which is good for society but problematic for many businesses. In fact, our business problem is often the opposite, too much innovation that's causing so much change that we can't keep up with it.

Thus, as innovators drive microeconomic change in specific markets and macroeconomic change in economies, they also trigger creative destruction in their search for commercial success and competitive advantage.

The only solution carries with it a fair amount of irony: to deal with the changes brought by innovation requires ... more innovation, both in the specific solutions we offer in the market, and also in our approaches to managing the entire process. Hence, a framework such as the one proposed in this book is itself a response to the underlying issues and challenges.

innovation and customers

But the innovator's role is only half of the economic equation. Customers are the ones who determine the value of innovations because they're the ones who pay for them. "Market behavior" is an aggregate reflection of every consumer's drive to find the most attractive offers, and to maximize value received for the cost incurred. As innovation is the process of creating higher value offerings, buyers naturally gravitate to innovative products.

Although perhaps "gravitate" is the wrong word. Perhaps it's more accurate to say that people are obsessed with innovations. The capitalist system depends for its dynamism on the market's appetite for better value, which has shown itself throughout history to be unbounded and insatiable.

Inherent in the dynamics of market demand is the process that drives competition through innovation. Waves of change are launched by innovators, and then countered by competitors who innovate in order to defend their existing positions, or to attack with ambitions of their own. All of this serves only to drive the process of change still that much faster throughout the economy.

It's clear that in this environment, the future of every firm is determined largely based on its ability to innovate. Innovation is therefore a mandate, an absolute requirement for survival.

And it's a problem. A serious problem, because it's very difficult to manage the innovation process well.

Nevertheless, as more business leaders understand these challenges, and understand the vital role of innovation in the well-being of their companies, their nations, and even human culture, effort is channeled toward innovation like water over Niagara Falls. The job at hand is to make those efforts pay off, which is what we'll explore in the following chapters.

chapter 1

why innovate

the link between strategy and innovation

"Trying to define what will happen three to five years out, in specific, quantitative terms, is a futile exercise.   The world is moving too fast for that. What should a company do instead? First of all, define its vision and its destiny in broad but clear terms.   Second, maximize its own productivity.   Finally, be organizationally and culturally flexible enough to meet massive change."[7]

Jack Welch

Innovation starts with "why" because knowing why critically informs and determines every company's strategy, and of course that strategy is exactly what should be driving all innovation efforts. And thus the "why" driving innovation is simple: change is accelerating, which means that we don't know what's coming in the future, which means more uncertainty than ever, which means we'd better innovate to both prepare for change, and to make change.

If I was wrong about change, if things really did stay the same, then your company could indeed keep on doing what it's always done, and there would be no need for innovation. If markets were

---

[7]   Noel M. Tichy and Stratford Sherman, *Control Your Destiny or Someone Else Will*. New York, Currency Doubleday, 1993. p. 245.

stable, if customers were predictable, if competitors didn't come up with new products and services, and if technology stayed constant, then we could all just keep doing what we did yesterday.

Good luck with that idea.

Because all the evidence shows that change is racing at you faster and faster, which means many new types of vulnerabilities. Technology advances relentlessly, altering the rules of business in all the markets that it touches, which is of course every market. Markets are not stable, customers are completely fickle, and competitors are aggressively targeting *your* share of the pie. So please ask yourself, "Are we managing with the realities of change in mind? And are we handing uncertainty?"

Since the alternatives are either to "make change" or to "be changed," and making change brings considerable advantages while being changed carries a huge load of negative consequences, then the choice isn't really much of a choice at all. You've got to pursue innovation, and you've got to do it to obtain long lasting benefits.

So what we're talking about here is the practice of innovation as a vital aspect of corporate or organizational strategy; the rest of this chapter explores how strategy and innovation are intimately linked and should be mutually reinforcing. The chapters that follow will then address the best practical approaches to achieving superior innovation results.

To give you a better idea of how this works in practice, let's take a look at Apple, Cisco, Blockbuster, IBM, and Coca Cola to see how their strategies have shaped their pursuit of innovation.

apple: innovating to achieve the strategy

Innovation by your competitors and by your own firm causes existing products, services, and business models, and indeed entire businesses, to become obsolete. Since innovation is the driver of change, and change is the most fundamentally important driver of business strategy, then it's not an exaggeration to say that innovation is the means of achieving strategy, as we find in the story of Apple's turnaround from the abyss.

When Steve Jobs was asked to return to Apple as CEO in 1997 after an absence of more than ten years, the company was, to put it bluntly, a mess. If you thought that the PC market was a war between Apple and Microsoft, it was clear that Microsoft had won big.

Apple's market share was about 5% and shrinking, and to many observers it seemed that the company was fading away. Its product line was an incoherent collection of 11 different computers, and there didn't seem to be a clear vision guiding the company forward. The board of directors was desperate.

But did Jobs have a vision for the 21st century, as he had had in the 1970s? Did he still have the magic?

We know today that he did, but imagine that it's 1997 and you're Steve Jobs, and you have to figure out how to turn Apple Computer around. What do you do?

The company's current product mix is a *fait accompli*, but defining the future path for product development requires you to make strategic choices. More than anything else, you need to anticipate what people will want when they buy new computers to make sure that Apple's future products will meet their needs. If you can figure that out, then you can devise a strategy to return Apple to relevance in the PC industry, restore the company's credibility as a meaningful competitor, and earn profits.

Given his reputation, it's easy to suppose that Jobs, the lone genius, figured it all out himself, but that's certainly not true. The Apple executive team must have studied the driving forces in the PC market, and in doing so they realized that the driving force in the industry was the fact that customers were using more and more different media devices with their computers.

MP3 digital music players, digital cameras, and digital video cameras were replacing old analog devices, and the transition was accelerating so fast that the computer makers weren't keeping up.

Companies were writing new device drivers, but many of them worked poorly and were difficult to install, so the annoyance factor was already large and growing. It could take hours to get a digital camera connected to a PC.

Remember the timing, because it's important to the story. This was many years before the iPod, and about a year before Napster, the pioneering digital music sharing site that inspired the digital music revolution. So the fact that the Apple team understood the growing significance of digital devices for customers was certainly an insightful act of strategic thinking. Describing this insight later, at the 2001 Macworld conference, Jobs commented, "This age is spawned by the proliferation of digital devices everywhere: CD players, MP3 players, cell phones, handheld organizers, digital cameras, digital camcorders, and more. We're confident that the Mac can be the hub of this new digital lifestyle by adding value to these other devices."[9]

Jobs decision to position the Macintosh as the customer's "digital hub," the computer that could connect to *any* digital device, input or output, would indeed make the Mac an indispensable tool, and while the concept became central to Apple's strategy, implementation required the company to develop innovative hardware and software tools to make it real. Innovation, in other words, became the means through which the company's strategy would be realized; for Apple to survive, innovation and strategy were inextricably connected.

Many technical innovations were developed to make it easy for customers to connect other devices to Macs, including software drivers, and new tools to manage digital libraries of photos, music, and videos. The strategy also required the company to develop a new operating system to support all of this functionality.

From a programming and design standpoint, none of these projects were simple, and Apple set high standards for functionality and usability, which of course only made the effort more

---

[9]   Leander Kahney. *Inside Steve's Brain*. Portfolio, 2008. P. 223.

demanding.   In fact, the commitment to these standards had evolved in the early days of the Macintosh, and they were still considered vital to the company's mission.   In 1974 Apple had published the first of what would eventually be many editions of a key reference book that expressed its underlying philosophy concerning the customer's experience and usability.   It came out under the deceptively simple title *Apple Human Interface Guidelines.*

The book presents the design principles behind Apple's hardware and software, and described the user experience that the computer, its operating system, and all applications were designed to achieve.   Apple started this work from a philosophical perspective, and attempted to embody its philosophy in the code that ran the computer.

The 1987 edition of the book begins by describing the "Apple Desktop Interface," the screen that you see when you turn on your computer, and then goes on to describe the philosophy and design principles behind it.

> "The Apple Desktop Interface is the result of a great deal of concern with the human part of human-computer interaction. It has been designed explicitly to enhance the effectiveness of people. ... The Apple Desktop Interface is based on the assumption that people are instinctively curious: they want to learn, and they learn best by active self-directed exploration of their environment. ... People are also skilled at manipulating symbolic representations: they love to communicate in verbal, visual, and gestural languages."[10]

The book went on to describe specific design principles and standards for look and feel.   To a significant degree Apple was successful in embodying these characteristics in the Apple operating system and many application programs, and the devotion that Mac users felt for their computers and the company was largely due to

---

[10]   *Apple Human Interface Guidelines: The Apple Desktop Interface.* Addison-Wesley, 1987. P. 2.

the ease of use they experienced; Apple had anticipated their needs and designed tools to meet those needs.

But Apple was not the originator of this philosophy. Apple's successes built on ground breaking work that was being done at Xerox's Palo Alto Research Center, PARC, where a collection of brilliant scientists who were trained in many disciplines had carefully developed the principles of personal computing, and then built the first genuine PC in the early 1970s.

Decades later, the design of Apple's iPod followed the same principles, and the resulting simplicity made the iPod the world's number one MP3 player within months of its introduction to the market. Apple's subsequent successes with iPhone and iPad were also based to a significant degree on its deep commitment to producing devices that were intuitive and easy to use.

It probably wouldn't be worth mentioning Apple's user interface guidelines if the pursuit of an optimal user's experience through good design was standard procedure throughout the computer industry. But during this period there did not seem to be any specific design standards underlying Microsoft's products, and the company was widely criticized for providing its users with genuinely awful experiences, such as the infamous "blue screen of death" that appeared when the computer crashed, which happened frequently. As the design approaches described in the 1987 interface guidelines have been copied both by Microsoft in its Windows OS and by Google's Android smart phone OS, it's clear that while Apple hasn't won all the battles in the industry, its philosophy, and the philosophy that was developed at Xerox PARC, has certainly won the war

The principles of effective user interface design were later evident in another Apple undertaking, it's chain of retail stores. When the stores were first announced, many experts in retail predicted that Apple would fail. "I give them two years before they're turning out the lights on a very painful and expensive mistake," retail consultant David Goldstein told *BusinessWeek*.[11]

Apple developed the stores so that customers could experience first hand how easy the Mac was to use. Consequently, the stores had to be located in high traffic shopping areas where people could just drop in and check out Apple's products. High traffic also meant high rent, which was another source of criticism when the concept was first unveiled.

Contrary to the dire predictions, the stores have been hugely successful. Apple now has more than 300 of them open worldwide. They reportedly draw more than two million customers a week, and Apple's store on Regent Street in London is said to be the most profitable store in the city; The *London Evening Standard* reports that by 2009 in that store alone revenue had reached £60million a year, or £2,000 per square foot, more than double the sum estimated for the nearby Harrods department store. The Apple store also became a tourist attraction in its own right.[12]

By implementing the digital hub concept in its computers, adding iPod and iPhone to its product mix, and opening its chain of stores Apple gradually gained (or regained) customers, enhanced its image, and increased its market share. Within a few years the company was no longer in danger of collapse, and it became once again a credible competitor in the PC marketplace.

Today Apple's share of the US PC market is growing, although it's still less than 10%. But the iPod is the undisputed MP3 world leader, with 70% of the market, the iPhone became the world standard design for smart phones immediately upon its launch, and the iPad may do the same in the tablet market. And 13 years after Jobs returned, Apple's total market capitalization recently achieved an insider milestone when the company's total stock value surpassed arch-rival Microsoft.

To summarize, without a focused and successful effort at innovation Apple surely would not have survived; the quality of its

---

[11]   Leander Kahney. *Inside Steve's Brain*. Portfolio, 2008. P. 208.

[12]   http://www.thisislondon.co.uk/standard/article-23737856-apple-store-most-profitable-shop-in-london-for-its-size.do

innovative efforts led not only to survival, but leadership. Innovation was thus essential to the company's strategy, and it was in fact how the strategy was executed, so much so that we simply can't imagine "Apple" without thinking about "innovation."

Innovation plays the same role for many firms.

Do you admire Google? Then ask yourself what role innovation plays in Google's strategy. It's obvious that we wouldn't admire Google, and in fact we wouldn't even know about Google if it weren't for innovation. The very existence of the company is based on a single strategic insight and on two critical innovations that made the strategy real. The insight was that as the number of web pages grew, the internet's potential as an information resource was surpassing all other resources for scale, speed, and convenience, but it was getting progressively more difficult for people to find the information they were looking for. People therefore came to value better search results, and Google's first innovation to address that need was its PageRank system, developed in 1995, an algorithm for internet searches that returned better results than any other search engine at the time.

The second innovation was a business model innovation, which turned the company into a financial success along with its technical search success. When Google's leaders realized in 2000 that they could sell advertising space at auction in conjunction with key words that Google users searched for, they unleashed a multi-billion dollar profit machine. The integration of these two innovations provided a multiplicative advantage, and Google's competitors are falling by the wayside as the company continues to dominate.

For example, in November 2010, Ask.com threw in the towel with only 2% of the market for internet search after trying for five years to compete with Google following its $1.85 billion acquisition by Barry Diller's IAC/InterActiveCorp. Diller wrote, "We've realized in the last few years you can't compete head on with

Google."[13]

Yahoo, a much bigger company than Ask, came to the same conclusion earlier in 2010 when it decided to position itself as a media company rather than a technology company, and outsourced its search function to Microsoft's Bing.

What other companies do you like?   Do you also admire Starbucks? Or Uber? Or Disney? Or Sony? Or Toyota? Or BMW? They're certainly innovators, and many of us appreciate them precisely because of it.

Or perhaps it's Cisco that you admire.   Let's look at Cisco as we consider another important strategic question, innovation or acquisition?

cisco: innovation or acquisition?

The generally-accepted failure rate for corporate acquisitions is in the neighborhood of 70%, meaning that about 7 in 10 acquisitions fail to deliver the expected value, and the acquiring company ends up worse off than before.

Cisco's operating model, however, is based on the idea that growth-by-acquisition is a good thing.   Since it was founded in 1984 Cisco has acquired more than 170 companies at a cost of more than $70 billion,[14] and contrary to the general pattern of failure, Cisco reports that more than 70% its acquisitions have met or exceeded expectations.

The existence of some of the acquired companies is not an accident.   Venture capitalists sometimes fund start-up companies that address new market opportunities in the specific hopes that Cisco will acquire them, which is also an example of how an innovation culture extends into the broader ecosystem surrounding

---

[13]   *San Francisco Chronicle*, "Ask.com layoffs spell surrender." November 10, 2010

[14]   https://en.wikipedia.org/wiki/List_of_acquisitions_by_Cisco_Systems. As of March 2017.

a successful company.

Whether it's a startup or an established company that's the target, one key to making these deals work well is Cisco's precise integration methodology.

"Acquiring other companies is an important strategy for Cisco to rapidly offer new products, reach new markets, and grow revenue. Since 1993, Cisco has acquired more than 120 companies, from small startups to large, well-established firms such as Linksys, Scientific Atlanta, and WebEx. Integrating the employees, products, services, operations, systems, and processes of acquired companies can be a daunting effort. With multiple acquisitions occurring each year, it became clear that Cisco could not approach the integration effort in an improvised manner, with different personnel and activities engaged each time. Instead, acquisition integration needed to become a standard way of doing business for Cisco employees. Cisco needed an integration approach that would be consistent across the company, repeatable for each new acquisition, and adaptable as Cisco began to acquire large companies with different operational parameters. Cisco has developed—and continues to evolve—a well-defined approach to integrating acquired companies. This approach encompasses the following elements:

- Formalized and centralized integration management through a designated team in the Cisco Business Development group.
- Cross-functional teams for each acquisition that plan, manage, and monitor integration activities across Cisco.
- Standard principles, metrics, tools, methods, and processes that can be repeatedly applied to new integration efforts, yet are adaptable to the unique issues and parameters of each deal. These standards are defined both at the corporate level and within the many Cisco departments involved in acquisition integration.
- Extensibility of the acquisition integration model to other

major change events, such as divisional consolidations, divestitures, or acquisitions by Cisco divisions."[15]

This is a Cisco marketing document, so the glowing feeling of perfection that the quote conveys should not be taken literally. Nevertheless, the approach makes sense, and of course the companies in Cisco's markets take it very seriously, having watched the company gobble up a string of very attractive firms over the years.

A modest example of Cisco's discipline showed up in its acquisition of Pirelli's Optics business in 1999. On the day that the deal closed, Pirelli signs were removed at facilities throughout Italy and Cisco signs went up in their place. This was reported as something of a surprise in Italy, in that the Italian culture was not accustomed to seeing things come off so definitively. While replacing a bunch of signs is one thing and managing a complex business is something else entirely, this was nevertheless a message to everyone about the seriousness of Cisco's intent, and the message was indeed not lost.

As the dominant company in its industry that had an attractive market cap of $110 billion and $40 billion of cash in 2010, and which had increased to $172 billion and $72 billion by 2017, Cisco is well positioned to continue its growth through acquisitions, while most of its smaller competitors simply don't have the capital strength or market dominance to be attractive acquirers.

In addition to its active pursuit of acquisitions, Cisco's internal R&D budget is more than $6 billion per year, so it maintains a good balance between internally-driven innovation and acquisition-driven innovation, and that is also a key to the company's strategic success.

---

[15]   "How Cisco Applies Companywide Expertise for Integrating Acquired Companies." A public white paper available at http://www.cisco.com/web/about/ciscoitatwork/business_of_it/acquistion_integration.html. Copyright © 1992–2007 Cisco Systems, Inc.

While Cisco is the leading company in many of its markets, the industry as a whole is still a young one. IBM's long history, on the other hand, illustrates the dangers that can come from prolonged success followed by the arrival of a sudden downturn.

ibm & blockbuster: dangers of success

Some companies succeed by focusing on a particular aspect of business performance, only to see the market shift its interest, leaving them holding an empty bag. When a new generation of technology emerges into the market it often initiates a major upheaval in the distribution of revenues and profits. IBM was a victim of this, and so was Blockbuster.

Blockbuster dominated the market in home video rentals, but when "video rentals" meant "going to the store to rent them" was displaced by mail delivery and then by video streaming, the company quickly tumbled into bankruptcy. Netflix captured the heart of the market, and Blockbuster kept its doors open only because video producers didn't want to lose an important distribution channel.

In a bitter piece of irony, it was recently revealed that ten years before Blockbuster's bankruptcy, the CEO of Netflix visited the CEO of Blockbuster in its Texas headquarters to propose a partnership that would bring Blockbuster's storefront retail and Netflix' internet-to-mail distribution into a single operation (this was years before video streaming was possible). According to a Netflix executive who attended the meeting, "They laughed us out of the office."

Ah, when the mighty fall, they fall hard.

Past success meant growth and profits, and as companies increase in size and scope the nature of management's challenges also change from innovating new markets to optimizing in existing ones. The farther top managers are from the realities of change, the more difficult it is for them to face up to the need to adapt.

Most large companies invest so much to defend their existing markets that they're slow to recognize new market structures. They remain committed to old products and services too long, and fail to develop new ones quickly enough.

Leaders of small companies, in contrast, are commonly in direct contact with customers as a natural part of their roles, and this helps them recognize the need for change (although they may lack the capital to execute it). But the increasing complexities that large businesses must contend with to achieve sustained growth lead them to multiply layers of organization. As the stakes become higher, the risks that the small company took as a matter of course are now subjected to more scrutiny, and reaction times slow. The mindset problems that I mentioned in the Introduction often set in, and more committees often exacerbate the problem. Managers must rely on second-hand information or their own memories of "how it used to be," and they lose touch with the voice of the market. More levels of management have a say in major decisions, and time lags in decision making are longer. In some companies "analysis paralysis" sets in, and the demands for ongoing administration of a by-now large business requires heroic attention.

In spite of everyone's best intentions, dysfunctional and bureaucratic behaviors grow, and often result in distortions to the flow of information that senior managers depend on. Corporate politics receives increasing attention, and emphasis shifts to internal events, while external factors are obscured.

Hence, generations of GE observers noted the vital importance of the company's corporate politics this way: "Many of GE's best managers devoted far more energy to internal matters than to their customers' needs. As GEers sometimes expressed it, their company often operated, 'with its face to the CEO and its ass to the customer.'"[16]

In this situation, significant innovations from competitors may

---

[16]   Noel M. Tichy and Sherman Stratford. *Control Your Destiny or Someone Else Will.* Currency Doubleday, 1993. P. 38.

find their way into the market without a compelling response, and even large firms find themselves in decline. Blockbuster's persistent focus on designing the retail store experience, managing locations, staff, and inventory, and optimizing operations occupied management's attention while Netflix perfected two new distribution options that Blockbuster ignored, video-by-mail and then video streaming. Having responded too slowly, Blockbuster ended up in bankruptcy.

IBM also experienced a life-threatening shift in its market when mainframe prices collapsed in 1993 due to the steady advance in the power of computer technology. Almost overnight, about $7 billion evaporated from IBM's revenue stream, and there was nothing the company could do but to collapse itself, or seek other markets. The company went through a gut-wrenching restructuring over the following decade, as CEO Louis Gerstner led the transformation of IBM from a hardware manufacturer into a services firm.

There are two aspects of the story that are particularly relevant to this conversation. First, it's quite rare for a company to transform itself to the extent that IBM did, and surely a great deal of the credit must be given to Gerstner. Most companies in this situation collapse and disappear, highlighting the "destructive" side of creative destruction. As a roadmap for transformation you'll have to look hard to find a better story than IBM's, and Gerstner himself has provided us with a compelling version of it in his book, *Who Says Elephants Can't Dance?*

The second key point is that long before Gerstner accepted the CEO's job, IBM's leaders understood that the market was changing, and they also understood what the company needed to do. They just didn't manage to actually make the necessary changes.

In a memo to IBM employees that he wrote during the summer of 1994, Gerstner noted, "We've had outstanding business strategies before. I've read them all, and they're remarkably ahead of their time. The problem was, we never fully implemented them. We sat in meetings, nodded our heads in agreement, and then went back to doing whatever it was we were doing before. So we agreed we needed to change, but we didn't change. We said we needed new strategies, and we created them, but we didn't implement them. We said we wanted IBM to remain the leader in our industry, but we didn't do what we had to do to retain leadership."[17]

This brings us back to the importance of mindset; believing that the elephant can dance, and then getting the elephant to believe that it can dance, and then actually dancing with it, are also heroic acts of management. Without a vision for innovation and a willingness to innovate, it will not happen, and in IBM's case it took a near-death experience and an outsider to bring the organization around to the necessary mindset.

And then once the mindset was in place, the actions must follow. Gerstner oversaw massive change in how the company operated: 200,000 people lost their positions at IBM, some before Gerstner arrived, and some after. The entire structure of the business was shifted to create a services capability that grew from $15 billion in revenues in 1992 to $35 billion in 2001, while net income shifted from a loss of $8 billion in 1993 to a profit of $8 billion in 2001.

Achieving this turnaround required that the entire compensation structure of the company had to change, its accounting and finance processes had to be reengineered, and its product development process transformed. Nothing was the same, except perhaps the name of the company.

IBM isn't the only company to have encountered a challenge of this magnitude, but it is one the few to survive the experience. For most that succomb, the corporate culture acts as a barrier. Practices and mindset that work so well during the success years get deeply ingrained, leaving the company's leaders incapable of grappling with the problems that lie outside of their operational expertise.

Gerstner notes, "I suspect that many successful companies that have fallen on hard times in the past – including IBM, Sears,

---

[17]   Louis V. Gerstner. *Who Says Elephants Can't Dance*. HarperBusiness, 2002. P. 323.

General Motors, Kodak, Xerox, and many others – saw perhaps quite clearly the changes in their environment. They were probably able to conceptualize and articulate the need for change and perhaps even develop strategies for it. What I think hurt the most was their inability to change highly structured, sophisticated cultures that had been born in a different world."[18]

coca-cola: a shifting market

Like IBM, Coke was a world market leader for decades, and developed a global brand that was and remains one of the most valuable in the world. (The marketing firm Interbrand ranks Coke as the world's #1 most valuable brand, worth $70 billion. Impressive for a company that earns about $31 billion of revenue each year.)

But by the 1990s consumers were concerned with their sugar intake, and developed a taste for water, juice, and teas. As a result, by 1995 the carbonated beverage market in the US grew only 3%, while sales of non-carbonated drinks grew 18%.

With its focus on defending the traditional soda market, Coke recognized change much later than arch-rival Pepsi. In fact, the two companies looked at the market quite differently. While Coke saw itself as a beverage company, Pepsi expanded it's outlook and began to focus on growing what it called "share of stomach," meaning the totality of the snack food products that consumers purchased.

To expand its reach, Pepsi acquired Gatorade, Quaker Oats, Frito-Lay, and Tropicana, and smaller brands including Lipton, Naked Juice, and Mother's Cookies. Together these brands achieved net revenue growth of 17% between 1996 and 2004, and Pepsi's share price grew by 46%.

Coke, meanwhile, saw its net revenue increase by only 4.2%

---

[18]   Louis V. Gerstner. *Who Says Elephants Can't Dance*. HarperBusiness, 2002. P. 185.

between 1996 and 2004, and its share price plummeted by 26%.

At which point Coke's board brought in a new CEO, Neville Isdell. Restating the painfully obvious in one of his first public occasions, Isdell remarked that, "We were too slow to change," and he set about to move the company beyond its strategic obsession with red cans of soda, and to change the company's culture by overcoming the widespread fear of failure, and thereby accelerate the development of the necessary innovations that would return the company to a growth trajectory.

•••

The stories of Apple, Cisco, Blockbuster, IBM, and Coke demonstrate the close relationship between strategy and innovation, and the important role that innovation plays in transforming the concepts of strategy into realities in the marketplace: none of these companies could have succeeded without innovation.

Apple's strategy of focusing on the user experience led to innovations in its product portfolio. Cisco's strategy of growth through acquisition led to innovations in organizational structure and process. IBM's strategy of becoming a systems integrator led to innovations in its business model, as well as the structures and processes that delivered that business model to the market. Blockbuster and Coke, on the other hand, did not see innovation as strategic necessities, and paid a heavy price.

The themes we've explored here also give us a foundation upon which we can now explore the meaning of "strategy" in a bit more detail.

defining "strategy"

According to the handy online dictionary (which, by the way, is itself an innovation, and one that has been quite disruptive to the traditional business of printed dictionary publishing), "strategy" is:

"The plan of action that is designed to achieve future goals."

That definition is not quite sufficient for our purposes, but it gives us a start. With the operative words *plan*, *action*, *future*, and *goals*, we see that effective strategists must anticipate and envision the future to define the best position to occupy in a competitive landscape.

What we add to concept of the "plan" is the need for an organizing principle, or a way to understand the broader patterns of change, and to locate our own goals in conjunction with the broader view.

Having a strategy that is coherent with the evolving external market then enables business leaders to make good decisions in the present that will likely lead toward achieving their goals.

As the focus of strategy is on grasping the essence of a constantly changing situation, and on *anticipating* the future, and the goal of innovation is to *create* the future, innovation is clearly an *instrument* of strategy. And as a key driver of adaptive change from within, innovation is an essential creator of future value for every organization.

From the strategic viewpoint, then, innovation is the means of gaining advantage, while from the operational viewpoint it is often the means of survival, the means of generating new efficiencies that lead to new profits, as I mentioned above. The most effective approaches to innovation will continually strive to address both the strategic and operational benefits, neither to the exclusion of the other.

Now let's translate these ideas into action, and explore a strategy framework we can use to link strategy and innovation from the implementation perspective.

taking action:
designing and implementing your strategic model

The first element in your master plan describes the connection between strategy and innovation in a way that will constitute an implementable and manageable process. Because this part of your plan relates to strategy, you have to focus first on understanding the outside environment in which your organization is competing, because what happens outside defines the context in which your strategy must necessarily play out.

If your organization already has a well-defined strategy then it may address the points that are explained below, and it merely needs to be adapted to the needs of the master plan.

However, if you lack a compelling strategic framework or you'd like to consider it again, my colleague Bryan Coffman and I have been developing an approach to help you think through these strategic questions, which we call Strategic Modeling.

the strategic modeling framework

Have you ever heard an executive say, "Our strategy is to double in size in the next 5 years"?

The problem with statements like this is that doubling in 5 years isn't actually a strategy, it's a goal. And while there's no question that setting good and ambitious goals is important in business, determining how you're going to achieve them in the real and very complex world is where strategic thinking really adds value. We have found that following the steps described below can be very helpful when you need to think through the design of strategy:

1. Define a point of view about the external environment.
2. Identify your current position.
3. Define your goals.
4. Design the strategic hypothesis.

define a point of view

Defining goals and executing the strategies that achieve them will occur in a world that you do not control. The uncertainty and unpredictability of the environment requires that you understand not only the market environment in which you're competing today, but also the way things are likely to unfold in the future. Therefore, the first element of the strategic model is a "point of view" about the world, and the market, and how they're changing.

Your "point of view" is a statement that articulates what's happening throughout the world that your organization inhabits, and describes why that matters. (To help you think this though, the next chapter provides an overview of some key driving forces that are impacting the world economy.) It explains the key characteristics of today's world, and anticipates what you believe that world will be like tomorrow.

And why bother with this?

Because defining your point of view about the environment in which you're competing is essential to developing an understanding of how it's evolving. When you think through the important things that you know about the environment, and then make predictions about how it's going to be, you enhance your capacity to learn, because the comparison between what you expect to happen and what actually does occur will help you identify which of your assumptions are correct and which are not. This, in turn, will help you to continually refine your views and improve your ability to make valid assumptions, predictions, and decisions.

Of course every manager has ideas and beliefs about the future, as these are the bases upon which all decisions are made. In fact, every decision is itself a prediction, as Dr. Deming points out, because the choice between one or the other alternative can only be based on an expectation about which will turn out better in the long run. The expectation is itself a prediction.

So making your point of view explicit merely brings these assumptions to conscious awareness, where they may be examined, tested, validated (or not), and improved upon.

Without a point of view, if such a thing were even possible, change could not be anticipated at all, and events would just come at you in a rush with no discernable pattern and no underlying meanings. Under these circumstances the function of management would be nearly impossible. But that situation is not acceptable.

Your stated point of view therefore describes how your organization will meet these challenges by defining your goals and plans for the future.

To prepare this point of view you'll explore the rate and types of change that are occurring in your marketplace, and the role and impact of new technologies, to help you anticipate the way the future is therefore unfolding. You'll examine how this is likely to impact your organization, and define how the organization will need to change to meet these challenges. You'll describe the capabilities you have now and the ones you're likely to need.

history

Because your point of view is a tool to help you create your preferred future, success requires that you understand both the present and how it came to be. Thus, to understand the current situation, anticipate the future, and define plausible strategic hypotheses it's essential that you understand history.

Stated from the other side, if you don't understand history you're probably doomed to failure. Karl Marx may have expressed this best when he wrote that, "Men make their own history, but they do not make it just as they please; they do not make it under circumstances chosen by themselves, but under circumstances directly found, given and transmitted from the past."

It's not a coincidence that many innovators are also thoughtful students of history, and a strong grasp of history will help you to become one.

Here are some history questions to consider:

- How did our industry first develop, and what have the major changes been over the years?
- What were the major crossroads or crucial decision points in our industry's history?   And how might things have turned out differently if those decisions had been different?
- What have the successful business models been, and how have they changed?
- What has caused the companies in our industry to change positions in the market?
- What stories from the past do we still tell today?
- What aspects of those stories are also reflected in our experiences of today's environment?

And as it is a tool for learning, please do not expect the predictions embedded in your point of view to be 100% correct. Actually, of course, there's no way that they can be. Things are always changing, and our understanding of the vast, external reality can never be perfect or complete, so there will be plenty of opportunities to improve.   Nevertheless, stating your models explicitly is essential to improving them, and to managing in a complex environment.

identify your current position in the terrain

Having defined your point of view about what "reality" is, you can now locate yourself somewhere inside it. Hence, your point of view can be understood as a map of the terrain of reality, and your location is a particular spot on that terrain.

Perhaps the terrain is a matrix, and since it defines a competitive environment, the key performance criteria in your market are likely to become the axes. Is your market price sensitive (what market isn't?); then price may be one axis. What's the other?

It may be product or service quality, differentiation, or perhaps fit with market need.

Once the terrain or the matrix is defined, what are the favorable and unfavorable positions on it?

What's your position relative to your competitors?

Now that you see where you are, it becomes possible to consider where you'd like to be. This is your goal, which is probably somewhere other than where you are now. Hence, while your current location has specific attributes, including your operational performance level, your competitive situation, and the way you're coping with external events and pressures, your preferred location will be different in some specific ways.

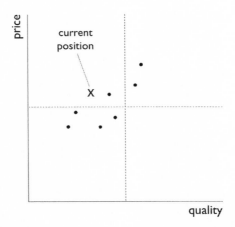

Figure 3

The Current Position
Dots represent competitors.

define the strategic goal

Many companies express their goals as a function of the competitive market. They want to be bigger, stronger, or better than they are today, and perhaps more successful than their competition. They also may express their goals in terms of capital markets, as they want to earn a better than average return on capital.

Some define their goals as an expression of their intent to serve their customers, or to serve their communities.

If you're in a period of hard times, such as IBM in 1992, or Apple in 1997, or Blockbuster in 2010, your goal may simply be to survive. If you do, and you regain a better position in the market, your goals will change and become more outwardly directed.

If you're Coke in 2004, your goal relates to regaining leadership in your market. And if you're Cisco, it may mean retaining and extending your position of strength by continuing to grow your firm, and continuing to lead your industry.

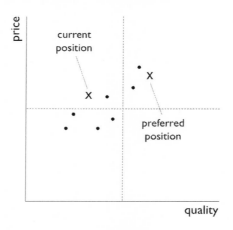

Figure 4
Strategic Goal: The Preferred Position

define the strategic hypothesis

It's one thing to have a goal, but something else to attain it, and something else again to remain there. To get from your current location to your preferred one will require a journey of some sort, and the nature and character of that journey describes much of the work you need to accomplish. And then retaining your desired position usually requires an enduring strategy to prolong your success, and thus the strategic hypothesis describes not only how you mean to get where you want to be, but also how you will create a self-reinforcing (virtuous) cycle whereby success leads to further success (we saw this graphic previously).

It's often helpful to express this work in the form of a hypothesis: If we do 'this,' then the result will be 'that.' Hence, we call this the "strategic hypothesis."

This will be a central theme of your innovation master plan, the driving thrust that shapes your choices as it informs the types of innovations you need to develop, as well as other strategic initiatives you may need to accomplish that lie outside of the scope of innovation.

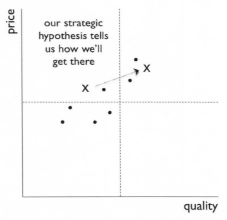

Figure 5
The Strategic Hypothesis: How We'll Get There

Because you mean to create a sustainable proposition, your hypothesis will be more than just an action item or a list of actions. It will be effective as an element of strategy when it leads to the attainment of objectives that are self-reinforcing, that close the loop. For example, if developing higher quality products leads to more profits, then those profits can be plowed back into still further quality improvements, and so it becomes a self-sustaining cycle (which, by the way, is the strategy that both Toyota and Honda followed to attain world automotive leadership).

A strategic hypothesis describes the iterative feedback loop that leads to more success, which means it's not just a once-and-done action plan, nor a glorified to-do list, which may not be easy to define nor to accomplish.

Further, the hypothesis should not be a self-evident tautology, such as, "more sales lead to increased market share," as there's no mechanism in that statement that says how to achieve those additional sales.

Nor is a strong strategic hypothesis a motherhood statement, nor a perfectly bound little package of business babble. Instead, it may be a couple of pages of detailed reasoning that may indeed have a central theme or organizing principle, and which will also provide considerable detail as to how the goal will be attained, and especially how it will lead to a world of self-sustaining improvement, growth, and success.

To summarize, then, what we've discussed so far is a strategic model consisting of these four elements:

1. Your point of view, which describes the world as it is and how you expect it to be.
2. Your current situation, your present position in the competitive landscape.
3. Your goals, the type of organization you'd like to be, and the performance you expect to achieve.
4. And your strategic hypothesis statement, the detailed expression of if-then statements that convey how you expect to get there, and the virtuous dynamic that your success will generate to enable you remain.

Now let's look at the challenges of the 5 companies I described above to see what this tells us about the strategic modeling approach itself.

testing the framework
apple

By 1997 Apple had been developing me-too products for nearly a decade, and although the company still had customers, they were running out of reasons to remain loyal by the time Apple's board asked Steve Jobs to return as CEO. The PC industry was quickly moving on, and leaving Apple behind, so Apple's current situation could be described as "approaching total irrelevance."

Jobs' first goal was simply to make the company viable again, but this required a strong sense of purpose and direction. As the leadership team studied the evolving marketplace, the concept of the digital hub took hold as an appropriate strategic goal for the company to target. The means of getting there, the strategic hypothesis, was that if the company could develop the right combination of hardware and software tools to enable customers to use their Apple computers as the easiest-to-use digital hubs for all their digital applications and devices, and if customers could be persuaded to try them, then the company would once again be relevant and important in the industry. And over the next 5 years that's exactly what they did. Profits were retained and reinvested in a continuing stream of innovations across a broader and broader set of needs, making the company's products indispensible to a growing set of users, until the company itself became an iconic representation of the best experience that consumer electronics could provide.

cisco

Cisco was born at a propitious time, and took the lead in its market almost immediately. The market grew at a very rapid rate, and given the rate of technical advances in the industry, the current situation could therefore be stated as, "a fast moving wave of technological progress and market growth," and Cisco was riding on the front of the wave.

But with so much going on across a wide range of technical systems and subsystems, the scope of progress was far too broad for Cisco's internal R&D capabilities to keep up with. Therefore, to achieve its goal of remaining in the lead as the industry continued its explosive growth, Cisco's strategic hypothesis could be stated as, "sustain success and lead the market, create an attractive equity position, and use that as a lever to expand our technical scope by acquisition." Or more simply, get in front and stay in front through clear vision and superior execution. A few early successes created enough momentum to make the strategy achievable.

blockbuster

Blockbuster grew rapidly with the video rental market, establishing itself as the unquestioned market leader through good timing and shrewd management. However, too much focus on the existing market structure of DVD rentals at its retail stores left it vulnerable to a new business model, mail order rentals, and then to a new technology, video streaming.

Its business deteriorated so quickly that it was forced into bankruptcy to avoid failing altogether. Its goal now is simply to survive, but it's an open question as to whether the company can even pull that off.

What's the hypothesis that makes survival plausible? Can Blockbuster catch Netflix? Does it have any useful assets that constitute a strategic strength? The stock market doesn't think so – from a peak of about $30 in 2002, it's now trading at about 8 cents a share, while during the same period Netflix has risen from about $10 to $200 per share.

So the two companies are on opposite trajectories. It will take some tremendous innovation successes to save Blockbuster, but in reality the company seems to lack any strategic assets, and it's probably too late.

ibm

IBM was confronted with a life-threatening crisis, the collapse of its primary market. Therefore, at the time its current situation was simply that the bottom had fallen out, and without a new business model the company would surely die. The leaders of IBM seriously explored the idea that company should be broken up in pieces and sold off, and Gerstner was brought in to sort it all out. While the board had a strong preference for keeping the company together, it wasn't clear if that could be done, and if so, how to do it.

As Gerstner and his team studied the situation, however, they identified two strategic goals which they believed could sustain the company as global leader, albeit a quite different company than the old Big Iron mainframe company. The first was that IBM could become the leader in providing services to its clients that integrated products from many vendors, whereas it had once specialized in providing products and servicing only its own; the second was that the rise of computer networks would create a need for those services to an unprecedented degree (which the success of Cisco, occurring at the same time, is also based on). The two hypotheses were mutually reinforcing, and in hindsight, correct.

Gerstner's managerial hypothesis was that he could get the elephant to dance quickly, that he could transform IBM's stagnant culture and its inefficient operations before the collapsing market exhausted all its cash and forced him to liquidate the company. He succeeded admirably, and returned IBM to a position of global prominence that far exceeded most people's expectations.

coca-cola

Coke focused so wonderfully on its critical core product that it didn't notice the world changing around it, and it's growth slowed to a crawl. The situation could therefore be stated, simply enough, as "the world changed but we didn't." The strategic goal for CEO

Neville Isdell was therefore to return the company to a growth trajectory and get its stock, which had dropped half its value in the preceding 5 years, performing at a level comparable to its main competitor, Pepsi.

Isdell diagnosed four major problems: lack of response to market change, as noted above, as well as mistakes in advertising, supply chain and partner management, and most lamentably, a lack of innovation. He specifically attributed the lack of innovation to the company's culture, which, much as Gerstner described, grew complacent as it grew sophisticated. The fear of failure set in, and as people became unwilling to risk mistakes in pursuit of innovation, innovation stopped.

Isdell set about to change Coke, his hypothesis being that fixing the four root problems would return the company to market leadership. But unlike the turnarounds at Apple and IBM, he was not so successful. When he retired in 2008, Coke's stock price was not substantially higher than it had been four years earlier when he publicly identified the 4 causes of the company's demise. It would seem, then, that the sophisticates outlasted the CEO.

But that might not be correct. Coke was indeed on the rebound until the financial collapse of 2008, when the value of the company dipped again as the entire economy slumped. Since then Coke has made significant progress under its new CEO, Muhtar Kent, and has just about matched the performance of its arch-rival Pepsico. Interestingly, Coke's market cap is now about 40% higher than Pepsi's, a good portion of which is attributable to the strength of the Coke brand; through all these difficulties the brand has always been managed impeccably (with the exception of the "New Coke" disaster), and brand management remains one of the company's most successful and important competencies.

Each of these stories maps well onto the strategic modeling framework, although of course these short versions don't tell us the gnarly details of how these transformations were achieved at the hidden levels deep inside each company, where policies, systems, and processes make the difference between success and failure. That stuff is usually kept secret, which is one reason why Gerstner's book on IBM is so interesting. (It's also very well written.)

Each of the stories also illustrates the connection between the four major elements of the framework, the current situation, our position, the goal, and the strategic hypothesis, that defines a set of priorities and actions for management.

They also highlight the importance of a well-considered view of the future. The winning companies are almost always clear-sighted and future oriented, while the losers often suffer from debilitating short-sightedness (so we're back again to the mindset problem).

While there's of course a massive amount of simplification here, the framework may actually be useful to you precisely if it helps you to simplify a massively complex reality into a story that you can act effectively on, and if those actions make sense as the future unfolds.

In addition to the steps I've outlined here, the strategic modeling framework also suggests that you examine the business processes that constitute the way you operate today, and then describe how these need to change to attain your strategic goals. The final element of the model is thinking through how you're going to persuade the various stakeholders that they must make the transition from the old ways to the new ways.

So while there's much to strategic modeling beyond this very concise overview, my intent has been to give you a way to think about the linkage between strategy and innovation that will allow you to formulate clear goals towards which your innovation efforts can then be directed. As I mentioned, the next chapter presents a brief overview of some of the major forces that are driving change in our world, and this may also help you to formulate a good picture of the contemporary world and define your own point of view.

the agile sprint

The agile innovation sprint approach is a great way to manage the innovation process to create maximum value in minimum time. This approach and its variations are becoming ever more common because they produce results that are significant and impressive. As I also noted above, you can use the same process to create your entire agile innovation master plan. Depending on the level of detail that your plan needs to attain, the sequence of five sprints can last a day, or a week, or perhaps a few chunks of days spread over a quarter.

At the end of each chapter in which I outline the five major elements of the master plan, I'll include some thoughts about the focus themes for the agile innovation sprint that pertains to that element. Here are some thoughts about agile strategy, and some questions to consider as you work on your own plan.

Understanding: What new knowledge do we need to create in the agile strategy sprint? Obviously, the key factors that compose your strategic model define a set of questions that need to be answered.

- Where are we now?
- Where do we want to go?
- How can we get there?
- How are our competitors trying to position themselves?
- What impact will external trends and technologies have on our markets?

Your means of developing robust answers to these questions will require research into the driving forces of change that impact on your organization from outside, and this is in fact the topic of Chapter 2. You'll also need to assess your own capabilities, as well as those of your competitors. And what about new competitors, the ones who you don't know about yet? They may be the deadliest, for they'll come at you in unexpected ways, perhaps by applying new technologies that they understand, but you don't.

This is indeed exactly how Uber and Lyft have transformed urban transport, and had a major impact on the taxi industry, among others.

Hence, you'll gather a great deal of information, and then unpack to identify the essential themes, opportunities, and challenges.

Diverging: What new ideas will our unpacked data set reveal? What new directions can we pursue? What new capabilities will new technology inspire us to undertake. Here we are imagining future possibilities on a grand scale.

- What would we do if we had access to unlimited capital?
- Who would be our ideal partners for future growth?
- Where can we recruit the talent we will need?

Converging: Let the analytic thinkers have a shot at this inspiring future landscape and help us to separate real opportunity from fiction and fantasy. Where are the immediate adjacencies? Which hills are too large to climb?

Prototyping and validation: Let us now compose a rigorous strategic plan, complete with financial models and projections, and let's test it on some rigorous and knowledgeable experts. What critical insights can we gather to help us refine our thinking and hone in progressively on the essential details. We iterate and refine.

And *voila*, look at that: it's done. Our agile innovation strategy is complete.

Innospective: Have we used our time and resources effectively in preparing our work? Has our team interacted smoothly? Have we argued passionately in advocating our differing views without losing sight of basic respect for one another? Have the ideators and the naysayers complemented one another? And of course, how can we do better next time?

the last word ...

The agile strategy sprint has brought you face to face with both the up and the downsides of research, forecasting, planning, and modeling. They are at once inspiring and sometime frightening, for the future is coming at us faster and faster now. And with it come ample opportunities for new creation, but also a possible train of destruction.

Indeed, the concept of creative destruction offers a compelling description of what's constantly happening in the capitalist marketplace. It's both a warning about the prevalence of change and a reminder of the inescapable need for innovation to respond to it. It's thus an invitation to become an innovator.

"Creative destruction" also accentuates the important connection between strategy and innovation, and perhaps it also helps you see that you must align your strategic efforts with the broader patterns of innovation in your industry. This may also give you insight into the specific innovation processes that need to run inside your organization.

If you follow the model that's presented in the following chapters you'll rise to the challenges of creative destruction by developing an innovation portfolio of initiatives and projects; you'll manage those projects to completion and success with a rigorous agile innovation process; you'll develop a culture of innovation to evoke the highest levels of participation from everyone in your organization while also engaging an abundance of outsiders in the pursuit of innovation. You'll also design and implement the infrastructure that enables people and systems to operate at the highest levels of effectiveness.

The design for of all this will be your Agile Innovation Master Plan.

And as you implement it, you'll see enormous improvement in the quality of your innovation process, and more importantly in the results you achieve. You may or may not become the leader in your market, but you should expect to achieve significant improvement in your competitive positioning, in the value of your brand, and in your prospects for the future.

These are the "whys" of innovation.

chapter 2
the driving forces of change

"Life isn't one damn thing after another. It's the same damn thing again and again."

Edna St. Vincent Millay

Either way you want to think about it, whether it's always something new or the same damn thing again and again, there's definitely a lot happening out there. And because it's so important to define a useful point of view and an effective set of goals, innovators and would-be innovators inevitably must develop a deep understanding of the key strategic issues facing their organizations and the history that has brought them into existence, in order to develop the right strategic guidance for the forward-looking innovation process.

In this chapter we'll therefore take a quick look at 6 damn revolutions, the macro driving forces essential to understanding the nature of change that's occurring around the world today. While these may or may not be the most pressing issues for your company, chances are that some combination of them will have huge influence on your situation, on the strategic choices you have available to you, and on your approach to innovation.

So while the purpose here is not to give you a comprehensive view of change in all its dimensions, I will highlight some topics that are broad and tremendously influential change drivers, and briefly explore how these issues may affect your organization. For your own purposes a much more detailed view of the driving forces will be necessary, so consider this perhaps a primer get you started.[19]

driving force #1: the digital revolution

1992 was a revolutionary year in politics and in business. In addition to the tightly contested presidential election between George W. Bush, Ross Perot, and Bill Clinton, corporate board rooms across America were confronting CEO failures at an unprecedented rate. Amex CEO James Robinson was removed when his board realized that he didn't know how to turn the company around from a disastrous slide. IBM CEO John Akers stepped aside in favor of turnaround specialist Louis Gerstner as IBM, too, faced a life-threatening situation. Robert Stempel of GM was fired, as were Compaq's Rod Canion, Apple's John Sculley, Kodak's Kay Whitmore, Digital's Ken Olsen, Goodyear's Tom Barrett, and Macy's Edward Finkelstein. In all, 16 CEOs of Fortune 500 companies were removed in 1992 and 1993, the biggest concentration of CEO removal in decades.

Why did it happen?

Change had arrived with a vengeance, in the form of cheaper computing power, which created a digital revolution that brought new forms of competition to America's largest corporations. IBM watched horrified as its mainframe revenues plummeted from $13 billion to $7 billion from 1992 to 1993, and as I mentioned in Chapter 1, the company had to lay off more than 200,000 employees.

While the digital revolution hit the computer makers first, it

---

[19] This discussion of the driving forces of change is adapted from my recent book *Foresight and Extreme Creativity: Strategy for the 21st Century*, in which you will find a much more detailed discussion of these forces, along with dozens of graphics explaining the key trends, and hundreds of footnotes if you wish to research the source data to support many of these statements.

then moved on to attack other companies too, because cheap computing power suddenly enabled small companies to deploy the computational resources that only big ones previously had, and a major barrier to entry abruptly disappeared. Companies all over the world lowered their operating costs, increased their IT capabilities, and improved their own business models by creating better products and services at lower prices. Many of these new players emerged from the edges of traditional markets, and because they came from the hidden edges they were able to develop and refine their business models without attracting the attention of the larger firms.

This new digital power has resulted in significant growth across the entire economy, but has also brought new competitors for the world's corporate giants, and thus new threats to Amex, GM, Compaq, Apple, and Kodak in the US, Philips, L'Oréal and Siemens in Europe, among many others.

This process of digitization also accelerated the trend toward larger-scale commoditization, as goods that had once been considered luxuries became so cheap to make that they became available at mass market prices due to digitized design, manufacturing, and distribution systems. This new computer-driven world of manufacturing and distribution became essential to the successes of Tesco, Carrefour, Wal-Mart, IKEA, and Home Depot, as they were among the first to grasp how to exploit the new capabilities of computers to help manage a tremendously complex global enterprise.

Today's Internet War between Google, Microsoft, and Facebook marks just another step in the digitization of the economy, showing us that the digital revolution will continue to change the tools we use to create and consume information, and will therefore continue to have enormous influence on which business models are successful and which are not. The revolution, in other words, isn't over yet.

Digitization impacts all aspects of the arts, entertainment, business, and society, and it's crucial to how products are designed, manufactured, and distributed. It's also essential to how consumers gather and share information, and how they get entertainment, as it is central to how companies manage their finances and operations. It's even a basic resource for farmers, who plow and fertilize their fields according to what they learn from satellites, and it also tells them how, where, and for how much they can sell their produce. This is as true in the corn belt of Nebraska as it is in rural India, coastal China, and central Brazil. In fact, there is no aspect of society that is not significantly affected by digitization.

One final example is the printing industry, which obviously has been impacted by the shift to digital media. But how much impact has this had, really? Well, between 2003 and 2010, gross printing industry revenues in the US declined precipitously, from $120 billion to $80 billion. During that period, 22,000 print shops closed, and in 2010 3 shops were closing each day. Today, if you're interested in owning a big printing press, a nice 4 or 5 color Heidelberg unit that would normally cost $50,000 or more, you can pick one up for cheap. How cheap? In many cases, it's yours if you'll just come and haul it away.

Who's impacted by this besides the printers themselves? It's the folks who deliver a lot of the stuff they print, the post office. And they're hurting, too. The total volume of mail that the US Postal Service delivered declined from 212 billion pieces in 2007 to 167 billion in 2010, to 154 billion in 2016, a drop of 27%, causing continuing losses in the agency. So if you've been wondering why the price of stamps is increasing, that's the reason.

In response, the USPS reduced total work hours by 63 million in 2010, equivalent to 36,000 full-time employees (out of a total work force of about 584,000), but still lost $5.4 billion through three quarters of 2010. The agency estimated that it will incur about $238 billion in losses by 2020 if Congress doesn't permit it to revamp its outdated business model.[21] Yes, there you have it, even the post

---

[21]   Hibah Yousuf, "USPS posts $3.5 billion loss as mail volume plunges." *CNN Money*, August 5, 2010.
http://money.cnn.com/2010/08/05/news/companies/US_postal_service_earnings/index.htm

office knows that innovation is mandatory in the digital age.

And what impact will continuing digitization have on your company?   Could a competitor undercut your cost structure by digitizing significant aspects of your industry's value chain?   Will a design, production or quality slip-up at your firm result in a tidal wave of internet-driven negative publicity that you must spend weeks and millions to counter?   (It did to Toyota.) Can you find new uses for computer technology to increase your sales, or improve your own operating efficiency?   Can you enhance or transform how you communicate internally, or how you communicate with customers?   And how about social media?   Ah, that's next!

consequence: social mediaization throughout society

Digital technology becomes progressively more significant as it's applied to more and more functions of life, business, and society.   Business today is inconceivable without the internet, and the countless software tools that we use to manage the modern enterprise.

And now hundreds of millions of people are using social media platforms like Facebook, Instagram, Twitter, and LinkedIn to communicate with one another, which constitutes a trend with enormous momentum, and perhaps enormous importance.

Facebook alone claims to have more than 1.9 billion active users as of May, 2017, 70% of whom live outside of the US.   If it were a separate country, Facebook would be by far the largest in the world.   People spend billions of hours per month on Facebook, and it offers more than 7 million applications from outside developers, which means that Facebook the platform is itself becoming major world market, an online example of globalization, and a powerful business force in and of itself.

Yet as a social phenomenon and an industry, social networking is so new that although the consequences seem to be important, they're also entirely unpredictable. It's impossible to know where these trends are going, or what they might mean two, three, or five years in the future.

Will it be expected that every business must have a presence on Facebook (or its newer, cooler offspring) in a few years, just as it's mandatory today for every company to have a web site?   It's entirely possible. But what else could it mean? Will social media become a force for social change, or merely a bunch of "places" to connect with friends? Will Facebook's new currency become a powerful economic engine, or merely a curiosity? Will anything be different when the number of Facebook users passes a billion?

These are among the questions that you should be asking and dialoging about with your colleagues to make sure that new forces and factors don't catch you by surprise, and also to position your firm to take advantage of new possibilities and opportunities.

consequence: globalization

Globalization as we experience it today is a consequence of digital technology, for digitization enables global commerce and global enterprises, resulting in a global economy that has drawn every nation into a single economic system, and through social media, many of us are now participating in a single mediated social system as well. As a result, every company's strategy must address a globalized market in which increasing numbers of people are participating in social and business communities that transcend national boundaries.

Globalization today means that Wal-Mart and Facebook are everywhere, but only twenty years ago the practices of global business were typified by the successes of Toyota and Honda. When these Japanese manufacturers started in the auto industry they specialized in low priced cars, but with a consistent focus on improving the quality of design and manufacturing they've moved steadily into more lucrative segments of the market. A big break occurred in 1973 with the first Oil Shock, as the sharp rise in oil prices suddenly created demand in the US market for their fuel efficient cars.   Almost overnight, both saw rapid growth in their shares of the US market as consumers looked for alternatives to American gas guzzlers.

Since then, Toyota has steadily increased its share in most world markets, and is now the leading auto manufacturer in the world.

But with globalization and expansion have also come new challenges. Maintaining high quality standards has proven difficult, and the safety problems with brakes, accelerators, and airbags reported over the last few years have tarnished Toyota's brand image and cost the company billions of dollars.

A more recent manifestation of globalization is the Somali pirate industry, which preyed on ships carrying goods past the horn of Africa between Asia and Europe. The exponential growth of world trade has vastly enlarged the total shipping market available to the pirates, who developed a sophisticated business model that reflected a fundamental understanding of globalization. For nearly a decade until the world's navies united to stop them, they applied sophisticated risk management decision-making models in their planning, and cleverly exploited the global financial system; when they succeeded in their high risk venture they earned large profits for themselves and their impoverished communities.[22]   In the Somali city of Hargeysa there was for a time a structured investment market for those who would like to invest in piracy, a market that in 2009 had 72 registered "companies."

Globalization also means that you may choose to have your next surgery outside of the US, as the popularity of "medical tourism" grows. More than 40,000 Americans journey each year to Costa Rica to have surgeries there (about 100 per day), and The Deloitte Center for Health Solutions reports that cost savings range

---

[22]   Chris Kohler. "Play Cutthroat Capitalism, Wired's Somali Pirate Game." *Wired Magazine*. July 27, 2009.

from 30 to 70% of US prices.[23] Dozens of countries are lining up to develop the lucrative trade in health care, as US providers steadily price themselves out of the market. Nearly a million Americans traveled overseas last year for medical treatment (more than 2500 per day), while about 75,000 people came to the US for the same reason.

With impacts throughout the manufacturing and supply chains, globalization is a vital driving force that has a great impact on the operations and positioning of every company. Your new iPad, laptop, or smart phone was probably assembled in China, where contract manufacturer Foxconn Technology employs more than 1 million workers, but at very low wages. After an unacceptably high number of suicides the monthly wage has reportedly been increased to $300 per employee.

The power and impact of globalization means that it's essential for every company to understand the current and future impacts of worldwide trends on operations, to develop a globalization strategy to optimize learning opportunities through exposure to various markets around the world, and perhaps also to extend its reach to new customers. As customer communities are also global, no large company can hope operate successfully without addressing global markets.

So what does globalization mean to your company? Can new competitors come into your market from elsewhere in the world and undercut your pricing? Or deliver better service? Or out-innovate you? If it happened, how would it unfold? What would you do in response?

consequence: commoditization

In 1992 Wal-Mart passed Sears to become the world's number one retailer. How did Sears allow this to happen?

---

23   Deloitte. "Medical Tourism Consumers in Search of Value." 2010.

First, Sears suffered from the arrogant assumption that it was invulnerable, and then its leaders fundamentally misunderstood the key competitive dynamics in the market (the mindset problem again), and allowed Wal-Mart to out-innovate them in three critical performance dimensions: cost of goods, cost of distribution, and pricing.   In essence, Wal-Mart mastered one of the critical forces that drives today's economy, commoditization.

There's irony in this, in that Sears itself was once a world champion commoditizer itself, but then like Coke and IBM, it got distracted by its own success.

In fact, commoditization has been an underlying economic force for centuries.   The industrial revolution lowered the price of everything to the point that middle class citizens of the developed nations live better material lives than the richest of kings and queens once did, and Sears, founded in 1886, played a big part in bringing this explosion of material wealth to people throughout the US.

Wal-Mart's business model is based on constantly increasing volumes at progressively lower prices in the mass market.   It built its national and then its global brand on continual price reductions, its "Always Low Prices" slogan plastered throughout its stores.

Another effective commoditizer, Ikea, has developed a similar approach.   This was explained to me by an employee in an Ikea store: "We look for companies that are in trouble, and we hire them to make products for us by the millions at ridiculously low prices."   (I'm not kidding; it's a direct quote.)

Commoditization continues to be an inexorable competitive force that is manifested in our times in many ways, from the Wal-Mart-ization of the world's retail supply chain and the accompanying outsourcing of manufacturing to Asia, to upheaval in the retail grocery business, to the outsourcing of computer services to India, to the precipitous drop in the price of computing power, to the cheap air fares that we now enjoy.

For example …

A&P supermarkets, also known as the Great Atlantic & Pacific Tea Co., operator of almost 400 supermarkets and 34th largest retailer in the US, filed for bankruptcy in December 2010. In a regulatory filing, the company cited a shift in consumer spending to wholesale clubs, drugstores and supercenters (i.e., commoditizers). In bankruptcy, the company plans to shed $380 million of pension funding commitments and retail lease agreements.[24]

Southwest Airlines introduced a commodity-oriented business model to air travel, and transformed the entire industry. Ryanair followed Southwest's model and took it even farther.

Deregulation of the telecommunications industry has dropped the price of phone calls to unprecedented lows, while cheap cell phones have brought convenience to more than 5 billion customers. During 2009 and 2010, an average of 60 million new subscribers signed up for services each month, and bought handsets too, but the wave is slowing down as the market gets saturated, and the focus of competition is shifting upstream to smart phones.

The financial services industry has also been commoditized, slicing margins and intensifying competition for thousands of banks, brokerages, and insurance companies.

Ever-cheaper computer chips have commoditized the entire computer industry, and thus IBM's explanation when it chose to sell its PC division to the Chinese firm Lenovo was that the company was focused on adding value, and simply didn't want to compete in a commodity industry.

---

[24]   Tiffany Kary. "A&P, Century-Old U.S. Grocery Store Owner, Files for Bankruptcy." *Bloomberg*, December 13, 2010.

The trend of commoditization is enabled and indeed accelerated because of digitization, and it will certainly continue during the coming years as an additional 2 – 3 billion people living in Asia and Africa are likely to join the ranks of the mass consuming middle class. This will drive intense competition in manufacturing and distribution as hundreds of millions of new households join the consumption party. The competition to serve these new customers will be fierce, and continuing downward pressure on prices will be intense. At the same time, the likely decline in the availability of natural resources, the dynamics of global supply and demand, and continuing advances in product design, manufacturing, and distribution will all have enormous impact on the dynamics of every industry.

The vital questions for you could be, "How is commoditization affecting our business today, and how will it affect us tomorrow?" It's inevitable that competition will drive prices down in nearly every market, so how will your organization respond?

driving force #2: climate change

Economic growth since the dawn of the Industrial Revolution around 1800 has been made possible by the consumption of fossil fuels – coal, oil, and natural gas – which enable civilization to accomplish work on a scale that was inconceivable in 1750, when animals, humans, fire, and a bit of water power were all that civilization had to draw upon to get work done.

However, as we now know all too well, burning all those millions of tons of fossil fuels has produced not only stunning economic growth and the globalization of human civilization, but the unfortunate side effect of excess carbon dioxide in the atmosphere, which is apparently altering the Earth's climate in significant ways.

As temperatures increase and ice caps melt, droughts are becoming deeper and more prolonged, storms more frequent and more intense, and even viruses and bacteria more prevalent and more potent.

Hence, the threats to humanity are significant, and as a result we can foresee that the increasing severity of climate change will lead to significant changes in the structure of the economy as nations around the world come to grips with climatic disruption.

driving force #3: the energy industry revolution

As the realities of climate change and the inescapable linkage to fossil fuels consumption become accepted facts of both science and policy, a key consequence will be the transition of the world's energy systems away from fossil fuels. Of course this is already happening, as wind and solar power systems become progressively less expensive and more productive, and more and more of them are installed worldwide.

However, as the fossil fuel industry have been the basis of the world's economy for the last 200 years, and has reached its current level of maturity as a result of trillions of dollars of capital investment in drilling and extraction and refining and distribution systems, and in the billion + cars and trucks making their way up and down the world's roadways, we should not expect that the transition away from fossil fuels will be an easy one. Instead, it will be difficult and perhaps also divisive, and certainly it will be economically disruptive.

driving force #4: urbanization and population

In 1800 about 3 percent of the world's population of one billion lived in cities. Two hundred years later, in 2010, about half of the total population of 7 billion lived in cities. The powerful trend of urbanization has been a major factor in the stunning growth of the economy, for it is generally in urban settings that people create technology, science, learning, and progress.

Interestingly, the trend of urbanization shows no signs of slowing down, and in fact demographers predict that if current rates continue, by the end of this century about 95% of the population will be living in cities, for the cities lure people with great consistency all around the world.

People move to the cities in search of economic opportunity for themselves and their families, and for education and health care and entertainment, and for mates.

It's also interesting to note that whereas farm families tended to be large, because on farms children constitute nearly free labor, city families are often smaller because children in cities are not producers, but consumers, and raising children is expensive. Four or five children are common for agricultural families; one or two children is more common in cities.

This is important because as the world urbanizes, birth rates drop, which implies that if we do indeed reach the point at which 95 percent of the population is urban, then the population explosion of the 20th century may become the population implosion of the 21st.

This will have significant social and economic consequences. Socially, it would mean the average age of the population will be increasing, meaning less workers and taxpayers, and more retirees. Health care costs for society as whole would therefore increase, but consumption of many other types of resources would decrease.

In fact, this would be nothing less than a fundamental restructuring of the entire world economy. For the last 200 years the economic system has been based on progressively more people moving to cities, joining the modern industrial workforce, paying taxes, setting up households, and having still more children to participate in the same process. This has fed economic growth worldwide, but it appears that this process is now coming to an end, not because of government policy or overall intent, but simply because urban families are choosing to have fewer and fewer children.

Already there are about 50 countries worldwide in which the

population is literally shrinking, perhaps most notably Japan, which is forecast to have a total population of about 65 million by 2100, down from more than 120 million in 2000. This will be a traumatic social and economic devolution for Japan, as its significance and power in the global community will inevitably decline as its population does also.

And is there a linkage between urbanization and population implosion in Japan? Indeed there is; Japan is already the world's most urbanized nation.

Over the next 90 years a lot of things could happen to alter Japan's population trend, such as changes in values that lead Japanese women to prefer to have more children, or changes in cultural values and immigration laws that lead to more net immigration into Japan than is presently occurring. But as of right now those things aren't happening, and if they don't materialize then Japan's population will shrink drastically, with fundamental impact on Japan's economic and social structures.

driving force #5: culture change in a turbulent world

When you put it all together you see a world in which a great many fundamental changes are occurring, and all at the same time. Digitization is transforming the economy, and with the coming of robots and AI the transformation will accelerate.   Meanwhile, climate change will force radical changes, and lead to the restructuring of the world's energy systems and perhaps the end of the entire fossil fuel industry much more quickly than some are prepared for.   And as urbanization continues, the global rate of population growth will likely decline to zero, and perhaps the world population as whole will even begin to contract.

In and of itself each of these changes is in fact revolutionary in scope; the realization that they are occuring at the same time suggests that we are in for a very turbulent ride. But it will also be a time of tremendous opportunity for innovators and entrepreneurs, who will seize upon the changing times to create new ideas, products, services, and companies that will both leverage and accelerate this broader process of societal change.

For example, one impact of digitization and the rise of social media is a sharp decline in the number of Americans who read newspapers, as electronic news sources replace the printed word. Electronic media bring the immediacy of disasters that occur everywhere in the world instantly to the palm of your hand, and in this way they seem to heighten the badness of the bad news. But if you do happen to look at a newspaper, take a look at the section that's called "World News" and you'll read about turbulence on a massive and widespread scale.

I picked a day at random, November 26, 2010, and that day's news from across the globe included stories about gang violence in Rio de Janeiro, drug violence in Colombia and Mexico, students protesting education cuts in Italy, social services cuts in Greece and Ireland due government debt crises, as well as political or territorial disputes between India and Pakistan, North and South Korea, Israel and the Palestinians, and Japan and China. That's not a complete list of the world's troubled spots, but it's enough to remind us just how widespread the turbulence is.

And then a few days later, WikiLeaks began releasing a set of 250,000 diplomatic cables, an action that some claimed was the beginning of a real "cyber war." And a few days after that, the government of Ukraine announced that they would soon be offering tours of the Chernobyl nuclear reactor site.[25]

(Honestly, I don't know if we ought to admire the chutzpah behind turning the site of one of the world's worst engineering and environmental disasters into a tourist attraction, or be appalled at the hubris.)

Another way to get a sense for the scale of turbulence in human society is by noting that apart from major instances of warfare,

---

[25] Maria Danilova. "Disaster area will be opened for tours." *San Francisco Chronicle*, December 14, 2010.

about 1.6 million people die each year in violent crimes,[26] which works out to about 4400 people per day, or sadly, about 3 per minute. 1.2 million more people are killed in auto accidents, and an additional 50 million are injured, according to the World Health Organization.[27]

In parallel with the violent events are many equally disheartening trends. For example, even more people die due to tobacco use, almost 14,000 each day, 5 million per year.[28] Many other unpleasant trends also afflict our society, including infant and child mortality, hunger and starvation, preventable deaths caused by treatable diseases, as well as trends that occur across even longer time frames, such as global climate change, increasing air pollution, and deforestation.

Other important trends emerge not from specific dangers, but due to changing social values.

In a compact and informative little book called *International Relations*, Paul Wilkinson summarizes his review of world affairs with this comment: "It would be entirely understandable if the reader felt somewhat depressed at this stage [of the book]. A brief survey of some of the major problems and challenges of international relations reveals that we live in a very dangerous world, and that many of the most serious threats to our peace, security, and economic and social well-being are the result of human actions."[29] Somewhat depressed indeed...

Ours is a turbulent world, and there's nothing to suggest that the turbulence will decrease any time soon. So in what ways is your organization vulnerable to political, economic, or social disruptions? And how can you protect your organization from the

---

[26]   http://online.sfsu.edu/~rone/Buddhism/FivePrecepts/AnnualViolence.html

[27]   http://www.who.int/violence_injury_prevention/publications/road_traffic/world_report/en/index.html

[28]   Majid Ezzati & Alan Lopez. "Estimates of Global Mortality Attributable to Smoking in 2000." *The Lancet*, 2003 September 13, 2003; 362: 847-52.

[29]   Paul Wilkinson. *International Relations*. Sterling, 2007. P. 170.

impacts of these changes?

Conversely, how many of these trends and challenges present innovation opportunities? Health care, environment, politics, news, social services, finance, aerospace, technology – innovations in all of these fields and many more will become central to humanity's response to turbulence, and it is our entrepreneurs and organizations that will develop these innovations and introduce them to the market.

consequence: acceleration
running faster to stay in the same place

Each of these forces and consequences – digitization, climate change, the energy transformation, urbanization, and social turbulence and the linked consequences of commoditization, social mediaization, globalization, and turbulence – is a strategically decisive issue that's central to everything that your organization must understand and plan for.   But as I noted, they are not occurring independently of each other. In fact, they're mutually interdependent, and they feed off of one another. As their impacts converge, the result is the potential for thoroughly disruptive acceleration and the amplification of their impacts in a way that is decisive and inescapable. And unpredictable.

Underlying all this change is a root cause, a very simple, entirely human, and utterly characteristic fact of the entire history of civilization: tool making.

It is the introduction and use of new tools that creates change, and humans are habitual tool makers.

Through our capacity and proclivity for making and using tools we change ourselves, our communities, our civilization, and our planet. What is commoditization, after all, but the use of new tools of production, communication, and transportation?   What is digitization but a specific form of tool to create, share, and store data?   What is social mediaization but a particular means of communication enabled by a particular type of tool? What is globalization but the spread of a common economic tool set across all the oceans to nearly all the peoples of all nations?

Our use of and attachment to particular tools then becomes embedded in social values, in mores and concepts of right and wrong. As a result, a great deal of the turbulence we experience is rooted in social disruptions caused by our expanding tool set; new tools and the values they evoke confront established social systems, values, beliefs, and attitudes that have been shaped during eras when different types of tools were used than the ones we use today.

But it's not just social values, of course. New tools define new economic realities, which fundamentally affect how individuals, families, and communities earn their livelihoods.

In the words of James Burke, "The more the tools, the faster the rate of change."[30]

And every day we're busy making new tools and bringing them to market as fast as we can, so as the resulting events increase in magnitude and trends gain speed, every company becomes more vulnerable to change.

Trends erupt from nowhere and expand rapidly to global scale, altering the perceptions of citizens and customers, reshaping markets. Similarly, new competitors arrive from anywhere in the world without warning, and unexpected events cause turmoil.

The significance of acceleration is entirely visible by observing the increasing impact of mass communications and social networking media that drive market fads. Hot products, music, and movies can draw the interest of hundreds of millions of people in only a few days, but a problematic side effect of these ubiquitous mass media is the collapse of the profit-making window. Movies that have the potential to be blockbusters have to be released with a massive burst of advertising that must send ticket sales skyrocketing in the first weeks, or their marketability collapses in disappointment. James Cameron's *Avatar*, for example, reportedly

---

[30]   James Burke. *Connections*. Little Brown and Company, 1978.

had an advertising budget in excess of $100 million, and earned ticket sales of more than $2.5 billion. More modest films that once might have stayed in theaters for months while gradually building their audience are now gone after a couple weeks, and almost immediately sold on DVD and through other channels, because building a theater audience patiently is no longer a viable business model for a media conglomerate (although it is still pursued by smaller firms).

Authors Margaret Mark and Carol Pearson refer to this as "collective speedup." They write, "People today not only move more quickly, they can also process information rapidly. If the pace isn't quick, they get bored. The media most facilitative of this desire to experience and know everything and do so instantly," are of course social and electronic media.[31]

driving force #6: counter revolution

All of this change also creates a sixth driving force, which is expressed by people who react to all this change with fear, resentment, and opposition. There has always been a strongly conservative segment of society that opposes change, and with the acceleration of change in our times, the voices of anti-change, nationalism and xenophobia are clearly reflected in recent politics. As change represents revolution, we are experiencing, in effect, a counter revolution.

Indeed, as of 2017, right leaning and nationalist leaders are in power in the world's four most populous countries, China, India, the US, and Indonesia, as well as in Russia, and nationalist sentiment was certainly behind the Brexit vote, and is playing a stronger and stronger role in politics throughout the European Union.

There can be little doubt that this trend is a reaction to change;

---

[31]   Margaret Mark and Carol S. Pearson. *The Hero and the Outlaw*. McGraw Hill, 2001. P. 85.

it remains to be seen whether this rightward tilt will be able to actually stop change from occurring.

taking action:
designing and implementing your response to acceleration

The organizational consequences of these factors are three-fold:

First, markets are changing faster than they ever have before.

Second, consumer preferences and attitudes are changing faster, too.

And third, managers are called upon to make decisions on progressively more complex issues, but they must be prepared to do so in significantly less time.

All this is forcing deep changes in how managers think and how they operate.

Change is now occurring so fast that traditional approaches to planning aren't effective. (Some say that they've never been effective, but that's a different story.) To cope successfully with this dynamic world, leaders have to find new approaches to thinking and managing, and new ways of gathering information, planning, decision making, allocating resources, developing strategy, and linking strategy to innovation.

So what's your process for doing this?

Is your team working on improving its decision making skills to handle more information in less time? Do you have systems in place to collect event and trend data in real time? Are you tracking the external factors that will affect your business over the next 5 or 10 years?

And what forces are driving change in your market? Are they easy to spot, or does change in your environment emerge on the fringes where it's hard to notice unless you're carefully paying attention.

How are you improving your processes to deal with the acceleration of change? How do you relate them to your innovation program?

There's always the temptation to try to predict where the key trends are going to take you so that you can lock in your strategy and make better decisions. Predictions, however, are notoriously and consistently wrong, so a strategy based on a prediction is highly suspect and may be dangerous. Fortunately, there's a better alternative.

scenario planning

The scenario planning process enables you to examine dozens or even hundreds of important trends and events, to identify the ones that are most likely to be critical to your future, and then to use these as the basis not of predictions, but of *scenarios*, or stories, about what might happen. Scenario planning helps people think about the future not in a narrow or deterministic way, but to explore a wide range of possible outcomes from current trends and forces, and then to identify the strategies that make the most sense for a variety of outcomes.

In this way the focus is not on a single future, a single outcome, or a single strategy, but on understanding how the possibilities will be shaped by future events that we know will be important, but which cannot be predicted.

This approach transforms planning into a learning process, and a method of increasing awareness about what's important, why, and what the consequences *could* be. As a result, leaders are better prepared to respond appropriately to future events quickly and decisively because they have already thought through many of the likely consequences, nuances, and combinations.

Scenario planning is often done in workshops that can involve dozens or even hundreds of people. Participants engage in rich and dynamic conversations about the things that matter today and may matter tomorrow. In addition to the value that comes through the dialog about strategy, these workshops also enable people to discuss ideas and concepts that they find most engaging, and perhaps most troubling, and to explore the positive opportunities as well as potential threats in a setting that's non-confrontational and is not geared toward producing a single definitive outcome. Hence, it's a very useful thinking tool for executives because it changes the nature of planning work from a simple "problem > solution" construct to a more robust perspective that involves "driving forces > scenarios > possibilities > strategies."

Figure 6
Scenario Planning to Understand Possible Futures

Our teams at InnovationLabs and FutureLab have led scenario planning activities with companies in health care, energy, education, financial services, aerospace, high tech, and government, and they always lead to new insights and a much deeper understanding of how change is unfolding, and of how organizations can be better prepared for the future.

For example, a detailed scenario planning project with a

leading oil company explored the future of the energy industry across all possible energy sources and a wide range of possible social and economic situations. One of the participants then went back to her own business unit and used the same techniques to address a major problem that the business was facing, but which they had so far been unsuccessful in grappling with. By developing a set of scenarios instead of trying to come up with a "solution" to the problem, her team was able to explore the issues in a robust way and discover possibilities that they hadn't realized, exposing creative options that led them toward an ultimate solution. Again, by moving away from a simple "problem > solution" construct they were able to see the entire situation much more clearly.

In addition to the benefits for planning strategy and innovation initiatives, scenario planning can also be used to launch trend-tracking systems that help organizations to gather relevant information on more trends from more places on the globe to get an early warning about emerging change.

the last word ...

Scenario planning isn't the only good tool for thinking about and planning for change, and it's not the only way to manage it. Other tools and approaches may be right for your organization, and some of them are discussed in Chapter 8, The Innovation Infrastructure.

The key point here is that change is indeed accelerating, driven by forces that are massive in scale, inescapable, pervasive in influence, and highly unpredictable.

So is it an exaggeration to say that the survival of your organization may depend on the ability of its leaders to make sound business decisions in the face of changing conditions? Perhaps, but maybe not.

Do you want to risk it?

Fortunately, there's no need for that. Building a better decision making system, and the information gathering and modeling processes to back it up does require time, but not necessarily a lot of capital outlay. It will be time well invested.

Dealing with accelerating change requires both a robust process for thinking through the strategic consequences of what's happening in your world, and also a process for turning insights into useful actions that benefit your organization. Those insights will help to shape the strategic goals you choose, and then guide the actions, policies, procedures, and structures that create your organization's future.

By applying the agile innovation sprint approach to the creation and expression of your organization's innovation strategy you can define the key performance axes, the key areas in which it is imperative for your organization to define its own future by creating the innovations – products, services, business models, and processes – that will enable it survive and succeed in an increasingly turbulent world.

Translating these strategic goals and imperatives into useful guidance for your organization's innovation process is the function of the innovation portfolio and of the innovation process itself, and these are the topics for the next few chapters.

chapter 3
what to innovate
creating and managing innovation portfolios

"I have missed more than 9,000 shots in my career. I have lost almost 300 games. On 26 occasions I have been entrusted to take the game winning shot ... and missed. And I have failed over and over and over again in my life. And that is why I succeed."[32]

Michael Jordan [in a TV commercial for Nike]

Innovation, like basketball, is inherently risky. You never know in advance who will win. Would-be NBA champions miss shots and lose games, while would-be innovators risk money and time, possibly a lot of both, to create, explore, and develop new ideas, hoping to turn them into innovations. But regardless of how good they are at the game of innovation, many of the resulting outputs may cost a fortune and never earn a dime.

The larger game of business in which innovation is pursued is inherently risky, too. You never know what your competitors are going to do, or what changes are coming to the market, or how soon your existing products and services will become obsolete.

From a manager's perspective this presents a daunting challenge and a critical dilemma that arises every day: in what

---

[32] http://www.youtube.com/watch?v=m-EMOb3ATJ0

aspects of my business should the innovation effort be focused? Should we apply ourselves to innovation in our products or our services, or our brand, or the organization itself, our leadership team, our technology, our capital structure, or any of the countless others among all the possible targets?

While any one among this broad range of possible innovation targets may be important, no target is guaranteed to be the right one to pursue, the one that will inevitably result in success. Consequently, it's far better to develop a portfolio of innovations-in-process that can be brought forward to create change, or to respond to change introduced by others. This is an approach that calls for taking modest and disciplined risks to accelerate learning, so that when it's time to take bigger risks they're informed by what we've already learned, and the likelihood of success will be much greater.

In this way innovation reduces the overall risk for the future of your organization by creating new future possibilities whose time *may* come.

In this chapter we address the *what* of innovation, the second sprint in the agile innovation process. The central organizing concept is the carefully designed collection of new ideas-in-progress, the innovation portfolio, through which an organization prepares its own future while also preparing to meet future challenges introduced by competitors. This is the innovation portfolio.

In subsequent chapters we'll get to the details of the development process, progressing from strategy to ideas to innovations, and after that we'll examine the development of the right organizational culture to do this work, and then the necessary infrastructure to support it.

purpose and method

The innovation portfolio has two *purposes*. First, it's a learning system that will enhance our efforts to achieve our strategic intents through innovation, by helping us to deal with the problems of uncertainty and change. Second, and at the same time, it also reduces the inevitable risks inherent in the innovation process itself, and the larger risks related to being in business in the first place, by organizing the process of creating new products, services, and business models for the future.

The *concept* of a portfolio is that it provides a proven method for managing assets in the face of uncertainty. Just as investors in all types of assets create portfolios to help them attain optimal returns while choosing the level of risk that is most appropriate for them, the innovation portfolio gives us a tool to do the same for the innovation projects we're working on.

The *method* of innovation portfolio management is to transform the strategic initiatives that we have already reasoned through in Chapter One into a learning process that consists of a disciplined and thoughtful experiments that balance failures at the small scale on the way to ultimate successes at the large scale. We will explore the nature of this type of failure in a bit, but first...

The *content* of the innovation portfolio is, of course, innovation ideas and projects, of which there are four different types.

the four types of innovation

It's obvious that a fundamental breakthrough is entirely different from a minor incremental improvement, even though both may properly be understood to be innovations. Toyota's hybrid Prius car, an example of a breakthrough technology, required years of intensive engineering innovation and trillions of yen of patient capital; the same company comes out every year with a new color palette for its cars, and changes the shapes of hoods, trunks, and headlights, which are of course entirely incremental changes.

These are the two obvious types of innovation, but there are also two other types that Toyota has used very successfully, as we see with its luxury Lexus and entry-level Scion brands. (If you are outside of the USA then you may not know about Scion, as it only existed in North America. It was a Toyota subsidiary that sold less expensive cars, which placed it at the opposite end of the market from luxury-oriented Lexus; but it did not survive the recession of 2008.)   Lexus and Scion cars include some breakthrough technologies as well as a great many incremental innovations, but more importantly they are also "new venture innovations" because they are entirely new brands marketed by separate companies. The specific intent of new venture innovation is to extend the Toyota Corporation's life into the future for many decades.

According to the consulting firm Interbrand, which ought to know since brand valuation is what they do, the value of the Lexus brand, meaning the brand identity, name and logo as assets in and of themselves, as distinct from the revenue of the company, was about $3 billion in 2006, but then fell due to the global financial downturn and the massive impact that it had on the auto industry; it will most likely rise again.

Further, Lexus aspires to be a different *kind* of car company by providing a different sort of experience to their customers, a better one of course, and in this respect can be thought of as a "new business model innovation" because it's pursuing new ways of providing better experiences to earn higher profits.

This brief discussion of Toyota has shown how the company applies all four types of innovation to the development of its future value proposition.

Breakthrough innovations are the technical foundations of new companies and new industries. We pursue breakthroughs to attain major competitive advantage. Toyota, as world leader in hybrid engine technology, has gained an enormous advantage from its investment in this particular technology. As of April 2016 the company had sold 9 million Prius cars worldwide.

Incremental innovations are minor improvements to existing business structures, processes, and products. We invest in incremental innovation to maintain or improve market share. Toyota, inventor of lean manufacturing, is also the world leader in incremental innovation, leadership that came about through a dedication to continuous improvement that has endured for decades, following on the pioneering spirit of its brilliant originator Taichi Ohno.

New venture innovations extend existing companies into new territories, either literally or figuratively. We create new ventures to expand into new markets for long term benefit.

And **new business models** are new ways of making money by leveraging new or different customer experiences. Like breakthroughs, new business models can also transform the structure of markets by changing customer expectations, attitudes, and buying patterns. Examples of new business model innovations include online retail, which is of course fundamentally different from brick and mortar retail. Each has its advantages, but as we have seen with the success of Amazon.com, online book selling dramatically reshaped the retail book business by forcing many local bookstores out of business entirely, and the huge national Barnes & Noble chain is operating under severe duress because consumer buying patterns have changed so much, while Borders collapsed entirely.

It's often the case that a particular innovation doesn't fit into only one innovation category. Sometimes a breakthrough innovation is so different from the existing business that it becomes a new company, and hence a new venture innovation. Sometimes new business models are also new ventures, while in other situations it's an existing venture that must find a new business model.

As you prepare your innovation master plan and develop your innovation practice, all four types of innovation will become relevant and important because more than one type of innovation is typically required to sustain success in the market. Long term survival will likely require all four.

This is true even when a technology breakthrough is what you're developing and what you plan to sell. An example is Xerox. Chester Carlson's technological innovation was a compelling breakthrough, and a testimony to his insight and persistence. The story also highlights the difficulties of forecasting the market for genuinely new products, as many industrial giants of the day, including IBM, Kodak, and GE rejected Carlson's offer to license his technology because they could not envision its future success.

When he finally did find a partner, you may remember that it was tiny Haloid Company that took him on. Together they soon discovered that getting the technology to market entailed far more than simply building new machines, and the success of the company in its early years was due as much to its innovative approach to distribution – leasing the machines on a per-use basis instead of selling them outright – as it was to the technology. So it was Xerox's business model innovation that enabled the technology innovation to succeed in the market.

Today, Xerox is not the dominant company it once was, and a small but important aspect of the Xerox story is that in 1975 the company was so successful and so dominant that it was literally forced by federal government regulators to license its technology to competing companies. With this strange and quite short-sighted turn of events the regulators proved to have a poor grasp on the vibrant dynamics of technology competition, and sadly the company's downward slide began. Within four years, Xerox's share of the U.S. copier market dropped from nearly 100% to less than 14%. Again and again we see the inexorability of creative destruction and it's many agents, some of them lurking behind you, in this case, tragically, in the form of Xerox's own government.

Xerox stock declined from a high of about $60 per share at the peak of the internet boom to around $12 in 2010, and further to $7 by 2017, threatened by creative competitors whose own innovations in distribution and technology have largely surpassed Xerox's. But ironically, the problem was definitely not that Xerox management, in those heady days when the company was the resounding market leader, had failed to recognize the importance of innovation. In fact, they funded innovation generously, and quite intelligently. Technical innovations that surpassed the efforts of most other companies were constantly being created at Xerox's legendary Palo Alto Research Center, PARC, from which an amazing string of enormous breakthroughs in many dimensions of technology emerged (as I mentioned above in discussing the turnaround of Apple).

At PARC the first really usable PC was developed, initially by the scientists who wanted it for their own use, after which it was turned into a product called the Xerox Star. Apple co-founder Steve Jobs was given a tour of PARC during that period, and what he saw in the Star inspired many of the design features and innovations that became Apple's Macintosh. The Mac was a huge success, and so was Microsoft's subsequent Windows operating system, which is also built on many insights and breakthroughs that originated at PARC. But the Star was not a success; in fact it was a resounding failure, for reasons that we will explore in Chapter 6, because they have mostly to do with Xerox's corporate culture.

Ford is another example showing the importance of pursuing multiple types of innovations. The original Ford cars of the early 1900s were certainly innovative for their automotive engineering, but equally important to the company's success was the innovative production process (the first vertically integrated assembly line), manufacturing standardization, the distribution system (the dealer network), the salaries paid to workers (double the standard wage of the era), and the company's pricing model, affordability. All of these innovations together enabled Ford to dominate the market.

Even Ford's choice of black paint was an economic innovation, part of his relentless strategy of minimizing costs. Fords were originally painted brown, until a company engineer pointed out that black paint covered better, and would therefore be less expensive. The point for Mr. Ford was definitely not the particular color, but rather his highly principled obsession with of cost control. He understood that lowering the cost of manufacture was the key to developing his company and the broader market, and he was absolutely correct.

So from 1903 through World War I, cost control was the driver, but in the 1920s the auto market was maturing and Ford's success as a cost-cutting pioneer wasn't enough, as customers began to choose cars for comfort and style rather than just cost and efficiency. GM had copied and largely caught up with Ford's innovations, and began introducing some of its own. A minor GM innovation with major significance was the availability of cars in colors other than black.

Ford did not adapt quickly, and began to lose market share as the Depression set in and his own inability to grasp change held the company back. The company was saved from bankruptcy by the enormous demand for military vehicles during World War II, but after the war was over the company was again too slow to adapt, and was nearly bankrupt again by the late 1950s.

The Ford story illustrates how each industry has its own rhythm of innovation, including both technical and non-technical advances. Some innovations are advances in materials and manufacturing, some in design and methods, some in branding and communication, some in distribution.

While Ford struggled, GM seized the advantage and held it for 75 years. But Toyota and Honda are the leaders now, based on decades of emphasis on quality, reliability, and design, and most recently on new engine technologies like Toyota's hybrid. GM's share of the American market declined from 50% in 1980 to less than 35% by 2000, and then to less than 25% by 2008, and 19% through the first 9 months of 2010.

We don't know which companies will lead the market in 2020 or 2030, but no one would be surprised if it's a different one than any I've mentioned thus far, because sustaining market leadership from one market structure to the next is very difficult and happens only rarely, and we can't predict when the market structure will change. I write that, and then along comes Tesla ...

Sears is another example of a leader that became an also-ran. I noted in the previous chapter how Sears grew arrogant and complacent, and lost touch with the innovation mindset that had characterized its early years. Wal-Mart, meanwhile, developed its business in smaller rural markets that Sears had abandoned or ignored.   Sam Walton recognized that change, in the form of interstate highways, enabled rural stores to lure customers from very large distances to regional shopping hubs with many acres of parking. (In France, the founders of the now-global retail chains Auchan and Carrefour had the same realization.) As Wal-Mart expanded, the company focused on cost control, and developed innovative approaches throughout its growing supply chain, thereby lowering its operating costs and making it strong enough to compete with Sears and K-Mart in urban markets. As Wal-Mart grew Sears became a second-tier retailer, while K-Mart was eventually forced into bankruptcy; in desperation, the two laggards then merged.

Sometimes entire product categories become obsolete, and the buggy whip is often mentioned as an example.[33] There was also, not so long ago, a thriving business in ice distribution throughout the US, but that went away when the electric refrigerator arrived in the 1920s and 30s. Business historians will soon be adding the demise of the music CD to the list of displacement stories, as digital music distribution takes its place. Likewise, the video rental business, epitomized in the US by Blockbuster, was made obsolete by video streaming by Netflix, Apple TV, Hulu, and others. And now streaming must go mobile, or it too will be left behind.

The key point of these last few pages is that companies don't

---

[33]   A buggy whip was a very long whip used in the days of horses and wagons (buggies, or carridges) by the wagon or buggy driver to help control the horses. It is often used as an example of an industry that declined rapidly, in this case as a result of the success of Ford's Model T auto. Buggy whip makers had perfected their product by the 1890s, but it was entirely obsolete by 1910.

sustain success by focusing on only one type of innovation, and likewise they won't be successful in the future unless they balance their innovation efforts across all four types.

Each type must be managed as a separate portfolio of projects that address the specific needs and opportunities that each type of innovation embodies, and taken together all four will also constitute the fifth portfolio, consisting of all the projects.

Each of these five portfolios will be carefully designed to balance offensive innovations, those that we think could change the market to our advantage, and defensive ones, those that we prepare in case we need them. We sometimes refer to these defensive projects as "spare tires."

spare tires

Do you carry a spare tire in your car? And a first aid kit? And do you have fire extinguishers in your home and office? Of course you do, (or if you don't, you know you should). You do this even though you hope that you'll never have to use them.[34] Similarly, some of the projects in your innovation portfolio will never be used, but you'll still have good reason to develop them.

The purpose of your portfolio is to prepare for a wide variety of possible future conditions, some of which will never actually emerge into reality. So while it's inevitable that some projects in your innovation portfolio will never become relevant to the market, it's necessary to work on them anyway because you won't know in advance which are which. These projects will therefore never return value in and of themselves, but still they're not failures, they're better understood as useful and prudent precautions.

---

[34] The invention of the "run flat" tire may make the metaphor of the spare tire obsolete. This would be a nice example of how innovation changes the game in the tire industry, and thereby affects how we think about an entire product category.

the necessity of disciplined failure

Some projects will have clear and immediate goals, when you can see direct application and a straight shot from concept through development to market impact. Other projects, though, may be important not for the direct results but for the learning that you will gain. Such projects often involve a high degree of failure, necessary failure. And concerning failure, it turns out that there's a lot to say.

For organizations to deliver on the promise of innovation it's essential that their employees have the skills to effectively generate ideas, insights, and innovations, to understand, diagnose, analyze, model, create, invent, solve, communicate, and implement. These are all skills that we might consider facets of "learning."

Naturally enough, any organization that thrives in a rapidly changing environment necessarily has developed the capability to learn and to apply that learning to keep up with the changing world. Hence we get Arie de Geus' insight that the company wins that learns fastest, and is then able to translate that learning into products, processes, and structures: "Learning faster than your competition is the only sustainable competitive advantage," he said.[35]

Learning faster must also lead to *doing* faster, and the capacity to systemically reduce cycle time is also a valuable skill. Toyota perfected cycle time reduction in its many-decades drive to reduce the time required to change production models on its assembly lines from days to hours, and then minutes; our interest is in reducing the time needed to solve problems and deal with complexity through innovation. At root what we're talking about, then, could also be called "the productivity of the innovation process," and a portfolio is certainly a productivity tool.

"Productivity," specifically, is the ratio of results obtained to investment required; in the auto industry it's measured as person-hours-per-car-manufactured; in a bank, it is cost per transaction;

---

35   Arie de Geus. *The Living Company*. Harvard, 1997.

and in a software company it could be person-years required to produce a new program, or debug it.

While these examples explain productivity in "production" environments, we're even more interested in attaining improved outcomes in environments that are full of unknowns, where the central tasks are to create new knowledge through learning, and to apply this knowledge to solve problems and create business opportunities. This is the classic domain of innovation, and here productivity is much more challenging to measure.

Innovation as an approach to learning, particularly as it relates to potential breakthroughs and new business models, entails uncertainty, and hence the necessity to try things that may not work, in order to discover what actually does work.

Figure 7
Possible Future Realities Outside of Current Reality

Further, preparing to meet and deal with the unpredictable future requires us to gain experience and knowledge through experimentation across a wide range of hypothetical situations. As they are hypothetical, many of them may never materialize, and as a consequence many of these experiments may appear to be "failures."

But if they've been conducted with suitable discipline and a learning outcome has been achieved, then they should actually be viewed as successes.

The degree of uncertainty that organizations face in the market will influence the breadth of failure that's necessary to pursue; the bigger the challenges and the faster the changes, the greater the breadth of failure you'll have to accept, or indeed, to embrace. So while you might think that you have to *endure* failure, the truth is that you need to *pursue* it.

The importance of these failures is so unmistakable and unavoidable that it's worth commenting about the mindset related to failure, and the prevailing cultural assumptions in our Western world.

Like you, perhaps, growing up in a success-oriented culture has indelibly planted in my mind the belief that failure is bad and to be avoided at all costs. If I fail it be may be a sign that I am a bad person, while success is culturally imperative, and a sign of goodness. We are obsessed with winners who succeed, and we scorn the losers who fail.

Causing failure is a further and deeper sign of inadequacy along any one of many possible dimensions of behavior, including poor preparation, lack of skill or talent, faulty reasoning, or bad judgment.[36]

Each of these deficiencies is inevitably uncomfortable and may be quite painful. Hence, when we fail in any of these ways we often feel angry at ourselves, and humiliated, and we may swear … "never to do that again. Ever!" Such is the stigma associated with failure, and the mountain of judgment that falls upon anyone who fails.

Now consider your own career. You aspire to be a top manager in a big company and you've succeeded at every stage of your career path along the way, from schooling to the big milestone of the "first job," through the ranks and all the way up. You knew what to do, or you learned along the way, you planned it well and executed on it, and you succeeded.

This is not, however, the way it usually works with innovation. In the pursuit of innovation, failure may indeed result from all these

---

[36]   Twyla Tharp. *The Creative Habit.* Simon & Schuster, 2003.

sources and their insidious combinations, but it is still necessary. It is desirable.

Why?

Because some failures are entirely essential steps on the learning pathway that leads from a universe of uncertainty to clarity, capability, understanding, and thus to ultimate success. This reasoning lies at the roots of the comment from Michael Jordan that begins this chapter so gracefully (I'll repeat it here so you don't have to turn the pages back to find it).

> "I have missed more than 9,000 shots in my career. I have lost almost 300 games. On 26 occasions I have been entrusted to take the game winning shot ... and missed. And I have failed over and over and over again in my life. And that is why I succeed."

He succeeds, that is, because he knows what causes failure and what causes success, because he has seen it from the inside, and has complete and operational knowledge.

And just as we play the basketball games and golf tournaments to discover who the winners will be, we go forward in life and in business day by day to meet the unknown. And if, in the face of the unknown, we have experimented, and tested, and failed at many possibilities until we arrived at ideas and innovations that make the most sense in a range of possible situations, then we are in a better position to succeed in the long run because we also have complete and operational knowledge.

But if we are intimidated by the fear of or possibility of failure, and we don't test the limits of reality, then we're almost sure to fail in the long run because we won't be able to respond quickly enough to unexpected events as they unfold. Having failed to fail, that is, we are not properly prepared to succeed.

Innovation's apparent dead ends, like Jordan's missed shots and lost games, are inevitable, necessary, and in fact should be valued as learning opportunities. As a matter of innovation methodology we are therefore obliged to pursue failure in order to learn.

Executing on this principle requires disciplined management of the entire process such that we make good choices, set up clear experiments, probe fruitful opportunities, and indeed learn from the outcomes and ensure that there are no dead ends in the innovation process.

But that's not stating the situation clearly enough. Failure is not just something you tolerate. It's an absolute requirement. Because to succeed at innovation you *must* fail.

Suppose you have a set of products and services from which you earn revenues and profits today. You know that at some future date, perhaps tomorrow or perhaps in years to come, those products and services will become obsolete, because your company or a competitor will introduce new products and services that deliver better value, that will cost less or perform better, or both.

The problem with this scenario is the uncertainty: you don't know exactly what those future products and services will be, or when they will be required.

So what do you do? You could guess wildly, using the dart-board method. But obviously it's better to make well-informed judgments, which you could possibly do by experimenting and testing a lot of ideas, developing from experience a reasoned hypothesis about where the market is likely to go based on a deep understanding of technology, consumer preferences, the economy, demographics, and competitive trends, as you hone in on the emerging future.

Accomplishing this requires that you try a lot of ideas in order to learn what works and doesn't work. This will happen in some sort of laboratory, whether it's a chemistry lab or a machine shop or a test kitchen, or even a spreadsheet. Some of the ideas will seem to succeed, while other will not. Some will need further elaboration and more detailed testing. You will learn from all of them; you may learn the most from the failures. As we have an athletic theme in this chapter, a comment by golfer Bobby Jones is very pertinent here: "I never learned anything from a match I won," he said. The winning, in other words, was the culmination of the learning process that was rich with non-winning.

Of course the end goal is to succeed spectacularly. The failures are the necessary enablers, the instances of trying and learning, learning and trying, that lead to the destination.

Innovation is therefore deeply and sometimes brutally ironic, and given this crazy cultural dynamic concerning success and failure, and the very heavy values and reactions that both of them evoke, it's no wonder that the mindset we discussed in the introduction is so challenging for managers to understand, and accept, and adopt.

As a matter of innovation culture, though, we must develop in our organization a rather different attitude about failure than considering it a life-defining stigma, the scarlet letter, "F"!

Notable aspects of that culture will include our attitudes towards uncertainty and ambiguity, as well as a highly disciplined portfolio management process, as we will explore below.

the degree of uncertainty

The type of innovation risk that's appropriate in any situation is linked to the market or markets in which you're competing, and the anticipated rewards you're pursuing. In rapidly changing markets, such as consumer electronics, innovation risk is inherently different than in slower-changing industries such as, say, road construction.

The faster the rate of change, the bigger the strategic risks, and the broader the range of possible futures that you must prepare for. This will necessarily affect the composition of your innovation portfolio, so the ideal portfolio of each organization will be different: Apple, NASA, Genentech, Union Pacific, GE, and Starbucks are all innovative organizations, but when it comes to their innovation portfolios it's obvious that they cannot be the same in content or in style.

This concept is reflected in many industries as the percent of revenue that is typically allocated to R&D efforts.   As these investments are understood to fund the future, the faster things are changing the more it may be necessary to invest.

The biggest investors tend to be high tech companies and pharmaceutical companies; in high tech, R&D investments are typically about 15% of revenue, while in pharmaceutical it typically ranges from about 15% to 20%.   The third category of big spenders are the major auto companies, which invest 4% - 5%.[37]

As you transition to this new attitude about failure, it may be useful to compare your company's innovation portfolio with a venture capital portfolio.   Venture capital investors know that it's impossible to precisely predict winning business ideas from among any set of well-conceived early stage companies, so they invest in 10 to 20 companies at a time with the expectation that a handful of them will eventually have a shot at greatness, and these successes will more than make up for the many failures.

To realize the potential of this analogy, many of the projects that constitute an innovation portfolio must mature and develop into robust investment opportunities, providing senior executives and board level directors with increasingly attractive new options. But not all of them will.   And along the possibly long pathway to the failure or success of any particular idea, we will be obliged to live with a great deal of ambiguity.

return on ambiguity

The proper design and management of your innovation portfolio will enable you to fail intelligently, and with rigor, and to extract the maximum learning from these experiences, and so to ultimately create the most value.

But this requires you to inhabit a land of ambiguity, and to remain there for as long as it takes to conduct experiments, fail

---

[37]   Barry Jaruzelski and Kevin Dehoff. "The Global Innovation 1000." *strategy + business*. Winter 2010.

sufficiently, and gain definitive insight into the future as a result.

Consequently, one of the defining attributes of successful innovation managers is the high degree of tolerance for prolonged ambiguity that is required to succeed. It's the nature of the job, and those who are not comfortable with ambiguity usually aren't good at it.

By managing their portfolios over time, executives who can live with ambiguity will significantly improve their performance by not forcing false clarity to come too quickly. And as they practice the disciplines of innovation management and learning they'll get in better sync with the evolving market, and get better at selecting and supporting the projects that do have the greatest potential.

Still, many projects must fail. In fact, a rather high percentage of them should fail, because failure is an indication that you're pushing the limits of your current understanding hard enough to be confident that you're extracting every last bit of learning from every situation, and that you're examining a wide enough range of situations as a way to prepare for a range of unanticipated futures.

As Norbert Wiener puts, it, "Invention and discovery are not calculable risks. In the first place, the really inventive mind must take chances. A long-time record of no false starts probably does not mean infallibility on the part of the inventor, but merely that he has not been willing to push his ideas as far as they merit. The baseball player without a record of errors is the one who does not go after the balls that he might barely pull down, but allows them to damage the record of the other fellow."[38]

burn down

Suppose you're sitting in an innovation portfolio meeting and discussing potential innovation projects. You want to determine the likely ROI on a set of projects, so you assess the risks, and

---

[38]   Norbert Wiener. *Invention: The Care and Feeding of Ideas.* The MIT Press, 1993. P. 145.

eventually you choose which projects to invest in. You compare the projected revenue stream for each proposed innovation with other uses for that same capital in existing business lines, and you decide that the current business can make better use of the money.

It's all completely rational and reasonable.

Except that you've likely just made a mistake, and perhaps a large one.

The mistake is that your current products and services are gradually (or abruptly) becoming obsolete, so future earnings from your current business will deteriorate. We call this the "burn-down rate," which reminds us that the house of current revenue is gradually burning down, and if you do no innovating then you'll eventually end up with nothing that people want to buy.[39]

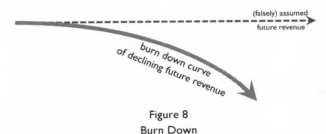

Figure 8
Burn Down
The specific profiles of your curves will be different.

The burn down rate varies significantly by industry, so you have to study the specifics of your own business to make a reasonable assessment. Are you in telecom? Then you already know that many (now most) cell phones become obsolete within months. But Boeing is still selling its 747 more than 45 years after it was first introduced (in 1970), although the current version 8 may be, finally, the last one.

That comment requires clarification, though, because the original 747 of 1970 and today's model don't even have the same

---

[39]   Eileen Rudden, Boston Consulting Group. She refers to it as the "discounted case flow trap." Clayton Christensen. *Innovation Killers*. Harvard Business Press, 2010.

outer shape. Though we still recognize it as a 747, just about everything has been changed, which is to say, innovated. The aircraft has been revised, system by system, from the inside out, with safer and more efficient technology throughout, through 7 generations of upgrades.

If Boeing had not made these changes, of course, then the 747 would have become entirely obsolete, so these investments were made in the interest of preserving the marketability of the product, and avoiding burn down. But if you don't factor in the burn-down, then your cash flow and ROI calculations are irrationally biased toward the existing business, and based on the obviously false assumption that existing revenue production will remain viable indefinitely.

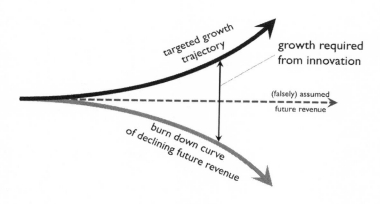

Figure 9
Burn Down & Targeted Growth
The vertical line represents the magnitude of the innovation challenge.

Hence, your portfolio management process has to account specifically for the rate of burn down when you calculate the revenue and profit growth that your innovation efforts must achieve. This may not be simple to calculate, but you need to understand when it is and is not fruitful to make incremental change to the existing business, to anticipate at which point it will be necessary to switch to something significantly different.

Here's a lovely example of someone thinking ahead and anticipating burn down. In describing the need to develop hybrid engine technology, Honda's head of engine development, Hideyo Miyano, commented that "We don't have much time." He estimated that within 20 years, gasoline engines would be pretty much obsolete, and he was consequently managing a large portfolio of projects to provide Honda with the necessary capabilities 20 years in the future.

What makes this particularly interested is when he said this. It was 1992.[40] Impressive, eh?!

manage portfolios *and* projects

OK, so as the future is unpredictable, and since one of the goals of the innovation portfolio is to explore broadly across the realms of possible future business, then as a consequence of this very exploration, the innovation portfolio absolutely invites failure. The Chief Technology Officer of a major global corporation put it succinctly when he explained his approach to testing new technology. He said, provocatively, "Our purpose is to fail."

Because only by failing does his team learn which new technologies work and which don't, and how they can best be used or how they cannot or should not be used. Failure is an explicit learning strategy, and so they run innovation projects to push the limits of reasonableness, knowing full well that failure is lurking, the inevitable and welcome companion of learning. Individual projects fail so that the portfolio as a whole succeeds grandly.

And therefore it would be unfair, brutally and self-defeatingly unfair, to punish innovation project leaders and portfolio managers specifically for the failures. Instead, they should be measured on and rewarded for the performance of a portfolio as a whole, not the performance of specific individual projects.

---

[40]   Karen Lowry Miller. "Honda Sets Its Sights on a Different Checkered Flag." *Business Week*. August 17, 1992. P. 45.

"Whole" means that they have applied the lessons of last year's successes and failures to create this year's successes, and this year's failures are expected to contribute to next year's successes. This will reward them for engaging in a vibrant learning process, for assuring that insights gained in any particular project are made to benefit all the projects.

This was brought home to me some years ago when I visited a research facility at P&G, and during the tour it was mentioned that one of the underlying management principles they followed was a concept called "kill'em quick." By this they wanted everyone to understand that if you happened to be working on a project and you discovered that it was a dead end, an impending failure, that the lab managers invited and requested you to let them know *immediately* so the project could be halted and you could be reassigned to something more promising.

Underlying this policy was the realization that, yes, failure is inevitable, and we're running a learning process here, and the sooner we all see failure coming, the sooner we can adjust our plans.

Practiced rigorously, this will progressively steer every portfolio towards success.

non-correlated assets

Starting in the 1990s and into the following decade, many banks and investment houses earned magnificent profits from mortgage-backed securities, and as the numbers grew this business became as addictive as a drug. The upside possibilities seemed unlimited, while the risks seemed miniscule; consequently, many shifted ever larger portions of their efforts to this lucrative market.

When the market started to stumble in early 2008, some industry observers assumed that the holdings of these firms were diverse and that because they owned many different types of securities in many markets they would be protected from catastrophe because even if one segment of the financial markets did poorly, which indeed they saw happening, the market as a whole would remain healthy.

They were wrong on both assumptions. What these observers had not understood, but which we all were to learn soon thereafter, is that many firms had concentrated too much of their portfolios and too much risk into this one type of asset. So when the mortgage backed security market failed, the plummet triggered a massively negative chain reaction.

One reason that it was possible for this to happen was that the market as a whole was largely unregulated. So in testimony before a congressional committee on October 23, 2008, former Federal Reserve chairman Alan Greenspan admitted that he had been "partially wrong" in his hands-off approach towards the banking industry. "I have found a flaw. It turned out to be much broader than anything I could have imagined. Those of us who have looked to the self-interest of lending institutions to protect shareholders' equity (myself especially) are in a state of shocked disbelief."[41]

The phrase, "much broader than I could have imagined" shows that Greenspan's understanding of portfolio theory may also have been lacking. This sort of catastrophic failure is precisely what he *should* have considered as possible, imagined that is. In practice, the "intellectual portfolio" of the uber regulator should by definition include an understanding of scenarios that are far broader than actual portfolio of behaviors that the regulatee, the market, can manifest.[42]

He told the House committee that he regretted his opposition to regulatory curbs on certain types of financial derivatives, those which left Wall Street banks facing billions of dollar's worth of

---

[41] Edmund L. Andrews. "Greenspan Concedes Error on Regulation." *The New York Times*. October 23, 2008.

[42] In cybernetic terms, we might technically consider this to be a problem of variety matching, in that the variety of the regulator has to exceed the possible variety of the regulatee, or in fact the regulator is doing a poor job. A good innovation portfolio must likewise dispose greater variety than the market can manifest, or it, too, is poorly devised.

liabilities. Committee chairman Henry Waxman then pressed him, with a distinctly ideological bent. "You found that your view of the world, your ideology, was not working?" Greenspan had no choice but to agree, saying that, "That's precisely the reason I was shocked, because I'd been going for 40 years or so with considerable evidence that it was working exceptionally well."

The line of reasoning that Greenspan chose exposed another portfolio management error, because he didn't account for how new behaviors unfold: ideas always work until they don't, at which point being surprised that they no longer do is evidence of poor preparation. Greenspan continued, "I made a mistake in presuming that the self-interests of organizations, specifically banks and others, were such that they were best capable of protecting their own shareholders and their equity in the firms." It turned out that regulations were necessary to assure that short term greed did not make the banks excessively vulnerable to long term risks. In fact, banking regulations are designed precisely to address this question, and those regulations had been non-existent.

The final irony worth mentioning here is that during the 40 year period that Greenspan refers to, the government, largely at his own instigation, went through a process of progressively de-regulating the banks and investment houses, allowing them progressively more freedom to pursue whatever markets they wanted in whatever way they wanted. And it was precisely the cumulative impact of deregulation that enabled the system to become so intensively concentrated into one type of soon-to-be-dysfunctional asset. So in his assessment of the possible behaviors of the market, Greenspan should have realized that deregulation was changing the very structure of the market, and therefore changing the nature of risk, and therefore requiring of the banks more self discipline if indeed they were also to be capable of self-regulating. (If he had looked, he would not likely have found much evidence of self-discipline.)

My point is not to belabor a debate over the correct ideological framework, but to use this story as a vivid example of how you have to think carefully about the principles of portfolio management, and study the contents of every portfolio in order for the portfolio to perform properly given a broad range of possible market behaviors. In the illustration below, the smaller circle represents the current behaviors of the market, which means that the design of the portfolio (whether it's an innovation portfolio or a regulation portfolio) has to encompass the possibilities in the bigger circle so that you are sure to examine and prepare for a wider range of possibilities since the exact future remains entirely unpredictable despite your persistent efforts to predict it.

Figure 10
A Wide Range of Possibilities
(The same image, by the way, was used on page 96 to make
a related point about possible futures.)

During the same period, Treasury Secretary Paulson also realized he ought to have anticipated a meltdown in the US mortgage industry. "I could have seen the sub-prime crisis coming earlier," he told the *New York Times*, admitting thereby that his conceptual framework had been inadequate. And this is the core of the portfolio design issue; it is a matter of defining the right conceptual framework.

Some observers did indeed foresee the problems, including the once-infamous and now-famous Brookesley Born, who was forced to resign as a regulator when she called attention to the growing risks.

Author and investor Nassim Nicholas Taleb put it this way in his pre-crash book, *The Black Swan*: "Regulators in the banking business are prone to a severe expert problem and they tend to condone reckless (but hidden) risk taking."[43]   [The "expert problem" is the situation of supposed experts knowing less than it appears they do.]

But they were in the minority. Greenspan and Paulson had a lot of company in mis-assesing the dynamics of the market. They and thousands of other bankers and investment managers had forgotten one of the key lessons of Investment 101, which is that healthy investment portfolios consist of "non-correlated" assets. The principles of correlation and non-correlation were worked out in detail in the 1950s by the father of portfolio theory, Harry Markowitz, who subsequently was awarded the Nobel Prize in Economics.[44]

"Correlation" means that two (or more) investments tend to behave the same way in any given set of market conditions. Investment portfolios containing securities that are highly correlated are riskier than portfolios with non-correlated securities, because they tend to rise and fall together. The rising part is welcome, but the purpose of a portfolio is to reduce risk, so creating a portfolio in which everything has the potential to fall together is a very bad idea and increases risk, which is exactly the opposite of what a healthy portfolio should do.

Hence, a "non-correlated" portfolio consists of a variety of assets that are expected to perform differently under any given set of economic conditions. If the market goes up, some assets will do better than others; if the market goes down, different ones will be the right ones to own. So the prudent investor owns both types in a non-correlated, or diverse securities portfolio, containing a mix of stocks and bonds from different markets and regions.

The validity of the theory was unintentionally affirmed on the grand scale of the economy as a whole by the collapse of the

---

43   Nassim Nicholas Taleb. *The Black Swan*. Random House, 2007.

44   Harry Markowitz. *Portfolio Selection. Efficient Diversification of Investments*. Wiley, 1959.

mortgage market and the chain reaction that followed, as it became clear that the affected firms had concentrated far too much risk into mortgage-based assets such that when the mortgage market turned bad, it dragged entire firms down.

To compound the problem, and perhaps to heighten the irony, it was the aggressive behavior of the investment firms and banks that drove the mortgage market into crisis in the first place by selling millions of families into mortgages that they could not afford, and the scale of the resulting damage was so great that it affected the entire economy, and triggered the recession.

This is the classic phenomenon of a financial bubble, which is indeed also a problem of excessive correlation. To jump into the rising market, investors abandon the principle of portfolio diversity in order to reap the seductive profits looming in front of them, and pay the awful price when the collapse arrives.

In the case of your innovation portfolio, non-correlation requires your firm to be working on potential innovations that address a wide range of future market possibilities in order to assure – and here is the key point – that the available options will be useful under a wide variety of possible future conditions.

Knowing as we do about the unpredictability of change tells us that the innovation portfolio should contain a wider variety of projects-in-process than the variety of our current set of offers in the market. In other words, our innovation pipeline should be actively engaged in exploring possibilities that are outside of the current market, so that if the current market should suddenly shift, we are prepared to respond.

If you talk with innovation managers at Nokia and at Boeing, to name two companies, you'll find that they are in fact working on projects that they know will never see the light of day; as of today, however, they just don't know which ones will eventually come to market, and which will not. Only time can tell them that, and prudence requires them to prepare. Nokia's set was, in hindsight, too narrow, and burn down became an inferno that also torched its stock price. Preparing a diverse innovation portfolio is exactly what

Nokia did not do (or at least they left out the smart phone from it), and which caused the company's perceived value to fall so dramatically when Apple mastered the smart phone paradigm and Nokia had no immediate response.

This also explains another reason that pursuing only incremental innovation is not a success strategy, as incremental innovations on existing products and services are useless when the market shifts in an entirely different direction. To borrow a familiar cliché, it's not desirable to be the maker of the world's best buggy whips when all the customers have switched to cars.

Or, like Nokia, to be focused on making mobile phones cheaper when customers want them to be smarter.

Hence, as Apple has seen tremendous success with the iPhone, Nokia's stock value plummeted even when the company was still the overall market leader by volume.

Or, like GM, which was focused on the annual styling cycle when customers decided they preferred improved design, higher quality and especially better gas mileage in the 1970s and again in the early 1990s, and yet again after 2005. (Here is a situation where a more robust appreciation for history would have served the company well.)

It does take a great deal of discipline to avoid falling into the trap of optimizing the current products and services for the current market, which is an example of dangerous correlation, and to recognize that non-correlated qualities and characteristics that may be different from what's needed and wanted today may become the romantic obsession of tomorrow's market. Mastering these new qualities and characteristics *in advance* is precisely the purpose of the innovation portfolio.

The need for non-correlation and therefore broad diversity in the portfolio also reinforces the need to explore and develop ideas across all four types of innovation. Hence, large companies will create and manage portfolios for each type of innovation, and hence there will also be a fifth portfolio that is an aggregate of the other four. The mechanics of creating these portfolios will be discussed in the next chapter.

Before we get there I will just briefly note that each different type of portfolio will be managed in a different process, by different people, who have different business goals, and who are measured and possibly rewarded differently.

Hence the thoughtful design of metrics and rewards is necessary to a well-managed portfolio, and your master plan also calls for you to the design the ideal metrics by which the performance of your portfolio should be measured.   The topic of metrics will be discussed in detail in Chapter 6, as it pertains to both the innovation portfolio and the innovation process.

In Chapter 4, which follows below, I'll describe a detailed process for portfolio design, and then in Chapter 5 we'll look at a design for the broader innovation process.

the agile innovation portfolio sprint

As noted above, it's often quite effective to create each element of your master plan by using an agile innovation sprint, and the guidance embedded in the model which suggests the cycle of *understanding, divergence, convergence, prototyping, validation,* and *innospection* provides a very effective process framework to assure high quality results and rapid progress.   For the design of your portfolio, the questions to ask in the *understanding* phase of the sprint have to do with current and future needs, capabilities, risks, and opportunities.   These questions are detailed at length in the following chapter, and at the end of the chapter I'll discuss the rest of the sprint.

chapter 4

taking action:

the ideal innovation portfolio

"There is money to invest. But practically no innovation."[45]
Former Russian President Dmitry Medvedev

To design the ideal innovation portfolio we begin with the work you did in Chapter One to define your future goals, vision and strategic intent, as we see that the purpose of the portfolio is to pursue them systematically despite the uncertain world, and to overcome the problem that President Medvedev laments, which is to find the right balance between investment risk and innovation output.

So now let's put the principles and concepts we've been discussing into action. We've defined a simple process for portfolio management consisting of only 127 steps, which will enable you to do this.

Oh, no, that's not right. Happily, there are only five steps…

Step 1:   Define the *Strategic Terrain*.

---

[45] Medvedev made this comment at a government meeting on modernization on January 31, 2011. A broader description of the innovation shortfall in Russia is reported in the article, "Dreams of an iPad Economy for Russia," by Lyubov Pronina, *Bloomberg BusinessWeek*, February 3, 2011.

Step 2:   Determine the *Performance Requirements* for the
          innovation effort.
Step 3:   Design the *Innovation Selection* process.
Step 4:   *Build* the Portfolio.
Step 5:   Make *Ongoing Improvements*.

Once you've chosen which projects to invest in, you'll manage them, continuing to learn as you develop new products and services that become the innovations. The details of that process are the subject of Chapter 5, the innovation process, but it's important to note that you've already begun working on it through the very act of designing your portfolio.

linear processes and non-linear thinking

The sequential nature of time serves us by preventing everything from happening all at once, but it also presents a danger when we're engaged in complex activities that involve learning.

The danger exposes the conceptual flaw in the process that I'll describe below, because if we understand that the process has to be a rigidly linear series of steps that must be followed in one and only one sequence, then we won't succeed.

Since the pursuit of innovation is a learning process, then it would be ludicrous to follow any set of steps slavishly and only in the same sequence each time. Instead, it's entirely plausible that you will learn something in step 5, say, that would affect how you would prefer to approach steps 1 or 2. This would naturally cause you to go back and revisit those earlier steps, and voila, the linearity is suitably disrupted.

(As a small but pertinent aside, how many times have you been in a meeting when an interesting idea came up in the conversation but it was decisively killed when someone said, "Well, yes, but we won't be able to deal with that until the next budget cycle, you know...." The "budget cycle" argument delivers the *coup de grace*, stifling even promising and perhaps important ideas / innovations from getting any attention now. This is not an intelligent approach, although it is common, because slavishly following a linear thinking process can decrease responsiveness and increase organizational risk.)

Writing and reading are also linear activities, as the words on the page or the screen are obliged to follow one after the other in sequence. But in your brain the words and concepts are anything but linear. The human mind is so powerful precisely because it works by association, as one idea or experience reminds you of another, and it is precisely these connections that lead to insights, which in turn lead to innovations; learning and problem-solving by association has been the engine by which civilization progresses.

Examples of this brilliant power of the mind are all around us, and a few examples may help to remind us of the importance of associative thinking.

On the way to discovering penicillin, Louis Pasteur was investigating the nature of antibodies and recognized a potential solution in a moldy petri dish, which many others had not recognized. He is rightly famous for his comment that "luck favors the prepared mind," as indeed it does; "preparation" is a process of pre-populating the associative links, without knowing which potential links may eventually lead to useful connections.

Let's take a practical glance at this – have you ever been in a brainstorming session that went flat? Chances are that happened because the set of possible solutions you were working with wasn't broad enough, that you hadn't pre-populated your thinking process with a diverse enough set of concepts and models to draw from. Good brainstorming requires good raw material, and you can't do it well with the same old ideas you've already heard a thousand times. Brainstorming does work when you see the problem or the solution set differently.

Archimedes, he who supposedly ran through town naked while shouting "Eureka!" when he saw the problem differently, was also inspired by associative learning, in his case concerning the nature of water displacement. While the specifics vary from story to story, the broader pattern is remarkably consistent: someone is working on a question or problem, and the solution is elusive. An unexpected event then occurs, which provides the previously-missing new information, and which illuminates the problem in a new way, and the solution is suddenly there in a flash.

Computers do not do this; only people do. And we do it all the time.

Steven Johnson explores this difference between computers and people in his book, *Emergence*. "The human mind is poorly equipped to deal with problems that need to be solved serially – one calculation after another – given that neurons require a 'reset time' of about 5 milliseconds, meaning that neurons are capable of only two hundred calculations per second. (A modern PC can do millions of calculations per second.) But unlike most computers, the brain is a massively parallel system, with 100 billion neurons working away at the same time. That parallelism allows the barin to perform amazing feats of pattern recognition such as remembering faces or creating metaphors."[46]

Johnson goes on to quote Ray Kurzweil's book, *The Age of Spiritual Machines*[47]: "Because each individual neuron is so slow, 'we don't have time ... to think too many new thoughts when we are pressed to make a decision. The human brain relies on precomputing its analyses and storing them for future reference. We then use our pattern-recognition capability to recognize a situation as compatible to one we have thought about and then draw upon our previously considered conclusions.'"

The act of pre-populating the mind with a large scope of relevant information and patterns is a powerful enabler of innovative results when we marshall that power in the search for new patterns.

---

[46]   Steven Johnson. *Emergence: The Connected Lives of Ants, Brains, Cities, and Software*. Touchstone, 2001. P. 127.

[47]   Ray Kurzweil. *The Age of Spiritual Machines: When Computers Exceed Human Intelligence*. Penguin Books, 1999.

So if we're going to do a credible job of managing innovation, then we have to enable and empower the mind's unstoppable associative capacities to reach their full flower, and not enslave its magnificence as though it were a dull, repetitive machine that can only do things in a rote fashion. Feed the mind richly to get richly innovative rewards.

In light of this I would also therefore simply like to remind you as you read the following passages, that it would be a mistake to follow a process like this, even one that's labeled step 1, step 2, etc., without paying attention to the nonlinear nature of genuine learning. Oh, and that reminds me – Chapter 5 also expresses a sequence of steps for the innovation process; please don't follow that one slavishly, either.

step 1: define the strategic terrain

In Chapters 1 and 2 we explored the strategic terrain in which your organization operates presently, and in which it may operate in the future. The agile strategy sprint you already completed (if you did) has given you a lot of insight about the threats and opportunities you face. This then becomes the essential context in which you will design your portfolio.

The intimate link between strategy and innovation is a two way street, as the possibilities of strategy will be informed by the possibilities of innovation, and likewise innovation efforts will naturally be directed toward targets you've already identified as strategic.

You also thought carefully about the action steps suggested there, so you've already grappled with the strategic factors, and you should have a clear picture of how the landscape is evolving.

Let me recap a few highlights here:

To manage the innovation process you'll have to understand the factors that are driving change in your industry, and assess how they're likely to impact your organization in the future. This will help you to get a better look at both your vulnerabilities and your opportunities.

Is technology driving your industry forward?   If your core products use computer chips, then the progressive improvement of chip performance creates strategic opportunities and risks for your firm. (Potato chips, however, are different.)

Or perhaps it's demographic factors, such as the aging of the population, that are central concerns.   In Chapter 2 I mentioned that in Japan the overall population is forecast to decline from about 130 million to about half that, 65 million, by the end of this century.   This will have a decisive impact on every Japanese company, and on every company doing business in Japan. (Does that leave many companies out?)

Do natural resources play a key role in your company's economic life? If you're in energy, mining, food, or chemicals, then resource cost and availability are at the center of your thinking.

Is yours a service business? Then do you know where you're going to recruit future generations of employees? And do you know how much training they'll need, and where they're going to get that training from?

Each industry, and within it each type of company, has it's own issues, and you've doubtless already spent a great deal of time thinking about this. (You're certain to spend a great deal more as time goes on.)   Your goal has been to develop a strategic perspective, a viewpoint that explains what's happening, and why.

You're not necessarily going to be right about it, and although it's probably more fun to be right, the point isn't so much about right and wrong as it is about improving your sensitivity to change, and being prepared to take action because you've already thought things through.

Then, when things do change (which they will), and one of your key assumptions is perhaps invalidated by subsequent events, you can say, "Cool! We didn't expect that! Now, what does it mean, and how do we have to adjust our thinking?"

Too often, however, the key strategic assumptions remain

hidden, and the consequences when they are overturned are therefore disastrous. So, by example, going back to the banking collapse, the two key hidden assumptions underneath the whole mess were that the mortgage market was permanently stable, and that the self-interest of the banking institutions constituted a valid mechanism for self-regulation. What actually happened was that the motive to earn amazing profits drove the underlying market away from sound practices and therefore towards instability, and the same lust for profits drove the banks beyond the limits of prudence and they put themselves at risk. Or, to put it bluntly, Greenspan's assumptions blew up in his face, and in everyone's face. Don't let that happen to you!

You also need to factor in your position in the industry. Cisco, as a leader in networking hardware, has different strategic options and strategic challenges than Juniper Networks or Alcatel, which in the current market configuration are chasing Cisco. Likewise, GM's options are different than Toyota's, and Southwest Airlines faces a different world than United, Air France, or Emirates.

Later on, when you've been running your innovation portfolio process for some time you'll naturally undertake periodic reviews, and you should revisit these factors to verify that your assumptions about them are still valid, and that they are the pertinent strategic criteria to consider.

step 2: determine the performance requirements for the innovation effort

A few pages ago we discussed the burn-down rate; it's a key element to assess as you design your portfolio, because it tells you what the innovation portfolios need to achieve in terms of financial contribution to your firm's growth in the short term.

So how fast is the market changing?

Will the rate of change in the market tell you how fast your products and services are becoming obsolete?

Can you draw a reasoned graph that shows the consequences of obsolescence, in the form of declining future revenues and profits?

Even if you can only guess, you still have to take a stab at it. We'll examine the specific nature of the changes in step 3 of the process, and learn from them what sorts of innovations might make sense to pursue. The purpose here is simply to give a specific form to your knowledge that things are changing and you'd better be preparing new sources of revenues and profits.

Knowing the rate of obsolescence will then tell you with at least moderate confidence how much new revenue and profit you'll have to create in the future simply to stay even with where you are now.

But of course it's not enough to stay even. Investors expect growth, and any company that doesn't deliver growth will be penalized. So your innovation efforts will have to not only replace the eroding revenues of existing products and services to prevent the pie from shrinking, but will also have to provide new revenue sources to grow the overall size of the pie as well.

So here in step 2, calculate the revenue and profit targets that your innovation portfolio should be designed to achieve.

You also need to know your cost of capital, and there is most likely a benchmark minimum ROI that all of your organization's investments are expected to achieve.

subjectivity

By now you understand that the decisions you have to make at each step of the innovation process necessarily involve assessments of risk and varying likelihood of success across a huge range of variables. There may be few facts to rely on, but a myriad of opinions and speculations, which is to say, a lot of guesswork. Hence, most of these decisions and factors are based on subjective judgments.

Consequently, the assessments and decisions that you'll make offer structure and guidance to your thinking process, and they must be made explicit so that they can be tested as you move forward through the process. Without explicitness, your process will lack rigor, and consequently it will be impossible to improve systematically.

to lead or to follow

A key factor that will influence your portfolio design is the realization that at any given time in any given market only a few critical value drivers are most important to customers, and your company may or may not be in position to deliver on those preferences. Whichever company happens to have the right mix typically gains a temporary advantage, with the emphasis on "temporary" since both technology and the market's needs often change, and usually without much warning.

But it's not just the preferences of customers that matter. The capital you have available will significantly affect your ambitions, and so will your intellectual property, the customer base you're currently supporting, and the capabilities of your team.

Despite all of these variables, though, there are really just three choices concerning your overall innovation strategy (although in practice they will naturally support many variations).

Option #1 is to lead.
Leaders create new products and services in advance of the competition, usually by anticipating the needs of customers, and thereby gain competitive advantage.

Option #2 is to follow.
Followers wait for other firms to set the pace and then they cleverly copy them. Lest your instinct is to think less of the followers, please note that many of the most admired firms in history have been successful followers, and it's a valid approach in many situations.

Option #3 is to choose a niche and defend it vigorously

The firms that have limited innovation resources usually have to choose a portion of the market where they can carefully cultivate a customer base and build some protection around their offer.   They may take advantage of specialized or local knowledge, or enhanced levels of service, or an offer that is so specifically targeted that customers are happy to remain loyal.

leaders

Some companies are so proficient at innovation that they take the lead in a market and remain there for extended periods of time; they lead the race wire to wire. Usually they succeed at this because they have effectively anticipated customer needs.

We have already discussed the enviable characteristics of many leaders, including Cisco and Wal-Mart, but almost all of them also faltered at some point in time, a list that includes Coca-Cola, IBM, Blockbuster, Nokia, Sears, and Boeing.

Maintaining leadership over an extended period takes a great deal of luck, or skill, or both, to create a defensible competitive advantage that endures. It requires exceptional discipline and a very strong innovation culture to adapt over extended periods, and while it can be done, and it's certainly worth aspiring to, the challenges should not be underestimated.

And as I have noted, the number one challenge is mindset.

followers

It's so tough to stay in front that many companies prefer to direct their innovation efforts in response to what competitors are doing. The difficulty of maintaining market leadership is usually high, and as time passes leaders see all sorts of challengers emerging from the dark, surrounding forests to lay claim to this or that part of their markets. Followers wait, and watch, and when something good emerges they copy it, hoping to leap past the originator, the approach that Peter Drucker labeled "fast-follower."

Spanish retailer Zara perfected the fast follower approach in the clothing industry by setting up a manufacturing and distribution system capable of producing the latest fashions very quickly, enabling Zara designers to copy high fashion styles and distribute the knock-offs to its stores worldwide within weeks.

In rapidly-changing technology markets, the evolution of the smart phone market shows the vulnerability of a leader's position pretty clearly. After its introduction in 2007 Apple iPhone was definitely the world-leading smart phone, but Android entered the market a year later, in 2008. By 2016, Android sales made up about 80% of the total smart phone market, while the iPhone's were about 15%.[48] While the Android phone's design owes a great deal to the iPhone, as the look and feel of the device is clearly a copy of the approach that Apple pioneered so effectively, Android's business model is proving to be much more effective in achieving market share than Apple's, but conversely Apple isn't too sad about its gigantic profit margins, and has indeed throughout its history made the strategic choice to opt for profit margins over volume.

Hence, while a current leader enjoys the front running position in an existing market structure, innovations and copies may emerge that signify changes to the market structure; would-be leaders are vigorously searching for these opportunities, and when they find one it often provokes a major change, a structural change in the market.

The transition between two structures is frequently the occasion when an established leader is displaced by a new competitor.

The emergence of the iPhone and its predecessor the iPod are both examples of structural change. The iPhone definitively altered the overall cell phone market, and so did the iPod. But shouldn't it have been Sony that dominated the MP3 player market? The

---

[48]   Savov, Vlad. "The entire history of iPhone vs. Android summed up in two charts." Jun 1, 2016. http://www.theverge.com/2016/6/1/11836816/iphone-vs-android-history-charts.

company had decades of experience in making brilliantly conceived and designed miniature music devices, having produced millions of tiny radios and Walkmans, practically inventing the category, and leading it wire to wire. And Sony owned BMG music, one the largest music publishing houses in the world. All it would have taken is for the company to put A and B together for Sony to dominate the MP3 era.

But Sony didn't do it; Apple did, creating the iPod and iTunes, which remain the leaders today, having so far turned back challenges from Sony, Dell, and Microsoft, among others.

It is worth noting that you could also say that Apple followed, copied, and outperformed Sony; how you frame it may just depend on your time horizon, and your knowledge of history.

The benefits of following are also evident in the story of Netscape and Microsoft. Do you even remember pioneering Netscape, which introduced the Navigator browser and rocketed to prominence in 1994? So many millions of people downloaded early versions of Netscape every month that the company was able to go public just 9 months after introducing its signature product.

Why did people choose Netscape? Simply because it worked better. This gave the company a brilliant head start in the browser market, which of course came to the attention of Bill Gates at Microsoft. Realizing what was happening, Gates quickly organized a crash program to create Internet Explorer, which quickly caught and then passed Netscape. Many observers have alleged that Microsoft used illegal business tactics to manipulate the market by forcing PC manufacturers to bundle Explorer with their machines while excluding Navigator, and there was a great deal of courtroom activity on this dispute. Nevertheless, by 1998 Netscape had lost its leadership position and had to seek refuge as a subsidiary of AOL.

AOL itself had pioneered the internet as a mass market medium, but was soon overtaken when free email services were introduced by clever start up companies that were immediately gobbled up by Yahoo, Microsoft, and Google. They displaced AOL's pay-for-access subscription business model, rendering it obsolete.

Meanwhile, Google's search algorithm was introduced in 1998, grew rapidly, and the company went public in 2004 and continued to grow quickly thereafter. The explosive success of Google's search engine made AOL's closed world and clunky interface obsolete, which rendered AOL's Netscape acquisition irrelevant; Netscape was eventually disbanded in 2003 ending a tumultuous ten year run, having been caught and passed by its competitors not once, but twice. (It continues to live on, however, in the Mozilla browser, which is embedded in Firefox.)

In 2008, with the internet world still evolving very rapidly, Yahoo spurned a merger offer from Microsoft based on its belief that it would do better on its own. But it proved to be a poor choice, as the company fell into decline while Google's search algorithm continued to produce better results than Yahoo, and Google's business model attracted more users.

With Google continuing to grow, Microsoft turned its attention to the search engine, and introduced Bing in 2009 in an attempt to take market share away from Google. After the first year, however, Bing remained stuck at 3% of the global market, while Google maintained 85%.

These are particularly fast moving markets in which it's rare for any company to sustain leadership indefinitely. So will another company be able to replace Google in the leadership position? As we see that innovations come in waves, leading to changes in the beliefs and attitudes of customers, and which in turn alter how they feel about various competing offers, it's entirely possible that one day Google will be pushed aside. Will it be Facebook? Twitter? Or a company that doesn't even exist today?

It's fascinating to see these changes occurring when you're on the outside, but often frightening from inside; no matter how enormous your competitive advantage is today, it may erode to nothingness tomorrow. Who's out there lurking, waiting to leap past your company?

own your niche

Not many companies have the resources to invest in innovation on the scale of Google, or Microsoft, or Cisco. But they do know that innovation is critically important to their success, and to their survival, so they invest in innovation selectively.

This is the third approach to innovation strategy, picking a spot where innovation can improve your business and focusing your innovation efforts there.   This strategy is available to every company, no matter how small, and no matter what the industry.

For example, can you innovate in hair cutting? I wasn't sure, until I realized that the national discount chains are indeed a business model innovation targeting people who want it done inexpensively. And recently I read that the founders of a hair salon in LA noticed that customers had basically two options, high end salons or discount chains. So they opened a service in the middle that was successful from the start by targeting the needs of their customers very precisely.[49]

Can you innovate in hotels? Of course. Hotel companies are innovating all the time to attract customers with just the right combination of comfort and style amenities, and frequent guest programs to create loyalty. Have you ever chosen a hotel for the loyalty points towards a free room (or an airline for the frequent flyer miles)? I admit, I do it all the time.

Can you innovate in food? This also happens all the time. The typical supermarket carries about 50,000 products, but the food industry produces 15,000 additional new ones each year.   It's shotgun innovation and trial by fire to see which products survive, from incremental additions to existing lines (a new flavor of Fritos) to entirely new product concepts, to entirely new retail chains like Whole Foods, which is also defining its own niche by focusing on health foods and rolling up local stores and regional chains to aggregate economy of scale.

---

[49]   *Entrepreneur* Magazine, Oct 10, 2010, p 20.

How about house cleaning? I didn't realize that anyone could innovate in house cleaning as a one-person business, because after all a clean house is a clean house. But then I learned about my friend's quite innovative maid, who brings fresh flowers each week when she cleans the house, and also cooks up some fresh bread or cookies while she's there, leaving her customers' houses smelling fresh. My friend says she'd give up Starbucks (OMG!)[50] before she'd give up her thoughtful and innovative maid.

These few examples are intended to show that innovation can indeed happen in every industry, and if you look carefully you'll see it occurring throughout your industry, too. But it's not happening in every company, and the stragglers are likely to fall farther behind.

the dreary stragglers

There are other approaches to innovation, but neither of them are appealing.

Some companies try half-heartedly but never succeed at developing innovations ahead of their competitors. Even their copies are uninteresting, and while they may have strong technical skills, they lack fire, or insight, or innovative instincts. Or perhaps they have a business model which casts them as contented followers rather than fast followers. These companies tend to become marginalized, and fade away as change accelerates.

And the last group consists of those that fail at innovation because they fail to try. They lack nerve, or talent, or awareness, and probably capital as well. These companies are not good bets for survival.

There's not much more to say about these two approaches, and so unless they get inspired to pursue innovation and make huge leaps in their skills they'll remain uninteresting from an innovation perspective, and vulnerable from a strategic one. They'll be

---

50   "OMG" is texting language used among young people that stands for "Oh my God!" In other words, a big surprise.

permanent followers, and many of them will be early casualties of change.

Companies and industries are too complex to merely select a single strategy to apply across the board. Inevitably you choose specific strategies for specific markets; in some you lead, in others you follow, and in others still you pick your spots or stay out of the innovation race entirely.

So the point of this discussion in terms of your innovation portfolio is to choose thoughtfully and explicitly. What, you should ask, does it take to be a leader in this industry? Do we have the capability to achieve that? Or are we better following, and copying? Or defending a specific niche?

step 3: design the innovation selection process

Once you have a perspective on how things are changing and which strategy you intend to follow, then you can decide what factors to emphasize in designing your overall innovation portfolio and selecting individual projects.

We often group these factors into three categories:

- External strategic drivers
- Internal innovation criteria
- Risk factors.

The three lists identify the criteria according to which you will evaluate the merits of individual ideas, as shown on the form a couple pages below.

By establishing the criteria in advance, you'll avoid the danger that a given idea is the pet project of a senior leader and gets supports beyond its inherent merits. Instead, all proposed projects will be evaluated (or re-evaluated, if this is a review session looking at an existing portfolio) according the same set of criteria, and the scores that they receive can be legitimately compared to each other.

external strategic factors

The external factors that you'll use to evaluate individual ideas and projects will depend on the characteristics of the specific industries and markets that you compete in. Develop a list of the criteria that are important for you.

As an example, these six, derived from the discussion in Chapter 2 concerning the driving forces of change, may (or may not) be relevant to your business:

1. Leverages the Digital Revolution
2. Leverages the Climate Revolution
3. Leverages the Energy Revolution
4. Leverages the Urban Revolution
5. Addresses Cultural Change
6. Addresses the Counter–Revolution.

Remember your list could be different … should be different.

internal innovation criteria

Here the focus is on the characteristics of a given idea and the capacity of your organization to transform that idea into a compelling innovation opportunity.

The following criteria *could* belong on your list; there may be others as well:

1. Uniqueness of the idea
2. Probability of technical success
3. Probability of commercial success
4. R&D cost to completion or to next decision point
5. Time to completion or to next decision point
6. Intellectual property protection or ease for competitors to copy
7. Durability of competitive advantage
8. Durability as an innovation platform*
9. Leverages existing competences and capabilities.

* I haven't yet discussed the concept of the innovation platform. Briefly, it's a basis on which other innovations can be developed, and may therefore constitute more desirable investment than a stand-alone innovation. For example, the core iPod technology concept is used in many different iPod devices, as well as the iPhone and iPad, because elements of the hardware and software of iPod enable a wide variety of devices to function. Similarly, auto companies typically design a basic frame, engine, and chassis configuration upon which they can then build many different coupes, sedans, and convertibles. On the outside the cars look different; on the inside they have significant similarities, which saves a lot of money in development and in manufacturing. Platform thinking was popularized by Black and Decker's power tools division, which developed a standardized battery system for tools that enabled it to significantly reduce development costs for many derivative power tool products.[51]

risk factors

Innovators face many potential types of risk, among them the technical risks that would-be innovations cannot be made to work, the financial risks of development cost or market acceptance (or more accurately, non-acceptance), the organizational risks of non-performance or the lack of requisite talent and skills, competitive risks if your competitor beats you to market or develops a superior offering, and of course the macro risks related to the driving forces of change.

Your appetite for risk is a function of many factors, which might include:

- The rate of change
- Your competitive position
- The historical or competitive rate of investment in innovation in your industry

---

[51]   Marc Meyer and Al Lehnerd. *The Power of Product Platforms*. Free Press, 1997.

Innovation Portfolio Evaluation	Idea or Project Name:					Project #

Step 1: External Factors

Strategic Factors: What are the key external, strategic factors affecting our business?	Weight (1, 2, 3, 5, 8)	Rating (1, 2, 3, 5, 8)	Score (Weight x Rating)
1. Leverages Digitization			
2. Addresses Climate Change			
3. Leverages New Energy Markets			
4. Leverages Urbanization			
5. Aligned with Culture Change			
Total			A

Step 2: Internal Factors

Internal Factors: What are the key internal factors affecting our business?	Weight (1, 2, 3, 5, 8)	Rating (1, 2, 3, 5, 8)	Score (Weight x Rating)
1. Implementability			
2. Uniqueness			
3. Brand Value Enhancement			
4. Speed to Market			
5. Leverages Existing Platforms			
Total			B

Reward Total

A + B / Out of ___

Step 3: Risk Factors

Risk Criteria: What are the key risk factors specific to this idea or project?	Weight (1, 2, 3, 5, 8)	Rating (1, 2, 3, 5, 8)	Score (Weight x Rating)
1. Technical Risk (it actually cannot be done)			
2. Market Risk (market does not accept)			
3. Concentration Risk (we become too concentrated)			
4. Timing Risk (we miss the market window)			
5. Financial Risk (too expensive)			
Total			

Risk Total

Out of ___

Sample Innovation Portfolio Evaluation Form

Figure 11

External Strategic Factors, Internal Innovation Criteria, and Risk Factors in the Innovation Portfolio

The criteria listed under each category are examples only. Yours will most likely be different. The external ones shown here are based on the topics covered in Chapter 2, The Driving Forces of Change. It's not necessarily the case that the highest scoring ideas are the best ones, nor that lowest scoring ideas are the worst, but the process of determining the scores should be informative in your discussion and decision making process.

- The strength of your balance sheet
- The personal views and attitudes of senior managers concerning risk
- The current economic situation
- Your perception of the overall risks and opportunities that your organization has before it.

weighting and scoring

Some characteristics are critically important to your business, much more important than others, so weighting the various factors will put emphasis where it belongs.

Determining the right weight is likely to be a fairly simple discussion, and it may not be difficult to reach agreement. However, if there is a wide range of disagreement then this may indicate that people hold differing assumptions about the structure of the market. This is a marvelous discovery, because if there are differing assumptions then someone is probably wrong, and you have arrived at a key point of learning. When you figure out who's right, and which assumptions are therefore valid or invalid, you may be able to make significant improvement in your basic underlying strategy or strategic intent.

However, you may need to devise a specific experiment in order to figure that out.

Another reason the scoring tool is useful is that when you review the portfolio on a periodic basis, perhaps quarterly, if any factors in the external environment have changed significantly you can reexamine the affected projects to see if the changes alter your scores, and by implication if some projects should be elevated in importance, or reduced. Perhaps changes in the external environment make a given project less attractive, or more so, such that a project which was only nice-to-have is now suddenly indispensable. Or conversely, maybe a project that was a top priority imperative last year is suddenly irrelevant. Projects may gain or lose perceived value and can be managed accordingly by adding or removing resources to accelerate results or stop the work entirely; this is a good thing, because it means that a disciplined process is helping you to optimize the use of your resources.

Note also the scoring model for the weight and rating columns – rather than a simple 1 – 5 score, we suggest you use 1, 2, 3, 5, 8 scoring. The purpose is accentuate the high scores and make them stand out strongly, as this has been shown to help considerably in the process of identifying the best options. (Technically this is known as Fibonacci scoring, named for the Italian mathematician, and widely adopted in Agile technique. This is also used in "planning poker," another tool from the software industry.)

So let's say that you're looking a portfolio of 25 projects, and everyone on your team has scored them, and the scores have been compiled so you know the average for each criterion, and you know the range. Further, everyone has chosen the two or three that they think are most important, and the ones they think aren't worth pursuing at all. There's a pile of papers sitting on the table that contains all this information.

Figure 12
Evaluating an Innovation Portfolio

First, please, put the papers on the wall so you can see all 25 at once (as you see in figure 12), and group them according to a criterion such as highest scoring to lowest, or group all the ones that anyone has selected for the top 3 list or their bottom list. Chances are there will be some that fall into more than one category; put those separately, maybe in the middle.

Now it should be much easier to see the patterns, and it's therefore possible to have a reasonable and fruitful discussion.

- Are there more projects than you can fund?
- Are there fewer good projects than you want?
- Are you weighted too heavily towards particular markets, or towards particular types of innovations?

All of this should be visually evident, enabling you to focus on portfolio design and decision making rather than just on the details of particular projects and personal preferences.

So let's say you've gone through this process and you've agreed on the 3 best projects. The others aren't right for now, but they may become relevant in the future, so the information about them is indexed and archived somewhere readily accessible so you can get at it later if you need to.

In the mean time you've got three possible new projects, plus a lot already under way. Now you need to look at them all together as a portfolio, and assess the risk – reward profile of the portfolio as a whole to make sure your risks are not correlated, and that your projects are sufficiently diverse in targets and in approaches.

Your confidence in the ability of your firm's innovation process and innovation managers to achieve the needed results is also going to be a significant factor. For example, a history of non-success may reflect extensive or prolonged incapacity, and will have already led to a bias towards acquisitions. Following processes as described here should begin to remedy the situation, and over time the results should improve and your confidence in it should increase. But that will not happen immediately.

As you integrate all these factors together in your thinking, an ideal portfolio will take shape, and it will be specific to your company and your industry.

There are two lenses to apply when planning a portfolio at this level of detail. The first is the balance between risk and reward, while the second concerns the balance between the four types of innovation.

the risk-reward matrix

A simple 2x2 matrix allows you to consider the balance between risk and reward, especially if you haven't already thought about the two together. The model is self-evident - the lower left quadrant is the wrong place to invest, while the upper right is usually very attractive.

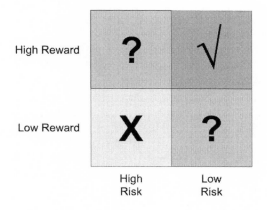

Figure 13
The Risk Reward Matrix[52]

(Note that for the moment we have probably set aside the

---

52   Some of the concepts presented in this section have been adapted from the book *Third Generation R&D* by Philip Roussel, Kamal Saad, and Tamara Erickson, 1991. Chapter 6 is particularly helpful.

benefit of the learning as a criterion (which we of course expect from every project) because now we're into assessing the financial and market perspectives. If we want to go ahead with a project because of what we will learn from it, absent the financial rewards, then that's fine, but we shouldn't weigh down our portfolio with those projects. Let's call them "pure research" and put them in a separate category.)

So what kind of risks are we talking about?

A given idea may not work out, which would involve cost to the organization in terms of lost investment of time and money.

Well, of course it might not work out, but often we've got to try to find out, and there's no guarantee that we'll get it right the first time.

That might lead to a second try, and then a third, etc., until we do get it right, and attain the eventual payoff. But it's also possible that any given idea leads to no specific payoff at all, that it's a dead end.

Ideally, how would you distribute your investment?

Some projects, strategic goals, or initiatives that are mandatory may not fall in the upper right quadrant, and they may even be in the lower left. How can you mitigate those risks?

Once upon a time we were working through the portfolio design process with a team of people who worked in a financial services company, and of course we introduced this matrix. Since they'd never used it before we tried it out with the ideas that they were already working on, the existing portfolio.

As we plotted the location of each idea, one after another, the warm light of awareness began to dawn around the room; the majority of the current projects fell into the least desirable quadrant, they were high risk and low reward.

Nervous laughter was followed by some chin rubbing. "Well," one of them said awkwardly, speaking for everyone, "That's interesting...."

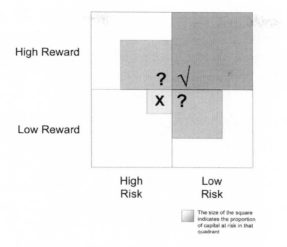

High Reward

Low Reward

High
Risk

Low
Risk

The size of the square
indicates the proportion
of capital at risk in that
quadrant

Figure 14
A Weighted Risk-Reward Matrix

Now that you know what you're aiming for, you have also established the necessary context to evaluate the projects that you're already working on.

Use the matrix to assess each project that's in the current portfolio. This will of course be subjective, but that's inherent in this process. The point here is to hone your judgment and to engage in a constructive conversation about what constitutes suitable reward and acceptable risk, and where individual projects fall on the matrix relative to the others.

The next step is to identify the quantity of funds that are currently committed to or being invested in each project in each quadrant. You can represent each project as a circle, with the size of the circle corresponding to the amount of money that you're planning to commit, or the amount already spent, depending on the question you want to address, as shown in figure 15.

This will show you the distribution of risk-reward across the entire portfolio, by project.

Lastly, you can now make a square in each quadrant to aggregate the individual projects, and size the square accordingly. This will enable you to see at a glance how your portfolio is distributed, both by number of projects per quadrant and relative investment per quadrant.

How does it look? Are you happy with the distribution, or is it out of balance?

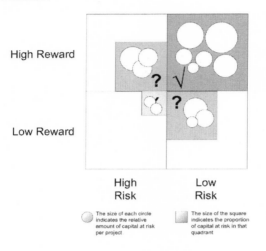

Figure 15
A Weighted Risk-Reward Matrix Showing Individual Projects
A circle represents each project in the portfolio, and the size of the circle corresponds to the relative capital investment it entails. The quadrant squares represent aggregate capital in that quadrant from all the projects.

four types of innovation means five portfolios

I've already mentioned the need for balance across the four different types of innovations, breakthrough, incremental, business model, and new venture innovation. You will go through the process above for each of the four types, and then again to aggregate them into the fifth, overall portfolio.

The majority of overall investment shown here is in Incremental innovations, and the balance distributed across the other three types. But what do the dynamics of your industry call for?

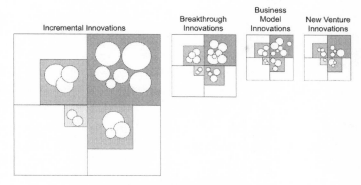

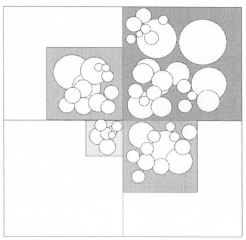

Figure 16
Five Innovation Portfolios

step 4: build the portfolio

Now all the diligent prep work you've done comes together. You're making decisions on your existing and proposed projects in order to determine which are most attractive. You document why you think so, so that as the work proceeds you can validate your assumptions and your decisions, or discover that it's time to reconsider based on what you have learned along the way.

The process I've described assumes that this will be done in a collaborative setting, involving a group of people who represent many different areas of expertise from within your organization, and who therefore can share their thoughts and assessments from many different points of view.

It will be very helpful to have a facilitator involved in designing and running this session. Regardless of how much we remind ourselves that it's a learning process, we also know that opinions may be influenced by factors including ego needs, idea-fixation, career path ambitions, pet peeves and pet projects, and personal visions of the future, so a neutral facilitator's guidance can help the effort to remain focused on creating future value for the organization as a whole.

The facilitator is likely to be someone whom we would call an "Innovation Champion," a term that will be explained in detail in Chapter 7. The role of the facilitator is not to comment on the merit of the ideas, but rather to help guide the process so that it's efficient for all participants, fair for everyone and each idea, and optimally productive for the organization. Facilitators also make sure that all the underlying information has been gathered – weightings agreed upon, assessments prepared, numbers aggregated and averaged, ranges calculated, and all those pieces of paper have been posted on the wall.

In the end, the actual decisions about going forward or not going forward on any particular project may reside with individual managers or small teams, but the input of a larger group should help to make the best possible decisions.

evaluating individual ideas

For each idea under consideration, the idea manager or idea owner should present an overview, the heart of the idea, to an evaluation team or innovation committee.

They can bring with them an already-completed data sheet describing the project, along with the information that I presented above as Table 1. However, sometimes the need to "fill out a form" is a barrier, and in that case you may choose to invite them to come and share their idea while team members or the facilitator document the salient points of their idea in the appropriate parts of the collection form.

The person or team that brings the idea should have been asked to think about the portfolio model, and should be prepared to state their opinions about where their project belongs concerning the type of innovation it is, and the quadrant on the risk/reward matrix where it resides. And they should be prepared to talk about how fast it can progress through the innovation funnel from idea (or wherever it is now) to completion. (The details of the funnel are presented below, in Chapter 5.)

The team should discuss the idea and the nature of the opportunity it represents. It's not necessary to reach consensus at this stage, as healthy disagreement about the future value of an idea is normal and natural.

- Does everyone agree about the risk-reward quadrant? If not, in what ways do they disagree?
- Can a small investment in experimentation resolve the disagreement?
- Does the group agree with the owner's assessment of risk? Can the scope of risk be validated in some way?
- How does the project affect to the overall Risk/Reward matrix? Is it an important contribution? Or is it too risky? Too slow?
- Is the potential return nicely attractive? Or insufficient?

All investments that are seriously considered should be plotted on the risk-reward matrix, and the totals recalculated to show what the new balance would be if the project were to go forward.

For each proposed idea, participants may also have creative ideas for improvements, further research, etc.

Other factors to consider may include:

- Timelines: Will these projects deliver value at the right time in terms of market demand and the pace of competitive innovation?
- Risk: Do we have the right balance of risk?
- People: Are the right people running or contributing to these projects?

Significant ideas or even good ones that are in need of further development could become the topics for focused workshops, during which the implications and possibilities will be explored in greater detail. This will also help the ideators to prepare the next steps, which may include business plans, customer research, tacit knowledge research, etc.

At Shell Oil, the game changer process was developed to help people with "big ideas" to explore these possibilities and turn the best ones into business plans that are then considered for funding by an internal venture board. Engineers are coached through the process, which occurs in a series of highly structured two day workshops that take place over a period of a few months.[54]

step 5: make ongoing improvements

By managing their portfolios over time using a process like this, a team of executives and their colleagues can significantly improve the portfolio's performance. And as they engage this type of thinking they get more in sync with the evolving market, and better at identifying and supporting the projects that have greatest

---

[54]   http://www.shell.com/home/content/innovation/bright_ideas/game_changer/

potential, and certainly better at shaping the future of their enterprises.

The organization also builds broad new capabilities in innovation as more and more people are drawn to participate in this process, which thereby nurtures the innovation culture that is the subject of Chapters 7 and 8.

While the first few cycles through the portfolio design process may have some awkwardness and even some false starts, like any skill this one requires practice to achieve mastery, and the benefits of mastery are so significant that the first unsteady steps are well worth enduring to attain the greater prizes that await.

the agile innovation portfolio sprint

What would an agile portfolio spring look like? It would in fact be a thoughtful effort to accomplish the work described in Steps 1 – 3 above.   Designs for the performance requirements and the selection process will be informed by the strategic context, and by the questions raised in those sections above. For each step you can identify a set of topics around which you must build your *understanding*, use these as the basis of a creative *divergence*, and then *converge* to an actionable set of concepts.

The work of *prototyping* and *validation* should probably be your initial efforts at Step 4, the building of the portfolio itself, perhaps through a few evaluation sessions looking at proposed ideas and seeking to classify them and select those with the top potential. Step 6, the *innospective*, will support your efforts to continually improve the contents of the portfolio as well as the ongoing conduct of your portfolio building process.

the last word…

During the early stages of the development of an idea, its future value is almost entirely a matter of speculation. As work is done to refine ideas in pursuit of business value, the key to success is learning, as the learning shapes the myriad design decisions that are inevitably needed.

The innovation process therefore seeks to optimize the learning that is achieved, and to capture what has been learned to improve the idea in focus, and for the benefit of the overall innovation process, as well as for the portfolio management process.

Innovation portfolio management is like venture capital investing, early stage investing, where it's impossible to precisely predict the winners, but nevertheless a few great successes will more than make up for many failures.

If we knew which projects were going to fail, then of course we'd stop working on them. But we don't know, and that's the charm of pursuing innovation, as well as its unceasing annoyance.

In fact, a healthy percentage of projects *should* fail, because failure is an indication that we're pushing the limits of our current understanding hard and persistently enough to be sure that we are extracting every last bit of value from every situation, and at the same time preparing for a broad range of unanticipated futures.

Given these factors, the process of creating, developing, and managing innovation portfolios shouldn't be handled from the CFO's perspective as a purely financial matter since these mandatory investments include a greater degree of ambiguity than most other forms of investment. Instead, the finance office and the chief innovation officer are partners in the process.

Discipline is essential to success, and so is encouragement. At Tata Group, one of India's most respected companies, an annual awards program for innovators from across the company celebrates dozens of teams that have tried and succeeded with new ideas. A few years ago, a new award category was added to the Innovista program, an award for projects that were not successful, but which constituted commendable failures. So when company chairman Mr. Ratan Tata stands up in front of an auditorium packed full of people to announce the award winners in the "Dare to Try" category, he sends an important message to the entire company about the necessity of innovation and the willingness of Tata senior management to embrace failure on the way to ultimate success.[55]

Dare to Try is defined this way: "This award is given to the most daring team which made a sincere and valiant attempt for a major innovation but could not obtain the desired results. We all know that 'intelligent failures' are stepping stones for path-breaking innovations. This award celebrates that spirit."

Since you're going to design your portfolio, you'll also design the criteria according to which you're going to assess its performance. What you measure in business has decisive impact on what your organization delivers, so as you proceed you'll need to think about what you really do need to measure. The topic of metrics will be taken up in detail in Chapter 6, where I'll discuss possibilities you may want to use in assessing your portfolio's performance.

Think of your innovation portfolio as a tool to help you manage risk and get the best possible return for the capital you have available to invest. It has to be designed thoughtfully, with due consideration for the strategic factors that are driving your business and your industry forward. Taken together, the projects that you select are the ones you believe most likely to enable you to achieve your strategic goals, to compete effectively and create competitive advantage, to grow your business, to sustain your success.

Implementation of the portfolio occurs throughout the subsequent stages of the innovation process, which means that it will take some time before you know if the portfolio you designed actually delivers the value you intended and aspired to.

Over time, as you manage toward this ideal portfolio, your team's ability to assess individual projects will improve, and the capacity to create value through the entire process will improve as well. As the projects that constitute an innovation portfolio mature

---

[55]   Please Google "Tata Innovista" for more information.

they will provide senior executives and board level directors with increasingly attractive new investment options, and thus a welcome (and expected) return on the invested efforts and funds.

chapter 5

how to innovate

the innovation process

"Great companies cannot be built on processes alone, but believe me, if your company has antiquated, disconnected, slow-moving processes – particularly those that drive success in your industry – you will end up a loser."[56]

Louis Gerstner

Innovation is obviously one of the key business processes that drives success.

It is, however, often misunderstood.

One of the major misunderstandings is the confusion between "ideas" and "innovations," as the following story will illustrate.

Not long ago I was talking with an executive who was dissatisfied with the innovation results his company was achieving. He knew that his firm wasn't producing enough innovations to meet their future needs, nor were they producing innovations of sufficient quality. Furthermore, their efforts to improve the innovation system weren't working very well. (I mentioned this situation earlier, and now I'll tell the full story.)

I asked him to explain to me how their process worked, and he

---

[56] Louis V. Gerstner. *Who Says Elephants Can't Dance*. HarperBusiness, 2002. P. 232.

told me about their elaborate system for gathering ideas from across the entire company. He was quite enthusiastic about this, and thought it was going well and would lead to success.

The person actually in charge of the project, the innovation manager, was a bright and enthusiastic young guy who was collecting ideas from many people at all levels of the company. But the executive then noted that most of the ideas were incremental rather than the breakthroughs they were hoping for. Furthermore, a lot of the ideas just weren't very good.

What he had, in fact, were not one, but two broken systems.

I recognized his problem, as I had heard the same story before. In fact, it wasn't even the first time I'd heard it that same week. It's a common problem, and in the last few years I've had conversations with dozens of executives – in high tech companies and energy companies, aerospace, health care, and consumer goods, and even universities and government agencies. They all complain that their innovation systems are broken; they know this because they're not getting good enough ideas.

The underlying problem that these executives share, the common root cause of their dissatisfaction, is that they think they can fix a broken "innovation system" with improvements to their "idea system."

It never works, because "ideas" are not "innovations," and "idea collection" is definitely not "innovation management."

Yes, ideas are certainly an essential part of the innovation process, but the distinction between ideas and innovations is missing, and there are other aspects of the innovation process that are essential to success, but frequently get insufficient attention.

Idea collection systems are based on the expectation that people will share their good ideas, but as this is happening at random, there's no reasonable basis to suppose that they really will be good ideas, let alone great ideas. Experience has shown that in fact what usually turns up are a lot of bad ones and old ones.

This should not be surprising if we've done nothing to stimulate or encourage breakthrough thinking, as opposed to incremental ideas, so of course most of the ideas that turn up are incremental. They arise during the regular course of the work day, when people are generally focused on getting their work done, so of course they pertain exactly to what people are doing at the moment.

To create a realistic possibility of breakthroughs and new business model innovations, and to improve the quality of everyone's ideas of all types, incremental and breakthrough and business model, you have to structure the process in a much more purposeful way.

And just in case you're thinking that success is a question of how much money you spend, please think again. Recent studies show that success at innovation is not a function of how much you spend on R&D, but rather on the quality of your process.[57]

This is the third sprint in the Agile Innovation Master Plan system. So here I'll describe the same process that I recommend to executives who want to know how to get better results from their own investments. Please keep in mind that the goal is not to get more ideas, but to get better ones, an abundance of great ideas that are fully aligned with your organization's strategic goals.

the innovation funnel

Given the uncertainties of the future, the nebulous nature of many ideas, and the additional uncertainties related to turning ideas into business value, it's obvious that a lot ideas are typically explored in the early, formative stages of the innovation process, they're studied, worked on, combined and recombined, edited in and out, up and down, and deeply massaged in order that the end result is a few completed, highly useful innovations.

---

[57]   http://www.booz.com/media/uploads/Innovation_1000-2009.pdf

Since there are many ideas in the beginning and fewer at the end, it's easy to visualize the innovation process as a funnel with ideas coming in the wide end on the left, getting magically transformed through a lot of hard but mysterious work inside, and then a few finished and magnificent innovations emerging triumphantly to market through the narrow end at the right.

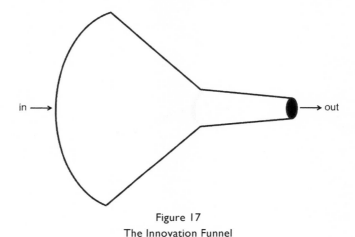

Figure 17
The Innovation Funnel

What happens inside the funnel are steps, or stages of work progressing from vague to very specific. At the end of each stage is a check point, a gate, and only the good ideas get past a gate and go on to the next stage. Companies may define the steps or stages differently, but the metaphor of the funnel consisting of stages endures, and "stage gate" models also endure because we know that we have to exert some influence over what happens inside the funnel since there's too much money, importance, and risk involved to leave it unattended.

But as the story above suggests, starting with idea collection really doesn't work at all, and in many organizations it ends up being counterproductive.

Ideas are of course the seeds of innovation, just as ore is taken from the ground as the raw material of steel, and waving fields of wheat provide the raw material for bread. But it takes a lot of preparation work to get raw ore from a mine and transform it into steel, and likewise there is work involved in preparing a farmer's fields to grow the wheat long before there's any grain to harvest or bread to eat. It's the same with innovation; we just don't start by collecting raw ideas, because we have a lot of preparation to do first to ensure that we get good ideas. It has to be a system.

a systematic process

Those who start their innovation process with idea gathering are starting in the middle, and as they haven't done the necessary preparation they probably won't end up with the high quality ideas they want. To carry the mining and farming metaphors forward, due to the lack of preparation they end up with a lot of useless dirt, or a pile of weeds, rather than ore or wheat.

We've already explored the principle that innovation must be a core element of every organization's strategy, which is the "why," and that is the beginning the innovation process. By clearly defining strategic intent we automatically steer towards development of new possibilities that could plausibly add value at the strategic level.

But this step is omitted if we jump headlong into gathering ideas, and it's why most of the ideas that come from unstructured idea collection efforts aren't very interesting, and therefore why the results are disappointing.

Here's the entire model.

step 1
strategic thinking

In Chapter 1 we discussed the linkage between strategy and innovation in detail. We began with the goal of creating strategic advantage, and thinking through specifically how innovation is going to add value to your organization's strategic intents, and how this will lead us to target innovation opportunities with the greatest potential to provide strategic advantage.

This is also the first step in the innovation process, through the translation of strategy into a set of specific intents and expectations.

step 2
portfolio management & metrics

In Chapters 3 and 4 we explored the design of your innovation portfolio, and discussed concepts including the four types of innovation and the five resulting portfolios, the nature of ambiguity, and the critical principle of non-correlation. This is step two of the innovation process.

We also discussed at length one of the important underlying facets of innovation management, the necessity of failure. Innovation is by definition doing something new, and as we proceed on the innovation journey we do not in fact know if we're going to succeed with any given project or effort, but we do have confidence that we'll succeed eventually because we will learn diligently.

Along the way we know that there'll be surprises, wrong turns, and attempts that will never come to fruition in and of themselves. So we manage innovation portfolios aggressively to balance the inherent risks of the unknown with the targeted rewards of success, to assure that our bets on the future are not correlated to any particular market structure, and to balance our pursuit of the ideal with the realities of learning, risking, and failing in order to ultimately succeed.

This is the sort of situation that drives many laser-focused executives crazy, but history has shown that there's no way to avoid it. The engaged and adventurous spirit, on the other hand, is thoroughly pleased by the very uncertainties that are encountered along the way, which is fine as long as you don't lose focus on the need to ultimately succeed, and as soon as possible.

Or in the words of Jonathan Ive, head of industrial design at Apple. "One of the hallmarks of the team is inquisitiveness, being excited about being wrong because it means that you've discovered something new."[58]

Behind these differing personalities lies the greater difficulty, in that people in the two roles often have problems communicating with one another. Like it or not, the operating executive has to put up with the adventurer, because without adventure there isn't likely to be innovation. The adventurer, for his or her part, thoroughly understands that delivering innovation is a strategic imperative, and is usually more comfortable with the uncertainties involved in getting there.

The crux of the portfolio as a solution is that by managing the entire collection of ideas and projects that constitute our innovations-in-progress as we would manage any investment portfolio, and by instituting the right metrics according to which we will diligently assess our own efforts and correct our course as needed, we have the best chance to arrive at our destination, competitive advantage.

Steps 1 and 2 together provide a platform and context for everything that follows, and thus they constitute the preparation stages, pre-funnel, or strategic alignment.

step 3
agile innovation process

The key outputs of step 2 are the design of the ideal innovation portfolio, which is what we believe, as of today, describes the right

---

[58]   Leander Kahney. *Inside Steve's Brain*. Portfolio, 2008, p 93.
       Ive made the comment at Radical Craft, The Second Art Center Design
       Conference. http://www.core77.com/reactor/04.06_artcenter.asp

mixture of short and long term projects across all four types of innovation that we anticipate will enable us to achieve our strategic objectives, along with our increasing skill at portfolio management. What we actually do will doubtless be different from whatever we envision today, but that's fine. We need clear directions in which to go, and we fully expect to learn along the way and change course as necessary, both as a result of what we learn, and as the outside environment continues to change and opens up both new threats and new opportunities.

The portfolio describes the ideal future products and services we'll target, but even if they're the right ones, we probably don't yet know how to make and deliver them, because if we knew, then we'd just do it and we wouldn't need an innovation process to get us there. So there is by definition a gap between what we know today and we *will* know once these new products and services have been discovered, developed, and applied. We compare our current knowledge with the knowledge we will need, and this shows us where the gaps are; filling them with brilliant new knowledge that leads to insights is the purpose of *research*, the third step in the innovation process.

As competitive advantage is the goal of innovation, however, and our competition is probably busy doing the same things, the knowledge we really want and need isn't going to be waiting around on the corner in a red suit for us to cruise by. Instead, it's probably hidden, and it may require considerable skill as searchers for the unknown for us to find it.

the knowledge domains

Although the gaps in our knowledge will almost certainly encompass a huge range of topics, it's also likely that our questions can be organized into either of two broad categories that we call "tacit" and "explicit" knowledge. Within each category there are two subcategories, and beyond that of course an infinite variety of pertinent subtopics.

Explicit knowledge is that which can be articulated and readily transmitted to others. It has been codified. Explicit knowledge domains are:

1. Science and technology, including the basic sciences, such as physics or chemistry or biology, emerging fields such as biotech or nanosciences, and applied fields like computing and the internet. These are abundant sources of new explicit knowledge.

2. Business disciplines, such as manufacturing, supply chain, finance, marketing, and communications are rich with explicit knowledge, as is knowledge pertaining to the current and observable *uses* that consumers make of products and services.

Tacit knowledge is difficult to transfer to another person, often because it includes unspoken or unrecognized elements or components. Tacit knowledge domains are:

1. Large scale social and economic trends that define the flowing and changing world of events, trends, beliefs, attitudes, and values, but which are often hard to track to a source, and which are highly unpredictable.

2. Customers often make choices according to unspoken needs, desires, and behaviors (which are also changing), and also according to the hidden *meanings* that products and actions contain for them.

The knowledge we seek will most likely be found in all four of these domains. We'll have to integrate together whatever we learn in order to create robust solutions, using new knowledge to transform a wide range of unknowns into knowns, and through which to expose significant new innovation opportunities.

In many situations, often the most interesting and compelling ones, the convergence of new science, technology, and business tools with social and economic trends and customer needs leads to the creation of new markets. Here the explicit and tacit come together, and it's where we probably want to be exploring to assure the future of our organization.

This is a tall order, though, and we've got to be careful not to underestimate the intellectual challenge as well as the management challenge of doing it well.

Let me offer some concise examples, just to ground this important concept in stories that that you may already be familiar with.

The most successful of the internet companies, including Google, Facebook, and Amazon, to name three, all exist because of a new technology (which is also a new tool), the internet (explicit knowledge), and they are surfing on (and have created) large scale social trends to fulfill previously unmet needs that address meanings that are important to users (tacit knowledge). eBay, of course, a new kind of consumer-to-consumer marketplace, has largely replaced the garage sale with something far more effective; Yahoo and Google have redefined how people get information, and how advertisers try to reach the very same people while they're getting information; Facebook is a new kind of community, and Amazon leads the way in the distribution of every kind of product imaginable.

More or less the same story could be told to explain the successes of Apple and Microsoft, and before them Xerox and IBM, and P&G, and Starbucks, and Wal-Mart. If we look by industry, we see much the same thing – airlines and aircraft manufacturers; energy companies; food companies; distribution companies; technology companies; even financial services companies, all use science and technology, and business knowledge (explicit knowledge), to address market trends and emerging and often undefined customer needs (tacit knowledge).

So let's explore what research in both areas could mean.

explicit knowledge

Research in the sciences and in technology follows a well-understood pattern. The exploration of basic concepts leads to suppositions about how things "could be," which then take the form of hypotheses. Scientists design experiments to test hypotheses, and then compare the results with their expectations. The name for this is "the scientific method," the disciplined approach to obtaining repeatable results.

In this way, explicit knowledge accumulates day by day, year by year, generation by generation. This has been the pathway of science throughout the course of human history, the process driving the growth of human knowledge. Newton famously remarked that he stood on the shoulders of giants, and then subsequent generations of scientists have stood on *his* shoulders, leading us to the present day when we all stand upon the towering edifice of the accumulated knowledge of civilization, a vast collection that continues nevertheless to grow every day through the efforts of countless scientists, scholars, and students.

The accumulating store of human knowledge is expanding at a phenomenal rate, now doubling every few years, and leaving us with an inexhaustible supply of facts, models, and concepts at our disposal. For example, about 30 million different chemical substances are known to exist, and new ones are being developed every day; perhaps one of them will pertain to your business.

For businesses, certain types of new ideas and knowledge are protectable through the patent process, which takes new concepts, expresses them in explicit terms, may result in competitive advantage and valuable assets that can be defended in courts of law.

And similarly, all the other domains of business knowledge contribute to our ability to design and manage global enterprises that serve millions of customers, and organize tens or hundreds of thousands of employees and suppliers into coherent operations that address market needs on a local or global scale to earn revenues and profits, constituting the economy.

tacit knowledge

Since businesses must have customers, and customers often make choices according to non-obvious criteria, our quest to understand who they are and what they want, and to understand the evolution of our society and the current and future values and needs of customers as large groups taken together as segments and markets, leads us to inquire not only as to how technology works, but also what users want and need to do with it, what it means to them, and especially what they'll buy, and why. Therefore, we also require another type of knowledge, knowledge about people, and their views, and the choices they make. We call this "tacit" knowledge.

Unlike the explicit nature of the hard sciences and many business disciplines, our understanding of human behavior is developed by the social sciences, including anthropology, psychology, sociology, and economics. These fields explore hidden and unspoken understandings, tacit understandings, which often constitute the most interesting and important aspects of human communications and human life. These are also the elements that compose human culture, the subtle and elusive factors that shape our values, beliefs, and attitudes, telling us who, at root, we are.

The accumulation of knowledge in the explicit domains of science, technology, and business is as old as humanity, and it's well understood. The tacit domains, however, while equally old, are much less well understood in the business context, so I'll describe them here in more detail.

While explicit knowledge of the sciences is shared through verbal and written expression and though communications media, tacit knowledge is almost always communicated subtly, through body language, and unspoken agreements, and through cultural norms and values that everyone who lives in a particular place and time automatically learns, although they are rarely discussed openly. As part of a community we learn what clothes to wear, and which flag to wave, and which car to drive, and what behaviors are proper and improper, and all that and much more expresses important aspects of our identity. The norms that we often feel compelled to conform to are our culture, communicated to us throughout the days of our childhood in thousands of ways that are spoken, but millions more ways that are demonstrated just in the course of living. Culture is the aggregate expression of the spoken and unspoken elements of a shared sense of who we are.

For most of us, the choices that define a cultural identity constitute "common sense," as they're what we feel, believe, expect, and even experience, although the concepts we use to organize our approach to "reality" are often beyond conscious awareness.

Cognitive scientist George Lakoff has put this very simply: "One of the most fundamental results in cognitive science, one that comes from the study of commonsense reasoning, is that most of our thought is unconscious - not unconscious in the Freudian sense of being repressed, but unconscious simply in that we are not aware of it. We think and talk at too fast a rate and at too deep a level to have conscious awareness and control over everything we think and say. We are even less conscious of the components of thoughts - concepts. When we think, we use an elaborate system of concepts, but we are not usually aware of just what those concepts are like and how they fit together into a system."[59]

In this comment Lakoff has explained not one dimension underlying the tacit dimension, but two. First, he says, too much is happening in our brains for our conscious mind to be aware of it all.

A good question at this point would be to wonder why so much of our experience remains beyond our conscious awareness. Studies of the human brain reveal that the sensory organs generate information at a prodigious rate, as the combined channel capacity of the nerves associated with the eyes, ears, skin, taste and smell systems is on the order of eleven million bits of data per second. Meanwhile, consciousness lags considerably behind at a paltry forty

---

59   George Lakoff. *Moral Politics: What Conservatives Know that Liberals Don't.* Chicago, The University of Chicago Press, 1996.

bits per second.[60]   This means that the brain is processing approximately 300,000 times more information than consciousness is made aware of, and by default our system of consciousness is therefore obliged to filter the flood of experiences into the limited capacity of our conscious awareness.

Lakoff's second point is that we organize reality into concepts, but we generally do so without significant awareness of where the concepts come from or how they fit together. We learn them as a natural part of our maturation, and they sneak into our being in such an insidious way that they are integral parts of us, so much so that we often cannot imagine our lives or ourselves any other way.

But people who were raised in cultures other than our own may indeed have been raised differently, and the "other way" that is inconceivable for us is entirely natural and normal for them.

Conflict between cultures then often arises when people have different and perhaps opposing concepts, models, or cultural norms. Religious, ideological, and political discord is often the result, which may even lead, as we see far too commonly in today's world, to war.

Conflict also occurs within cultures, often when change occurs in the broader environment that causes the prior norms to be in opposition to a new reality. Hence, technological and social change often leads to generational conflict when succeeding generations may have vastly different experiences of what reality is, or views of what it should be, from their parents and grandparents. What constitutes "proper behavior" comes into dispute.

A somewhat trivial example of this, but one that you may well be familiar with, is social etiquette around texting. It seems that many people in their twenties, for whom texting is an integral part of their experience, think it entirely normal to send and receive text messages any time, including during conversations, meetings and meals. However, many people in their fifties, for whom texting is not at all a part of their way of life, find this rather offensive.

---

60   Manfred Zimmermann. "Neurophysiology of Sensory Systems." *Fundamentals of Sensory Physiology*, Robert F. Schmidt, ed. Berlin, Springer-Verlag, 1986. p. 115.

A non-trivial example of this type of social conflict is the conflict that we know as the uprising of Tiananmen Square, which gave all the appearances of a cultural conflict between youth and elders, underlain by different views of history and of the future. (Although it may also be explained as a more traditional power conflict between those who had it and those who wanted it.)

Either way, it remains difficult to resolve disagreements when our beliefs are assumed rather than studied, and the roots of our values are hidden, which is precisely what we mean by "tacit."

This discussion is important because these tacit factors are often most critical to the success of innovation efforts, in that the design of every innovation must address the tacit factors just as it must also address the explicit ones.

Therefore we need to conduct research that exposes these hidden elements; we call this "tacit knowledge research."

What we wish to accomplish through tacit knowledge research is to develop a detailed understanding, or model, that explains how people think, and why they think as they do, and thus why they make the choices they make in any particular situation as it pertains to our company, our products and services, our industry, our future, and our innovations. This sort of investigation is quite different from the hard sciences, and requires different tools.

A reminder of tacit factors in product design is provided by the simple example of the humble car key. Today it's the standard design that a single key both opens the doors and starts the car, and since the key is symmetrical it works facing either direction, which assures 100% success putting the key in the lock or the ignition, 100% of the time. But for decades, American car makers provided one key for the door and the ignition, and a different one for the trunk. These keys were non-symmetrical, so the teeth were only on one side of the key, and it fit in the lock only one way. So imagine that it's a dark and rainy night, and you're fumbling for your keys while getting soaked, because you forgot your raincoat. You have only a 25% chance of getting the right key into the lock correctly, so three chances in four of getting wetter and more uncomfortable.

Eventually the Japanese innovation, the single, symmetrical key, became standard, because it works so much better.

From the perspective of the product designers, in this case the key and lock designers, the insight that leads to a symmetrical key comes from studying the experiences of end users. Here is a person with key in hand trying to get into the locked car, and the designers observe what happens and think through the factors that will make that experience as easy as possible.

50/50 Chance   100% Chance

Figure 18
Sensitivity to Tacit Knowledge Improves the Design of the Humble Car Key

While this is a simple example, the type of thinking that it requires is useful in an infinite variety of innovation challenges of far greater subtlety and complexity. We wish to expose tacit knowledge that is embedded in the experiences of individuals and in the collective psyche to understand the elusive factors that will enable us to design the best possible solutions. To gather this knowledge, researchers often conduct detailed interviews with people who represent a particular set of relevant characteristics, such as age, socio-economic group, job type, a particular interest or avocation, or a geographic segment, etc.

For example, we may want to learn about the needs of aging Baby Boomers:

• Will people age 50 or so be interested in this particular product?

- How can we design it to meet their specific needs?
- What meanings do other products in this category convey?
- Is there already a product or service on the market that addresses this need?
- Can we improve on it?
- How should we market it so that customers become interested in it?"

Researchers have discovered, however, that just asking questions like this is unlikely to yield good results precisely because so much of our experience occurs without conscious awareness. So we need a different approach.

ethnographic research

A highly productive method of exposing tacit knowledge is the discipline of ethnography. Originally developed as the branch of anthropology that focused on understanding human culture, ethnographers perfected their discipline by immersing themselves in cultures other than the ones in which they were raised, and decoding the patterns of belief and interaction to give us valid models of how others live.

They've also been working for the last few decades to understand not only the unique characteristics of humanity's diverse cultural heritage, but also the previously unrecognized attitudes, behaviors, and experiences of those who live in the world's great metropolises and participate in the global economy. This is the search for knowledge that businesses can transform into commercially successful products and services.

One of the notable places where the marriage of ethnography and business first emerged was at the same Palo Alto Research Center I've already mentioned, Xerox's marvelous lab near Stanford University, where a multidisciplinary team of those working in the hard and soft sciences developed an amazing set of technologies, including the first really usable personal computers (mentioned above), laser printing, Ethernet, and countless other innovations that found their way into Xerox copiers and computers.

Today, ethnographers are working for many companies. One of them is Intel Corporation, which is exploring the rapid spread of computing in China, an obviously important future market for the company. On an Intel web site, the intent of its ethnographic efforts is described this way:

> "Our purpose is to explore fundamental paradigms and phenomena of everyday life to help Intel think critically about how people, practices, and institutions matter to technological innovation and to conceive of provocative experiences in the future. We use social science methods, qualitative and quantitative, to generate insights, models and demonstrations that help reframe 'what matters' to internal and external partners."[61]

This graceful language includes some important distinctions. The focus on what matters to "people," "practices," and "institutions" encompasses three of the most complex aspects of the human experience, and Intel's efforts to learn more about them involve a considerable degree of sophistication. This ethnographic work has been the subject of articles in the *Harvard Business Review*, *BusinessWeek*, and other publications, but the company is just one among many that use ethnographic research to deepen their understanding of the tacit factors that influence their customers' views of the world.

For our purposes as innovators, the distinctions between tacit and explicit knowledge are vitally important. But to execute on our projects we also need a deeper understanding of how we actually develop and use them in practice.

This is where the agile innovation sprint comes into play as a

---

[61]   http://techresearch.intel.com/projecthome.aspx?ResearchAreaId=3

core element of your firm's innovation process. We introduced the basic concepts in Chapter 1, and here we'll return to the discussion and add a considerable amount of additional detail to you guide the effort in the most effective way possible.

the agile innovation sprint

Recently we set about to understand how the recent breakthroughs in Agile software programming could be carried into the more general work of innovation, and the result was the highly successful book *Agile Innovation* which I wrote together with Moses Ma and Po Chi Wu. We then started looking even more deeply, and in this section, which was mostly written by Moses, we describe the process in a considerable degree of detail.

•••

The core Agile process for innovation-related work is called an "innovation sprint." This process fuses the design thinking approach that was developed at Stanford University's d school (the "d" stands for "design") with the time-boxed, iterative workflow process as Agile software developers have defined it.

The merger of design thinking and Agile was first proposed in our book *Agile Innovation*, and has since become very popular. It's being used widely throughout Silicon Valley, including at Google, Nest and many others firms.

At root, the innovation sprint is a systematic process for understanding current and future market needs, creating brilliant new ideas, tracking, reviewing, and assessing them to assure that strategic priorities and the ideas are brought into alignment, developing, testing and validating them, and thus it is a disciplined process which assures that the best ideas are identified and brought forward for development.   Hence, this approach breaks down complex thinking, design, and creative tasks into a logical sequence of six stages that support our quest for optimal solutions by melding the art of creative thinking with the science of sound management.

As we saw in Chapter 1, the Agile Innovation Sprint looks like this:

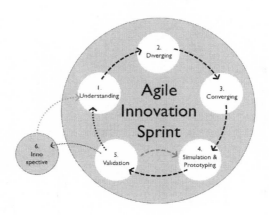

Figure 19
The Six Stages of the Agile Innovation Sprint
The output of understanding, diverging, converging, simulation & prototyping, and validation is new knowledge about the future, as well as new products, services, business models, and processes. The output of the innospective is improvement to our process of innovating.

phase I: understanding

To discover or invent great new products and services you have to learn to see the world differently. That is, you'll have to see what *could be* rather than what merely is. So you can never be contented and satisfied with the current state of knowledge and practice.

To see differently, you'll have to learn to change the way you go about looking, which means you'll also have to change the way you think. Or, as they say, "If you always do what you always did, you will always get what you always got."

Since "what we did" and "what we've got" isn't going to cut it in the era of exponential change and hyper-competition, we are compelled to find the critical differences. Hence, we must understand the future, and the means to doing so is to continuously expand our methods of perception. Consequently, the initial phase of the Agile Innovation Sprint is perceptual: using a wide range of observation tools to gain a profound understanding of the current and future needs of your entire market ecosystem, which includes users, customers, and markets.

The description presented here builds on the prior edition of this book, and if you are familiar with that work you will notice that we have shifted some of the terminology as we have elaborated on the basic process model. Previously we had understood this process to be a four-step sequence, Needfinding, Modeling, Ideation, and Prototyping. But practice in this field is evolving rapidly as many people are engaged in refining and developing these core approaches. Hence, what you read here is an updated version.

how "understanding" works

As an example let's look at a recent project for a consumer products company whose goal was to double the size of its business over the coming five years. The company had a lot of ideas, but they all seemed to be unsatisfying incremental, so they initiated a project to explore the tacit factors behind customer attitudes and views about their core product and the entire category in which their product belonged, in the expectation that this would enable them to understand how the market was evolving, and thus help identify breakthrough growth opportunities.

After exploring the strategic issues facing the company, and arriving at some conclusions about the strategic framework for the project, a team of ethnographers then interviewed members of 50 families in three cities over a period of a few weeks to explore their views and values in great depth. Unlike focus groups, which are usually conducted in a neutral and sterile office environment, these interviews took place in people's homes, where it was more natural for people to discuss the product and lifestyle choices they make, their views on various topics including personal care and exercise, and a dozen additional themes related to consumer and lifestyle choices they're making today, and which may offer insight into the choices they'll probably make tomorrow.

A peek into pantries and storage closets discloses what they'd bought, and the researchers asked them to talk about their choices. As there's often a difference between what people say and what they do, examining what they've actually bought and talking about it often reveals hidden thoughts and beliefs.

It's also common for people to describe their lifestyle habits based on what they think the researchers expect to hear, or on stereotypical notions that they apply themselves even when it's not so much the case, the actual boxes and cans on the shelves disclose what they've really chosen; this is one of many nuances that highlights the importance of the tacit dimension, of getting beyond what people say to get a clearer picture of their real beliefs and choices.

As I mentioned above, this phase of the tacit research process is sometimes called "needfinding," the search to understand hidden and future needs.[62]

The search for new needs does not occur exclusively in the structured setting of an ethnographic research study; it can also happen on "trend safaris," when we go for a walk along main street or at the mall, looking for new products and marketing ideas, and when browsing the internet, or looking at catalogs, or even watching this year's Super Bowl ads and exploring what messages the advertisers are intending to convey.

---

[62] For an excellent and detailed description of the research process that is summarized here, please see the award-winning paper "Innovation as a Learning Process: Embedding Design Thinking" by Sara Beckman and Michael Barry, *California Management Review*, Fall 2007.

Central to effective work here is the art of thoughtful and thorough observation. Ethnographers are trained to notice things that others may not be aware of. For example, the now-famous Oxo brand of kitchen tools were created to make it easier for people with arthritis to cook. And to the company's great surprise (and joy), it turned out that arthritics weren't the only ones who prefer tools that are easier to handle.

So we would say in this case that the industrial era "natives" remained unaware that skinny handles are harder to use, and fat handles much easier, until more than 100 years after the industrial revolution began.

In the understanding phase we are seeking a complete grasp of the customer's experiences by exposing the hidden knowledge and assumptions about which we have previously been unaware, such as the difference between fat and skinny cooking tool handles. Researchers therefore look for clues that may mark unsatisfying issues and problems we might then label as: hard-to-use; gaps in service; needs that are not met; and workarounds when people have to go to unusual extremes to solve problems, because all these situations may expose innovation opportunities, as indeed they have for Oxo.

Clearly one of the key goals is to discover "tacit" or hidden needs throughout the operational eco-system, because as Oxo discovered, it is these hidden, unspoken, or unarticulated needs that often provide the keys to creating genuinely new products, services, and business models. Consequently, the initial phase of the Innovation Sprint requires that you apply your perceptive skills by using a wide range of observation tools and methods to gain a profound understanding of these hidden needs. This applies to everyone in your market ecosystem – your customers of course, and also your future customers (who may be different than your current ones), as well as your partners, suppliers, staff, and all other stakeholders.

Leading marketing practitioners and product designers know that it's mandatory to study user behavior and user needs quite deeply before leaping into the product design process. The intensity of study that is required has increased with the increasing complexity and sophistication of both the products (technology) and of the customers (ever more enabled and engaged).

As I mentioned, research activities like this are not done in laboratory settings, but in real life situations where people are engaged in their day to day activities, and where the full context of their actions, attitudes, and aspirations may be revealed through what they do and say. Frequently those experiencing them (a customer, perhaps) is not consciously aware that this dimension of their own experience is even occurring, and so it's up the observer to discover what's going on, and what could be improved.

And while we certainly engage with existing customers in this research, we also talk with non-customers. Sometimes we refer to these two groups as "core" and "edge" markets.

exploring core and edge markets

Throughout the process of developing our understanding, it matters a great deal where we choose to search. In this context we make the distinction between "core markets" and "edge markets." Core refers to markets, services, products, and customers that are well understood, "typical," and already targeted. "Edge" refers to special uses, extreme uses and also non-users, groups that are not considered typical, and often not considered at all.

In traditional practice, we want to understand our core customers, just like we want to master our core competences. But in the forward-looking process of searching for innovation opportunities, we may learn much more from the edge than we can from the core.

Learning about the edge, however, may require us to spend time with people whom we don't think of as our typical customers, and may also require us to understand a much different thinking process than the ones we're accustomed to: the arthritic kitchen tool user is indeed such an edge customer.

A brand that developed itself entirely on the edge was Toyota's Scion, an example of business model innovation as well as new venture innovation that I mentioned in Chapter 3. The Scion brand was not targeted at Toyota's traditional customers in the US, mainstream baby boomers, but at their Gen X, Y, and Z children and grandchildren.

Before launching the brand, the Scion development team studied these new consumers by visiting their own communities, which were, from Toyota's perspective, edge environments: tattoo parlors, street rallies, alternative rock concerts, and inner cities where the company had neither a presence nor much experience.

As they spent time with their future customers, the Scion team began to understand how to develop a new brand identity to address the worldviews of these new customers. Team leader Jim Farley participated in many of these conversations, and it was during a 2 hour conversation with a security guard that the final brand positioning for Scion came into focus.[63]

With a target market consisting of young buyers who were generally not established with families and careers, people who were making the transition to adulthood, the Scion team came to realize that many of them still saw themselves as outsiders. Hence, the brand identity of Scion clearly displays the rebel attitude, which you may have noticed if you saw the company's striking advertising. "Often Misunderstood," said one billboard, reflecting a common feeling among teens and twenty-something year olds.

Scion reinforced its rebel positioning by becoming the (only) automotive sponsor of an American tattoo festival, among many similar promotional efforts where they worked to build viral buzz around the brand. Their efforts were very successful, as first-year

---

[63] "Job 1 for new Ford executive: Selling EcoBoost." Associated Press, January 6, 2008.
http://www.msnbc.msn.com/id/22527986/ns/business-autos/t/job-new-ford-executive-selling-ecoboost/

sales exceeded forecast by 300%.

By creating an edge brand for edge customers in an edge market, Toyota expanded its customer base into a key market segment it had not previously penetrated; in 2008, 70% of Scion buyers were new to Toyota.

In these times of rapid change it's obviously risky to focus only on a core market, because markets shrink and disappear with astonishing speed. Exploring the edge may help you to identify the future, and to target innovations that will enable your company to adapt to new markets and emerging market requirements.

The Scion story is a great example of how some brilliant insights led to great outcomes, but if you follow the automotive industry you also know that there's a twist in the story. In 2016 Toyota announced that it was shutting down Scion, as the initial success did not endure through the crushing recession of 2008. That downturn hit Scion buyers particularly hard, sales plummeted, and the brand identity that worked brilliantly in 2005 did not resonate in 2009. The driving forces change, which I described in Chapter 2, led to the demise of Scion.

This speaks directly to another critical dimension of understanding that you'll need to develop, the current and future competitive landscape in your marketplace. Who are your current competitors, and what is the structure of competitive market? How are the various competitors positioned, and how do you offers compare with theirs?

For Scion, the critical competition turned out to be the used car market, which is where their target customers turned when even a low-priced new car became out of reach. In another structural shift, American used car prices held strong, and bank lenders began to pursue the segment much more aggressively than in the past. Used car loans of 4 and even 5 years became common, although they had once been unheard of. When there is a structural change in the economy, all of the players have to adjust their strategies.

An additional key element is the impact of technology, and it's particularly important to gain a deep understanding of the ways in which new and emerging technologies may impact on the future business landscape. This was of course the first of the driving forces of change that were described in Chapter 2, and we all know how technology is continuing to alter both the structure of the market and the expectations of its users.

So let's say that you've done a brilliant job of gathering insights from customers, non-customers, and edge customers; that you have solid data on the current and expected future economic patterns and structures, and you've even got a good sense of how the technology landscape is going to shift. What do you do with it all?

"unpacking"

The multi-dimensional observations that your research revealed is at present a rather large collection of observations, impressions, facts and factoids, opinions, and speculations. Now you have to identify the underlying patterns, which will lead you to recognize both threats and opportunities. Hence, the other half of understanding is sorting out what it is that you've learned. We often call this "unpacking," or "modeling," because here the goal is to transform identified needs into useful and actionable models of the customer's frame of mind, as well as pain points, problems, trends, and opportunities.

"Unpacking" is a term used in clinical psychology that means carefully sorting and distinguishing the rich complexity of emotional experiences. Here we are extending its meaning to encompass not only the critical emotional dimension of tacit needs and end user experiences, recognizing and understanding the intense emotional forces, hopes, and dreams, the energies that are central to transforming tacit needs into the basis of great designs, but also including the market, business, and technology dimensions. What we're after is an integrated understanding of the present and the likely future.

Understanding

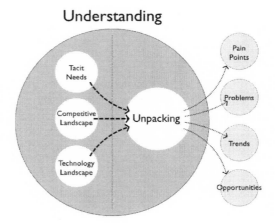

Figure 20
Understanding By Unpacking
Research into tacit, or hidden needs, the competitive landscape, and
current and emerging technologies are key inputs that we have to then
"unpack," or decode, from which we then can clearly identify the pain
points that need to be addressed, as well as the problems, relevant
trends and key opportunities.

During the unpacking process team members present and
discuss their observations and impressions, and through discussion
they seek a shared understanding of the research findings and
priorities. These they then translate into agreed upon "pain points"
and "problem statements," which become the conceptual bases of
the innovation work going forward.

Pain points and problem statements are concise expressions of
the needs, challenges, and goals of customers and other
stakeholders – both conscious and unconscious – which will then be
translated into ideas for the design of new products, services, and
business models.

Here's an example: during the early days of the Internet we
were tasked with producing a vision paper for a "unified internal
desktop" for a financial services firm. Senior managers wanted to
validate the ideal of a standard internal desktop using HTML, and

were focused on the cost savings that could be achieved by using a standard navigation and presentation layer to integrate the many stove-piped applications then in use throughout the organization.

During the understanding phase of our work we asked subjects to recount a "day in their life," and a common thread emerged that many people were turning their computers off at break time to get coffee, and drilling down more deeply we discovered that it took between 30 and 60 minutes to log into all the various databases and portals the organization had created. The concept of a "single sign on" was only then being invented, and employees simply assumed that waiting nearly an hour to get back to work was "just the way it is." The entire organization had formed a blind spot around this process. Digging deeper still, this also revealed that a core element of the cultures was "no whining or complaining." Interestingly, the complaint-free culture was therefore impeding the possibility of making important process improvements and innovations. Looking for blind spots and rituals that don't make sense is key to successful research.

Another tip to accelerate your research process is to look at the dominant business models in your industry – the sacred cows. Explore more deeply to identify underlying and perhaps long-held core beliefs about how value is created, and then consider how changes in markets, mindsets, and technology can enable new ways to create value. A recent example of this is Uber, which killed the sacred cow of taxi medallions and exposed a huge opportunity to create value. Another example is PayPal which decided to simply pay its customers directly for referrals and expanded its referral base enormously by doing so.

Uber and PayPal were willing to kill those sacred cows, and that's what you should seek to do also. Dissect the most important and long-held beliefs into their supporting notions: How do experiences about customer needs and interactions, technology, regulation, business economics, and ways of operating underpin core beliefs? How have core beliefs slowly turned into self-limiting beliefs?

While the first half of understanding focuses on gathering information about hidden attitudes and expectations, the unpacking work that comes next synthesizes these findings into concise and logical expressions that describe how people make decisions. Knowing how people decide, whether those decisions are conscious or unconscious, enables us to then shape a value proposition that will meet their needs.

In our project with the consumer products company, thinking through the needs as identified in the interviews disclosed some interesting surprises. The researchers learned in the earliest interviews that consumers think about the product category somewhat differently than the company's executives thought they did, and that consumers also had a different understanding of the product's key benefits. Consequently, researchers explored these themes in even greater depth in later interviews.

Thinking through these differences led to key insights about the way the market seemed to be evolving, which turned out to be an early warning about an important shift in the structure of the entire market, a shift of considerable significance for the company.

Specialists from inside and outside the organization also helped model these changes, as the team looked for evidence in related fields. They also explored possible business structures, supply chain models, marketing concepts, financial projections, and risk assessments.

Insights gained through modeling still need further refinement before the more specific work of product development. Once you've unpacked your extensive observational inventory you should have a clear list of pain points, problem statements, trend maps, and tacit needs. What we do with them now is use them as a basis for coming up with opportunities and solutions through brainstorming and other creativity techniques.

Figure 21
Example of Upacking in the Understanding Process:
The Self-Image of a Troubled Community

This example was taken from another research project, and simplified for inclusion here. Drug dealing is a persistent factor in this community, and the self-image of many community members is largely influenced by the uneasy relationship between insiders and outsiders (shown on the horizontal axis), and the ways that insiders and outsiders try to influence community members (shown on the vertical axis). The research sponsor was a social services agency, and the findings revealed how it was perceived in the community: as outsiders who judge and try to change the community members. This was a not a formula for success, but knowing this, the agency could then work to position itself more positively in the minds of community members.

phase II: diverging

At the beginning of the book I mentioned that many would-be and novice innovators start the innovation process by coming up with new ideas. I mentioned that this is actually not a very good practice, because what they generally end up with is a random collection of mostly useless ideas.

But now you see what's much better – a very targeted collection of deep insights into the multi-dimensional market space creates a super solid foundation upon which we can now do some tremendously effective ideation. This is what we do when we "diverge," that is, when we think about the great ideas that our research inspires and stimulates.

So yes, *now* we get to the ideas.

Pain points, problem statements, trend maps, identified tacit needs are all elements from which you and your team can begin generating solution ideas, which is the divergent process of exploring what *could* be done across a very wide field of possibilities. This is classically known as "brainstorming," but that's just one of a great many approaches that could be fruitful here.

We know that great innovations are often stimulated not so much with a focus on coming up with the "right answers" as it is by asking the right questions. Such questions are "ideation lenses" or "innovation perspectives" that boldly illuminate the challenges, problems, shortcomings, and needs, and goals. And when these have been nicely illuminated the ideas tend to flow readily along.

One way to stimulate the formation of great questions is to apply the process called multi-visioning, during which we adopt a particular perspective for inquiry for a short amount time, perhaps 10 – 15 minutes, and then we switch perspectives. Through multiple iterations we sample a variety of perspectives and engage in coming up with ideas from each perspective. This often leads to a lot of promising ideas, and it's fast.

Successful divergence results in a vast inventory of possibilities, which are sometimes recorded on post-it notes. When we display them on a large surface, the wide range of ideas can be viewed and assessed at a single glance.

The goal is usually to turn an underlying limiting belief on its head, which may lead to a radical new hypothesis about how to create value:

- What if people who shopped in discount stores would pay extra for designer products? That's what Target discovered.
- What if consumers want to buy electronics in stores, even after Dell taught them to prefer direct buying? That's what Apple created.
- What if LED technology puts an end to the lighting industry as a replacement business? That's what Philips embraced.
- What if lumber and hardware and home improvement are really one business, not three? That's what Home Depot pioneered.
- What if everyday drivers could become part-time taxi drivers? That's what Uber invented.

This is the kind of thinking you need to do: investigate deeply, think broadly, and dare to be different.

Do you remember the executive I mentioned at the beginning of this chapter, the one who had confused his idea gathering system with an innovation system, and who was also unhappy with the quality of the ideas his system was collecting? Well, hopefully now you understand his problem.

It's simple, actually – his company's process started in the middle, with the divergent thinking of ideation, instead of at the beginning, with strategies and structures. To summarize briefly, the master plan framework calls for us to arrive at divergent thinking after clarifying goals and intent, designing a portfolio, and then researching to fill the important gaps in our knowledge.

But his company, like so many others, skipped portfolio design and the understanding portions of research. With no solid picture of the current or future needs of customers, and no clear understanding of the important tacit factors, what they got was a random collection of ideas instead of a strategically focused set. Would those omissions lead to concepts that were likely to be weak? Of course.

So what kind of diverging ideas are we looking for? Well, it depends ...

Universal Search Methods	Outside-in & Peer-to-peer
1. Questions.	1. Open Innovation
2. Ethnography	2. University Partnerships
3. Innovation SWAT Team	3. Customer relationships
	4. Customer Research
Trend Gathering	5. Joint Research
1. Competitor Intelligence	6. Idealized Design
2. Economic Forecasts	
3. Trend Safaris	**Future Dreaming**
4. Market Analyst Reports	
5. Think Tank Studies	**Idea Hunting**
6. Advisory Boards	1. Customer Surveys
7. Conferences & Trade Shows	2. Learning Expeditions
8. Periodicals	3. Insight Workshops
9. Structured Reading	4. SWOT
10. Success Stories	5. Creativity Techniques
11. Periodical Scanning Services	6. Scenario Planning
12. Online Trend Tracking	7. Pattern Analysis
13. Weak Signal Research	a. White Space Mapping
	b. Technology Roadmaps
Problem & Solution Finding	c. Profit Pattern Analysis
1. The Learning Curve	8. Brainstorming
2. Root Cause Analysis	9. Drucker's Tough Questions
3. Systems Thinking	10. Idea Rooms
4. Collaborative Design	11. Idea Vaults Or Repositories
5. Design Methodology	12. After Action Review
6. Ideation Workshops	13. Customer Visits
7. Corporate Strategy	
8. Quality	**Appreciative Inquiry**
9. Open Space	

Table 1
48 Ideation Methods
For more detail please see Chapter 6 of *Permanent Innovation*,
one of the companion volumes to this book.

Does our strategy call for process improvements to lower our costs because we're competing in a commodity marketplace? Then the innovation process has to help us do that.   Do we need breakthrough new products and services to compete in dynamic markets? Then innovation must help us find them. Do we need new business models to help us adapt to rapidly evolving conditions and changing customer needs and expectations? Then innovation must give them to us. Are we too concentrated in a core market? The innovation must expand our view into the edges.

Often when discussing ideation, people automatically think of brainstorming, which is a process groups use to take a bunch of information as the basis for coming up with new ideas. Brainstorming is fine, but there are a lot of other approaches to explore, dozens of ways to generate ideas. In the companion to this book, *Permanent Innovation*, I've offered a detailed discussion of ideation that covers seven major approaches and then organizes them into 48 different specific processes as shown on the facing page.

the ideation sandbox

These processes are tools to bring to your "ideation sandbox." A sandbox is a special place where pliable sand and the fertile imaginations of children create limitless possibilities for exploration and discovery. This is the ideal destination for children's wildly irresistible creative play: a sandbox can be a rocket ship or a sailing ship, a tea party or the princess's valentine ball, a mighty fortress, and perhaps a fancy resort hotel, all within the space of minutes, as children imagine themselves in various iconic roles, as heroes, champions, parents, explorers, kings and queens, scientists, doctors, and soldiers through endless improvisation, imagination, role playing, negotiation, and interchange.

Our sandbox for grown-ups is the realm of endless 'what if...,' the place where many explorers congregate, discuss, and discover together. It's brainstorming. It's tinkering. It's wondering. It's arguing, sometimes, but in a good way, as we gather the needs and models and knowledge and discoveries that our tacit and explicit research has exposed, exploring what it all might mean for existing and future products, services, processes, and business models.

Figure 22
Diverging
Three Breakout Teams Working in Parallel on an Ideation Challenge

spontaneous ideation

This doesn't mean, by the way, that we dislike spontaneously generated ideas.   In fact, we love them!   We encourage idea development and idea sharing everywhere in our organization and across all aspects of the business.   In fact, we expect it.   We maintain a system that encourages people to share their ideas, and there are coaches who they can talk with to help define and develop their ideas, and we'll certainly give those ideas good attention. (The coaches are probably "innovation champions," whose role is described in detail in Chapter 7.)

And we also systematically engage our customers as innovation partners, and invite them to share their thoughts, needs, and ideas. (Our open innovation approach for doing this is described in Chapter 9, as part of the innovation infrastructure.)

So while randomly generated ideas are welcome, and perhaps important and necessary, we know that they're not sufficient. We're not counting on people to randomly wake up in the morning with great ideas that will shape our organization's future, and we're not waiting for that to happen.   Instead, we're structuring a disciplined process to create great ideas, and to turn them into business value.

And what do we do with the ideas we come up with?   We combine them, and recombine them to create even more possibilities.   But why bother with that?

creative combination

In any ideation process the first ideas that come out are almost never the best ones. Ideas have to be mixed and blended, combined and recombined, to find the gems that will *really* work, so an important part of the ideation process is called "creative combination," where we take ideas and mash them together.

This is also how a great many innovations originate, although not from a single innovator's effort, but from the accumulation and integration of progress over time, and then the combination of disparate elements into new systems and solutions.   As scientist John Holland points out,

"Many of these new combinations come about through cross-breeding of successful patterns from diverse areas or disciplines. The internal combustion engine represented a major innovation in that it created a mobile source of power. The building blocks for the internal combustion engine had been around for a very long time, including gear wheels and the carburetor. The innovation was the combination of these building blocks to yield an entirely different result."[65]

James Burke tells a similar story about the telephone.   He points out that Alexander Graham Bell's invention was a synthesis, and a brilliant one, of work done by a series of scientists over the

---

[65]   John H. Holland. In presentation the Credit Suisse First Boston Thought Leader Forum, 2000.

previous 100 years, including Dane H. C. Oersted, Englishmen William Sturgeon and Michael Faraday, German Hermann von Helmholtz, and Frenchman Leon Scott.[66]

We apply the same approach in a compressed time frame by taking the results of ideation, both systematic and spontaneous, and adding research findings from both the hard side (science, technology, and business) and the soft side (tacit knowledge) to stimulate us to develop and explore a broad range of recombined ideas across a wide range of internal and external topics. We work with an abundance of material that is not so raw, and much of it is already and automatically aligned with our strategic intent because it came about as a result of the direct linkage we have forged between strategy, portfolio design, and research.

During our consumer products innovation project, some new concepts emerged from our discussions that appeared to address new needs, and therefore would possibly be successful in the changing market structure that was also emerging.

Market research gathered from public sources suggested that the strategy of a major competitor was also shifting, which implied that the competitor's own research into these same market dynamics may have been helping them to recognize that a shift was taking place. This had significant implications not only for the specifics of the product development we were focusing on, but also for the strategic direction that the company would pursue for the coming five years, and its competitive positioning vis a vis astute and well-managed competitors.

This is an example of how learning in the heart of the innovation process influences our thinking at other steps as well; the product management team went back and reexamined the innovation portfolios now that a new strategic threat had been identified.

---

[66]   James Burke. *Connections*. Little Brown and Company, 1978. P. 78.

phase III: converging

The purpose of diverging is to come up with a very large number of extraordinarily great ideas. It's naturally followed by convergence, which is when we identify the best ones, or "the spine of the story" we're seeking to tell, the central core of the innovation narrative that explains who the customers are and how we are creating unique value for them.

In our consumer products innovation project, creative combination had resulted in clearly defined and bounded ideas for future products, services, business models, branding, and even customer communications.   The funnel metaphor was clearly evident here, as hundreds of ideas had been proposed and explored, dozens modeled in detail, tens have been mashed up in creative combination, and finally eight detailed concepts remained, the result of our process of convergence, in which we seek to understand the essence of our emerging story.

The spine of an innovation story is not just a core feature set or the "minimal viable product," but the meaning of both as part of the overall vision that connects with users at an emotional level as well as a practical level. Entrepreneurs must only understand not only what their invention/innovation does at a functional level, they should also strive to understand why it *matters*.

We seek to identify this spine by using clustering and multi-voting techniques to identify which themes or directions are most promising, and thus to pinpoint the key elements of the narrative. We can gather ideas by moving the post-it notes around to cluster similar themes into related families of topics, which often then forms the spine itself. Multi-voting with sticky dots gives a voice to each team member, and ensures that more forceful speakers cannot dominate the conversation.

At this point we may find convergence on a single idea and story spine, or we may have identified a few major alternative possibilities that we then need to explore in more depth, in order to arrive at the one that best crystalizes our intent and is most likely to result in the creation of maximum value.

The story spine must link the user's objectives – tacit and explicit, emotional and practical – together into a single coherent thread, which then pushes the underlying concept forward to the full expression of its meaning. Hence, we focus not only on the what, but equally or even more importantly, on the why. The spine thus acts as a compass, guiding the direction in which the energy of the innovation team will flow constructively.

In the Converging stage we have focused and narrowed the design to what we believe will be the most viable solution or solutions, thus enabling us to figure out what needs to be built, tested and validated.

phase iv: simulation & prototyping

What did we then do with the eight concepts? We had to find out what consumers really thought of them, and if they would in fact address the tacit needs that were exposed. So the next step in the research cycle is simulation and prototyping, the process through which we translate product and service ideas into tangibles that we could see, touch, taste & smell (especially if it's food), and certainly use.

This step is critical to transforming concepts into workable forms that can be evaluated not only for fit with the needs and desires of customers, but also for manufacturability and packaging, or service delivery, as well as for design refinement and cost modeling.

Nothing is more compelling than a good working prototype, which appeases even the most wary and pragmatic stakeholder, because they, too, can then see, touch, and understand for themselves. The additional value of prototypes lies not just in their persuasive value, but in the fact that working prototypes validate underlying concepts by making them actually work, thus demonstrating feasibility, even if it's just in a crude way. Hence, in this phase the team fleshes out their designs to a level of detail sufficient to affirm the core design direction in way that is not just hypothetical, but tangible.

experimentation and failure as prototyping

The concept of an experiment in the hard sciences is defined by the scientific method. It's an activity done to "try something," and in a rigorous setting the attempt is made in relation to a specific hypothesis about what the outcome will be. Since the scientist explicitly predicts the result before conducting the experiment, he or she then compares the results with expectations to discern the validity of the hypothesis. The progress of science therefore comes as a result of failures and successes, where the outcomes are compared with expectations, and an explanation for the causal connection is provided in the form of an underlying theory, and then validated through subsequent testing.

The quality of learning outcomes is significantly enhanced by engaging in a rigorous cycle of prediction > test > result, because it forces each experimenter/innovator to make their assumptions explicit, and therefore discussable.

Edison's famous experience with the light bulb illustrates the necessity of systematic failure, and also the social myths that grow around it. In looking for the best material for the light bulb filament Edison's team tested a lot of materials; most of them, of course, didn't work, or didn't work well.

When he was interviewed later, he was asked about "failing so many times." The journalist was of course expressing the common attitude that an unsuccessful experiment must equate with a failure, and therefore with disappointment, a value-laden viewpoint about the stigma failure and the joy (and necessity) of success.

But Edison interpreted the process differently. They were not failures in his mind, because with each one the research team had learned something specific.   Identifying such a difference of perspective, and exploring the underlying values and experiences that would lead anyone to one or the other attitude about experimentation, success, and failure, is exactly the sort of thing that would interest an ethnographer; it is definitely tacit.

When I looked on the internet for a definitive version of the filament story I found "quotes" identifying the number of those experiments ranging anywhere from a few hundred to many thousands, which tells us that Edison's story of "failure" is still an icon in American culture that is still being told and retold, and reformulated.   Perhaps this is because it addresses a concept that we're still grappling with as a society, and we haven't finished re-telling it, and revising it as we do so.   This is also an example of the tacit dimension of human culture.

If the product of your work isn't a "product," but an innovation master plan, then the prototype isn't a physical thing, it's probably a simulation of the business model.   This may be done using Excel, or through what if analysis, or in a Business Model Canvas.   Some have even used tools like chem lab pipettes to simulate cashflow through a business to simulate the model.   One of our friends has participants act out a Star Trek scenario, complete with yellow and red alerts.   Yet another way is to use business model simulation software, which our partner FutureLab enables using technology disruption maps to drive simulations to test business strategies and models.

However you approach them, remember that prototypes and simulations are compelling ways to formulate still better questions, and identifying the right questions is at the heart of the path to optimizing any design.

Remember also that various elements of a prototype can vary in fidelity.   The parts that model what must be validated or implemented sooner may need to be more detailed than the rest of the prototype.   We refer to this as high fidelity vs. low fidelity prototyping, and a typical prototype will combine high and low fidelity elements as required by the logic of what needs to be demonstrated to gain the required knowledge in a just-in-time modality. After all, some questions simply cannot be answered until others are fully in place and operational.

phase V: validation

Once you're done with your prototype or simulation you'll show it to real users, to gain their feedback.

So in our consumer product example, the ethnography team went back to the field to show concepts to consumers and get their reactions. People were excited about some of the concepts, while others were rejected outright. Overall, the net result of these tests brought the picture of a changing market into clearer focus and helped to pinpoint the best opportunities.

The fact that some of the tested concepts worked well and others failed is entirely to be expected, and it's a positive outcome. If all the experiments had succeeded then it would have meant that the range of ideas that we tested would have been too narrow; to ensure that a healthy innovation portfolio does indeed include concepts that probe beyond the range of the current market, the concepts that are tested in prototyping must go beyond "reasonable" to help identify the exact location of the boundary.

The Scion team had a similar problem, because their new brand was specifically directed at a market that they were still learning about. Consequently, they decided that while the brand would consist of three different models of cars, a coupe, a boxy van, and a sedan-like compact, they also recognized that since they were still learning about the preferences of the target market, they would have to choose body styles that pushed the limits of what were considered acceptable from a styling perspective, with the explicit expectation that one of the three models would fail in the market. This, they reasoned, was the best way to learn for sure what would work for the brand, and what would not. They were therefore prepared in advance to discontinue any failing models fairly quickly after the Scion launch.

Prior to the launch they designed a simple but powerful experiment: each team member made a prediction as to which model would fail, a fun, informal, and important test of their understanding of the market. As it happened one of the styles did indeed fail. But it wasn't the one that anyone had predicted; instead, the failure was the most "conventional" of the three cars. This, they understood immediately, meant that the rebel attitude preference of the market was even further advanced than they had realized, and that the market was absolutely ready to embrace the image of the rebel attitude that the brand concept was expressing. The failed style was replaced within a year, and their marketing efforts pushed further into edge territory in embracing the rebel positioning.

The purpose of such experimentation is to determine where the boundaries are, and because these boundaries actually exist only at the tacit level, it's necessary to venture beyond where you *think* they are to be sure you know where they *really* are.

If a prototype addresses genuine and unfulfilled needs in a genuinely value-adding way, it will feel to users like the heavens opened, and for you it may be that vast opportunities suddenly become conceivable, as new ways to interact with customers, organize your operating model, partner up, create new ways to virally market, or generate revenues start emerge with a fury. This is validation on steroids.

Embodied in an innovation may be a new business model, a description of a whole business system, or better yet an entire eco-system that provides rich, compelling and fulfilling experiences to customers. Such a business model describes how those transformative user experiences are created, delivered and evolved in alignment with the changing needs and preferences of customers.

This is what you seek to articulate through validation, to rise above individual products and services, to look for the meaning of those products and services, and the value-creating meaning of your relationship with your customers.

Validation is thus a sanity check on your dreams and fantasies about where potential value may lie, an opportunity to realize exactly how close you are, and how far you still need to go, or if perhaps you need to pivot to a different approach. Hence, this has elements in common with the observational field work you did in Phase I, except now its "validation ethnography." Whereas before you were looking for insights into the needs and expectations of customers, and particularly the unspoken ones, now you circle back to some of those same customers and explore with them the newly created value proposition that you have achieved through your prototypes.

Functionally, this often means that you'll need to conduct interviews with people as they use your prototype. Do they like it? Do they love it? Do they hate? Do they understand it?

To integrate your findings, you may ask yourself, How do our learnings reinforce the narrative thread that is part of our concept? What are the additional stories and observations? What did we learn about the flow of interaction, the key learnings?

phase VI: the innospective

The final phase to the innovation sprint process is the "innospective," the retrospective assessment of the innovation process that has been completed, the results that were achieved, and just as importantly, an opportunity to consider new ideas for improving the Agile Innovation process itself.

This is of course an essential way to improve the capabilities of team members, the performance of the organization, and the results that overall innovation process achieves.

Your entire team should participate, and everyone should be expected to share their highs and lows, and to reflect on and share the lessons they have learned through the process. Were the tools adequate? Was communication within the team effective? What worked out exceptionally well? Where did we fall short of our own expectations? What worked and should be kept or refined, what didn't work and should be dropped or fixed... and what out of the box ideas can we come up with to disrupt and renew our own Agile Innovation world?

what is and what could be

As we look at the overall process diagram for the Agile Innovation Sprint, one observation that immediately jumps out at us is that the left side of the diagram is concerned primarily with what is – understanding the current situation, and using that understanding as a basis for creating what then lies on the right side of the diagram, which is what *could be*.

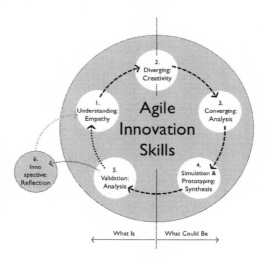

Figure 23
What Is and What Could Be

Our knowledge of the present informs our visions for the future, and as the cycle continues our vision also impacts on how we think about present reality. Present and future are thus part of an iterative cycle through which we decide on our aspirations.

And of course this is the essence of the innovation journey – our entire purpose is to create what can and should be, and by definition this also must be better than what is.

In summary, then, the Agile Innovation Sprint is a powerful tool you can apply to give useful structure to the innovation process, while still enabling a wide range of quite useful and creative explorations. Balancing these two, the need for rigor and the need for creativity, is a central challenge of all innovation efforts, and the Agile Innovation Sprint provides a compelling model that can be readily adopted. We've seen it work marvelously well in our own work, and we're confident it can work for you, too.

leveraging your team

Our understanding of the Agile Innovation Sprint has been heavily influenced by leading Silicon Valley educators and innovators Michael Barry and Sara Beckman[71] who I mentioned above. They observed that the research process draws upon quite different skills in each of its stages. This reinforces the importance of teams, because the complementary skills of many individuals can be thoughtfully composed to balance each of the different types of requirements.

People who are skilled at the identification of problems and pain points are observant, empathetic, and innately curious. They habitually explore new ideas, and they especially want to know why people make the choices they do.

Once we get to "unpacking," however, the strongest contributors are often those who like to take in a wide spectrum of what may appear to be unrelated information and find the common

---

[71]   These descriptions of the types of thinking at each stage is also adapted from the award-winning paper, "Innovation as a Learning Process: Embedding Design Thinking" by Sara Beckman and Michael Barry, *California Management Review*, Fall 2007.

threads that tie it all together. This is a quite different cognitive process than needs identification, so people who have strengths in these two areas should probably work together on a project team.

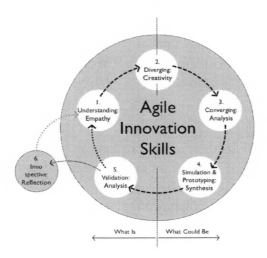

Figure 24
The Four Core Skillsets of the Research Cycle
Those who excel at *Understanding* through observation have very high empathy, while unpacking often draws on analytic skills. *Diverging* is a form of creative expression, while *Converging* is also analytic. *Simulation* and *Prototyping* require synthesizing and condensing complex ideas into tangible forms, and *Validation* is also analytic. Reflection requires a new perspective, and it's rare if not impossible to find people with all five of these skills, and perhaps foolish to try, as innovation is in any case best done by teams with complementary skills and a variety of perspectives.

Divergent thinking ideators are different still. They like to take conceptual information and see how a wide ranging set of needs and models can be brought together to solve practical problems. They're perfectly content to explore the patterns that link dozens of ideas, and find the points of inspiration that define the best possible solutions.

Those strong in convergence are often analytical thinkers who can eliminate extraneous themes even when they're emotionally appealing, to assure that our focus remains on the absolute priorities.

Those who build good simulations and prototypes like to make things, to tinker, to translate ideas into a tangible, physical or virtual form of some kind, while validators are, again, often strong analytical thinkers.

Of course you should have all of these types of people on your innovation teams so that they can combine their strengths to achieve the best results. And it will be most natural for them to apply the diverge – converge model throughout each stage of their process, focusing progressively toward specific choices and solutions that express the best thinking that leads to the best innovations.

sociology, demographics, economics

Regardless of what the actual number of experiments/ failures/tests really was that Edison conducted, it's the underlying principle of experimentation that we're really interested in – we test a hypothesis to discover the result, to it find out if it works or it doesn't, and through that to determine the validity of the underlying theory. In the end we're looking for the right theory, or explanation, because we want to act on it.

Therefore, we also conduct experiments in situations where we know the result but not the cause, and for which we therefore have a result but not an explanation.

In Chapter 2 I mentioned the declining population of Japan, a trend evident simply by the fact of Japanese women having fewer babies. Two intriguing questions are, Why is this happening? and What will the consequences be if it continues?, questions that seek to identify the unknown cause or causes. As these are questions of serious importance to the Japanese nation, social scientists are actively seeking answers. These will perhaps relate to the values and beliefs of Japanese women of childbearing age, and their family members, attitudes about careers and leisure time, about financial resources and family sizes, about their own culture and the future. But there could also be a medical cause, as yet unidentified.

Regardless of the cause or causes, if the trend continues then the consequences of declining population will be dramatic and decisive across all aspects of Japanese economy and society, with effects rippling outward from Japan to its Asian neighbors and across the oceans to the Americas and Europe.

For example, with a much smaller population, the Japanese market for Japanese manufactured products, including cars, electronics, food, and just about everything else, will be so much different than today that Japan's economy will be completely restructured. Housing prices will probably drop due to lower demand, and perhaps home equity for many owners vanish with shrinking prices. And will riders in the Tokyo subway experience spaciousness, instead of the crammed feeling of being sardines in a can, as they do today?

Japan's population will be aging, and every year more people will be retiring from the work force than are being born. Medical advances could extend the average life span by a decade or more, or perhaps indefinitely, amplifying the disparity. The labor force will have shrunk by more than half, so fewer than half of the jobs being done today could possibly be done then, unless every worker took on two full time jobs, which seems highly implausible. So who will be taking care of huge population of aged people if there aren't even enough people to work in the factories and the stores? Or will all the factories be entirely automated, and all the stores will be entirely self-service? If the factories are automated then maybe there will be sophisticated robots doing all the work, so perhaps no Japanese person will have to actually work at all.

Or perhaps everything will turn out completely differently. Eighty years is not so far into the future to be a topic for serious demographics, but no matter how these trends eventually unfold the implications will be important not only in 2100, but in the intervening decades, and not only in Japan.

Because as of today it's not just Japan that is experiencing a significant and steady decline in its population; 59 other nations are also at or near the point of shrinking populations, including Germany, Italy, Spain, most of Eastern Europe, Russia, and most of the other countries of the former Soviet Union.

Excellent research performed by clever researchers will explore the root causes and develop models to explain why, all of which will be essential for companies to succeed in these changing situations, and for society itself to grasp the reasons for changes that are occurring, and to make the policy decisions necessary to respond effectively.

I've focused this discussion about research by describing tacit knowledge and social science research because it's not so well or widely understood, but of course scientific and technical research is of course equally important for innovation.

So what must you do?

You must have a disciplined, systematic process to collect, model, and integrate new knowledge, both explicit and tacit. Naturally there must be people working in clearly defined roles to do it.

Success at each of these steps requires that people and teams work iteratively, developing and testing ideas and concepts, thinking broadly and then narrowing the focus, and then broadening again. These two modes of thought are embodied in the Agile Innovation sprint stages referred to as "divergent thinking," when we expand the field of view, and "convergent thinking" when we narrow and choose. Both modes are essential, and often our way of working through them is sequential – diverge, then converge, then diverge again, etc.

Throughout the research process, then, we have examined two different types of knowledge, the tacit and the explicit, in four broad categories, all of them essential to our efforts to create the future through innovation:

- An understanding of the new technological possibilities that are embodied in new scientific discoveries, developments, and methods.

- Knowledge of business practices across all the disciplines.
- An understanding of how society and its markets are evolving.
- Plus a view of future wants, needs, and motivations of current and future customers, as well as their beliefs and attitudes, focusing especially on new or previously hidden insights.

Together, these factors will converge to define changes in existing markets as well as new white space opportunities where new markets are already developing or are going to develop.

The output of research is needs identified, models of the hidden values and attitudes that underlie those needs, concepts that address the needs and models, and validated prototypes of the concepts. Together, these outputs express our knowledge about a wide range of important strategic issues, which may include emerging technology, societal change, and customer values. It informs us about what customers value today and will value tomorrow.

who?

At some point it will occur to you to wonder who's been doing all this research, modeling, ideation, and prototyping.

Technical research in the hard sciences is of course the domain of trained scientists, and if you have an R&D department that's probably where it's taking place or being coordinated. You're also working with other firms and perhaps universities to master the new scientific concepts and technological trends.

Tacit knowledge research, on the other hand, may not at first glance appear to be the responsibility of R&D, but actually it could and perhaps should be. If this requires a redefinition of R&D's overall role, that's OK, as narrow definitions of the role and purpose of R&D will limit its effectiveness if the current definition says that its role is only as a source of technical solutions.

R&D's role should encompass the entire scope of innovation, beginning in the strategic conversation, across both the hard and the soft domains, and in all four types of innovation, and certainly not just technology. If this constitutes a shift for your organization, then executing it will largely be a matter of refining your organizational culture, which we'll explore in Chapter 7.

Through all of this work, a tremendous expeditor of the effort is the right innovation infrastructure. While a poorly designed infrastructure can slow innovation work down to a crawl, the right tools can accelerate the progress significantly. This is the subject of Chapter 9.

The goal of all the work you've done so far is to understand why customers make the choices they do today, and what they'll want, need, and buy tomorrow. You've researched, thought, ideated, prototyped and tested your way through a tremendous breadth of territory, and by now some concepts have emerged that are absolutely compelling. You have accumulated a powerful set of knowledge about the worst and best innovations ideas, and you should know what makes the worst, worst, and what makes the best, best.

For convenience, you could organize your findings into five categories:

- **Forever failures**, ideas that you don't think deserve to ever again see the light of day. (But don't forget them, or they'll keep coming back again and again.)
- **Eh**, the ideas that could work, but which no one has any enthusiasm for.
- **Interesting**, as in "that's interesting," but nothing more.
- **Not yet**, ideas that are intriguing but whose time hasn't yet come; it may one day.
- And the *Yes, we gotta do this!* ideas. The ones you've got to implement *right now* because the brilliant flash of insight has

illuminated your viewpoint, and it's thoroughly backed up with abundant research. Your team knows what it is and why it'll work.

step 4
insight!

As you crystallized your work on these utterly compelling ideas, the light bulb over your head flashed brightly, and you knew you were on to something important. Eureka! The innovation and the target are mutually clarified; you understand what the right value proposition is for the right customer. While you may not feel quite like running through the street naked, you're pretty excited nonetheless.

Since you have diligently formulated and evaluated your ideas, you've moved way beyond just an intuitive feel for the rightness of these concepts; you have prototyped and tested, so you have documented evidence.

So it all fits together: evidence, experience, intuition, and tests have converged to *insight*.

As a step in the innovation process, insight isn't so much an activity as it is a peak achievement, a pause when everything comes together, and you look around at your teammates and by making eye contact everyone knows – this is it! We have a model that predicts the future. (By the way, the knowledge and meanings exchanged through eye contact are also a tacit phenomenon.)

While we may not fully understand how to implement our insights, that's why the next steps are innovation development and market development, to address and answer all the many questions that lead to successful implementation.

Nevertheless, we're now in a position to make choices about the projects that we definitely want in our portfolios, the ones we're going to invest in more heavily.

A few pages ago I mentioned that some people mistake ideation for the beginning of the innovation process. Others think that the beginning is the point of insight, and they use the icon of the light bulb to represent the entire process. But that's probably not the best model either. As you can see, in the well managed innovation effort we expect insight to come about as the result of the preceding processes and activities. Hence, insight is the *outcome* of a dedicated process of examination and development, not the beginning.

It doesn't occur because someone randomly had a good idea in the shower; it does occur because individuals and teams of people have been looking diligently and persistently for it.

Please note that the actual moment of insight may well strike someone in the shower, or while out jogging, or like Einstein, while riding his bicycle or playing the violin (he did both when he was working on a problem and had reached the point of saturation). But the necessity of the preparation leading up to that moment is the point that I'm emphasizing. Having carefully prepared ourselves, we cannot say when and how inspiration will strike, but the necessity for creative thinkers to cogitate and incubate, and let the assembled facts sort themselves out is well understood.

As with ideas, this doesn't mean that spontaneous insights are unwelcome or inconceivable, but from the perspective of innovation management we're not going to simply sit and wait for insight to arrive. Instead, we're going to pursue it aggressively in an effectively managed innovation process by engaging in careful formulation of our strategy, through portfolio design, and of course through many different types of research. Let me just remind you again of Louis Pasteur's comment that "Luck favors the prepared mind."

Insight, as a step in the innovation process, may thus mark the moment in time when there's a meeting that involves an innovation team and senior management. Perhaps it's a portfolio review when new ideas and projects are discussed, and next steps agreed upon. The main point is that while research has been an iterative inquiry of exploration and development, at some point in time you have arrived. You collect your suitcases full of learnings, discuss them, make decisions, and disembark from research and shift to development.

The remaining steps of the innovation process are innovation development (5), market development (6), and sales (7), but they hardly need to be described in an innovation book, as the important principles and practices in these business processes are so well developed and widely understood that there isn't much to add to what's already been said and written about them. The descriptions that follow will therefore be brief, and I will mention a few books in each category that I have found particularly helpful.

step 5
innovation development

You've got a strategy, a portfolio and research findings. They're captured in concepts that were prototyped and tested, refined through many iterations, and that led to insights, from which you made choices. Now is the stage where rapid prototyping leads to completed innovations.

Innovation development is design and engineering to transform great concepts into finished products, services, and business designs. This should be an integrated, multi-disciplinary process that includes the researchers who still probably understand the ideas best, because they've already done so much work on them, as well as people with deep knowledge of the relevant business domains, which may include manufacturing, distribution, branding, marketing, and sales.

Market Development, labeled as step 6 (and described below), occurs in parallel with Innovation Development, because the two jobs are mutually interdependent. The decisions you make in preparing the innovation for market, and in preparing the market for the innovation, require total coordination and alignment.

Still, can you make the new product or service actually work from a technical perspective? At scale? Step 5 is where you do ...

or you don't.   Yes, there are still risks and unknowns here, and there are still concepts that may ultimately fail to make it to the market.

Nevertheless, here we pursue everything that's required to transform ideas into finished products.   We engage in extensive engineering and lab testing, build advanced prototypes, design packaging, test assumptions, talk to customers, again, this time to learn their reactions to very specific designs, products, processes, and services.   We'll also interact with potential customers and non-customers to see how they respond.

And as we develop innovations, we build very detailed business models and write business plans.   In summary, we do all the stuff that's necessary have to turn a great concept into something of business value.

Some innovation development resources I have found helpful include:

- Fumio Kodama. *Emerging Patterns of Innovation.*   Harvard Business Press, 1991.
- William L. Miller and Langdon Morris.   *Fourth Generation R&D: Managing Knowledge, Technology, and Innovation.*   Wiley, 1999.
- Everett Rogers. *Diffusion of Innovations.*   Free Press, 1983.
- Philip Roussel, Kamal Saad, and Tamara Erickson.   *Third Generation R&D.*   Harvard Business Press, 1991.

project management

Project management skills are very important here.   You're probably juggling the time of some specialists whose skills are in high demand on many projects and in line operations, so making their contributions as effective as possible is critical to maintaining the credibility of the innovation process, and to sustaining their willingness to participate even though they already have heavy schedules.

It is often at the project management stage that the existence of the innovation has been disclosed to customers in the ongoing effort to engage them as innovation partners, and to maintain their loyalty in the face of competing offers. Consequently, delivery commitments may also have been made.

In this situation, with the company's brand image now on the line, project managers must be, in the words of former Lucent executive René Van der Hulst, "relentless." He adds, "It is essential to involve customers in setting priorities, in deciding which features to prioritize in the event that choices must be made, and in pushing through the last minute decisions that seem always to be necessary."

And it's also important to be willing to kill projects that, in the end, even after all this effort, are *still* not going to be successful. Give them a respectful burial, learn everything you can from the experience, and move on.

The output of this step, accomplished in parallel with step 6 (below), is completed innovations, ready for market.

step 6
market development

Innovation managers can't be focused only on products, services, or administration to the exclusion of the critical relationships between these elements, and the equally crucial interactions between companies and their customers.

So branding and market development play critical roles in the innovation process too. For example, in the 1970s Nike redefined the nature of competition in the sports shoe and apparel business by transforming star athletes into marketing icons, first with runner Steve Prefontaine and later of course with Michael Jordan. In so doing Nike created new markets for its shoes and clothing, and surpassed Adidas to become the global leader in a ruptured market.

Nike's core innovation was turning its sports brand into a lifestyle statement, and providing the products that linked the self-identity of its customers with world class athletes; this comes close to the ideal when we're talking about the company-customer relationship, and Nike pioneered it.

The driver of this relationship-building is market development, which proceeds at the same time as innovation development because although they handle different questions, the learning obtained in each is fundamentally important to the other.

The market development process addresses the universal business problem of how to introduce innovations into the market. It begins with brand identification and development, continues through the preparation of customers to assure that they understand, and hopefully choose this innovation, and is structured throughout as a learning process to capture new insights and ideas that may emerge as a result of the interaction with customers, non-customers, and potential customers.

An important underlying issue is that just because the innovation team got the new products or services out the door doesn't mean that your organization has the capacity to effectively market, sell, deliver, or service them. Therefore, in addition to the outward facing aspects of market development, this is also the phase where necessary internal capabilities are put in place.

Xerox provides a cautionary tale about market development. As I mentioned earlier, a very clever team of Xerox PARC scientists invented the first really usable personal computer, which included a great windows interface, a mouse, a laser printer, and Ethernet. It was already a mature technology in 1973, far earlier and much better than any of the young PC competitors could offer.

Unfortunately, the PARC team was not able to communicate the meaning or significance of its monumental achievement to their senior managers across the country in Connecticut. As a result, Xerox marketed the device as a terminal emulator for accessing the company's timeshare mainframe computers, which totally missed the real market opportunity. So while we ought to think of Xerox as the genuine PC pioneer, we instead think of companies like IBM, Apple, and Microsoft. Xerox was there first, but the company's management didn't realize where they were, and weren't able to capitalize on their amazing accomplishment.

John Warnock was a member of the PARC team and went on to be co-founder and Chairman of Adobe; he said this about the communications gap between Palo Alto's creative geniuses and the company's top managers.

> "None of the main body of the company (Xerox) was prepared to accept the answers. There was a tremendous mismatch between the management and what the researchers were doing. These guys had never fantasized about what the future of the office was going to be. When it was presented to them they had no mechanisms for turning those ideas into real live products. You were talking to people who didn't understand the vision and yet the vision was getting created everyday within the Palo Alto Research Centre. There was no one to receive that vision."[74]

So during market development we make sure of alignment and capability throughout our organization by organizing our work around what our customers really want, and helping them to understand how our offers could meet needs. The key outputs of market development are a prepared marketplace and a message that fits it.

Some market development resources I have found helpful:

- David Aaker. *Brand Leadership*. Free Press, 2000.
- Margaret Mark and Carol S. Pearson. *The Hero and the Outlaw*. McGraw Hill, 2001. (This one is very good.)

---

[74] http://design.osu.edu/carlson/history/lesson16c.html
The parent web site, compiled by Wayne Carlson at Ohio State University, is a tremendous reference site for the history and future of the computer.
http://design.osu.edu/carlson/history/lessons.html,

- Geoffrey Moore. *Crossing the Chasm.* Harper Perennial, 1991, 1999.
- Al Ries and Laura Ries. *The 22 Immutable Laws of Branding.* Harper Business, 1998.

step 7
selling (or delivery)

It's likely been a long journey, but now the financial return from the entire process comes through the successful sales of the new products and services. Or in the case of process improvement innovations directed internally, we now reap the benefit of increased efficiency and productivity.

We improve our brand and our build reputation as customers appreciate and admire the value that we offer. They tell their friends. We grow. We're very pleased with our successes.

But we don't stop there. Tomorrow we have to do it again because competitors are still after our market share.

For those not in the commercial sector, but rather in government or the non-profit domains, step 7 isn't necessarily selling, but rather its complement, delivery of value to the community in some form, such as new or improved services for citizens or support for an underserved segment of the community. While technically it may not be selling, it is the equivalent conclusion of the innovation cycle.

Useful books on selling are harder to find, as most of the titles in this genre are not strategic in nature, but rather deal with problem of motivating the sales force, which is a constant challenge due to the amount of rejection that they must endure. One book that I do find useful is:

- Harry Beckwith. *Selling the Invisible.* Warner Business Books, 1997. (Technically this is actually a marketing book, but it also has a lot to say about how to organize the sales effort.)

taking action
designing and implementing your innovation process

I've already discussed the inherent problems of language, of words on paper and visual diagrams, and the description of a process shown in 7 steps. This may unfortunately reinforce the illusion that it's a linear and sequential process.

But you know that new awarenesses, inputs or creations that occur in any step of the process could well impact how we think during any other step. Hence, we may make new discoveries, important ones, during the stage labeled "research" that could have fundamental impact on "strategy" or on "market development," or indeed on any other part of the process, and on aspects of our business that may not be involved in the innovation process at all. Most importantly, perhaps, what we learn in "sales" could and should significantly influence each of the preceding steps.

So while it's easy to visualize these seven steps as a sequence from 1 to 7, especially since that's how I wrote it, it would be a mistake to think of it rigidly this way.

And yet despite these limitations, in some respects it does indeed make sense to think about the process in a linear fashion because that's how projects have to be managed. They're born in strategic discussions, organized in portfolios, examined through research, initiated by the ideation phase, and continue through the subsequent steps until there is some form of conclusion and validation and economic return, or when they are abandoned.

The map can therefore be a useful, indeed essential tool for managers, and throughout this work we have to maintain both concepts in our minds, the non-linearity of a robust thinking and learning process, and the linearity of well-run project management process that is one and the same.

The capacity to simultaneously hold two different images of the very same process is characteristic of the innovation process itself, as we must continue to hold differing, and perhaps even conflicting interpretations of new and emerging data, information, and concepts until we gain sufficient knowledge to be sure of the most effective interpretations. We will be obliged to hold two, or perhaps many possible interpretations in our minds until we know, and that may take quite some time.

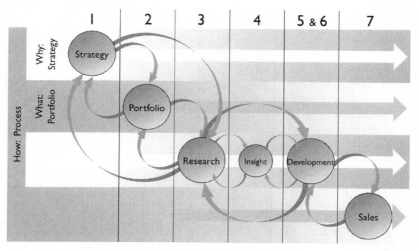

Figure 25
The Innovation Process
The looping arrows indicate feed forward loops to help people working downstream to anticipate change, and feedback loops from outputs back to inputs, representing lessons learned now applied to improving results. The arrows are more symbolic than realistic, as there will ideally be continual interaction between people working in various steps of the innovation process as they learn and share with others. Although the sequence of steps from I to 7 suggests that the innovation process is linear, the arrows moving from left to right and back indicate that all aspects of the process actually occur in parallel as multiple projects progress simultaneously.

Indeed, it's one of the characteristics of good and great organizations that this sort of ambiguity-laden learning happens at all. Conversely, it's a debilitating defect of those that don't succeed that we would call a learning-impairment. Developing the capability to learn is a key topic of the next chapter, which focuses on the people and developing their skills, which is integral to the innovation culture that they are building together.

the last word...
input, process, and output

If we look across the seven steps of the model it's clear that there are three distinct segments.

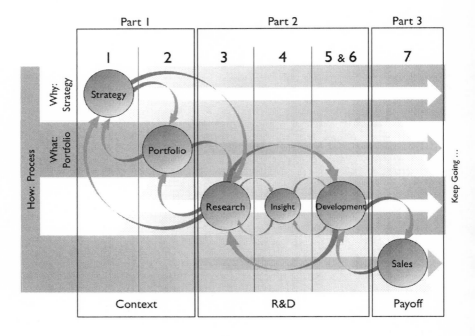

Figure 26
Three Parts in the Innovation Process
Context (input), R&D (process), and the Sales (or delivery) Payoff (output)

Part 1, Steps 1 and 2 define the context through the design of Strategy and the ideal Portfolio, and the definition of Metrics.

These Inputs define the scope, outlines, and structures for the innovation effort.

Part 2, Steps 3 - 6 is the heart of the Innovation Process as it is classically understood, which includes Research (as we have seen, its constituent steps are the agile innovation sprint, *Understanding, Diverging, Converging, Simulation & Prototyping, Validation*, and the *Innospective*), leading to Insight, and then to Innovation Development and Market Development.

Part 3 is the economic payoff as output, Sales, where the innovation process earns economic value for the organizations that create and manage them.

the agile innovation process sprint

This chapter on the innovation process is by far the longest in the book, and for good reason – this is the process you'll use (or some variation on it) to actually produce the innovations that your firm will eventually become known for. This is how you'll create future value for your customers, constituents, citizens…

The agile process sprint you conduct to organize and define all of the elements needed to make this work will largely focus on adapting the agile innovation process to your needs and your culture. What does "understanding" mean for our future markets? Who are the ideators who can drive divergent thinking? Who will help us converge on the best ideas without stifling our creative spirit? How do we simulate or prototype?

The answers to all of these questions depend in large part on the type of organization you are. Do you create and deliver services, or knowledge? Do you design and manufacture electronics, or foods? Are you a ministry of a government, or a social services non-profit? Each of these differing contexts will call for variations or hybrids of themes and concepts that we have described in this chapter.

And yet hopefully at the same time the consistencies are also evident. Some core set of process steps and forms of content will indeed empower the people throughout your ecosystem to make innovation a real and compelling part of both your organizational culture and its operational, market-facing reality.

... and managing the process

At some point you'll be thinking about who ought to be managing the innovation process, and the answers will depend somewhat on the type of organization. It will also depend on if there is an R&D department or not, whether there is a Chief Innovation Officer or not, the scope of the innovation portfolio and the amount of capital at risk, and the rate of change that the organization has designed its portfolio to meet.

Some of these questions will be discussed in Chapter 7, when we explore the innovation culture and the essential roles that have to be played to evoke innovative behaviors across the entire firm. One of the roles we'll discuss in detail is that of the Innovation Champion, who takes day to day responsibility for shepherding innovation projects and coaching innovative thinkers to turn their ideas into useful and valuable projects that will benefit the organization.

To support the efforts of effective and proactive managers, we also recognize that it's not possible to actually manage a process that you cannot or do not measure, which means that as a disciplined business process innovation has to be measured. So now that we have a model of the innovation process itself we can talk about how to measure the results in each of the steps. This rather large topic is the subject of the discussion that follows in the next chapter.

chapter 6

taking action:
designing and implementing your master plan
through

innovation metrics

or, how to measure the innovation process and its
results

"Measure what is measurable, and make measurable what is
not so."

Galileo

Like everything in business that involves the investment of
capital and time, innovation should be a disciplined process that has
to be measured so that it can be genuinely managed. This isn't
news, but it is nevertheless problematic, because measuring
innovation in the wrong way, or measuring the wrong aspects of it,
can be a genuine detriment to its progress.

Further, there are a lot of ways to measure innovation
productivity, so choosing the right metrics requires some selectivity.
Process-oriented metrics typically consider the means, such as the
number of new ideas proposed or new ideas introduced. They also
consider organizational outcomes such as increased capabilities
with existing or new technologies, which makes them potentially

useful as indicators. Financial metrics are focused on ends, the results, and include ROI-based models to track financial performance, or the proportion of sales or profits from new products. Given the many possibilities, it takes some effort to sort it all out, which is my purpose in this chapter.

the dilemmas of innovation metrics

Unlike most other forms of business measurement, innovation metrics present problems for the process that has to be measured. We might call this an "innovation uncertainty principle," as many of the assessments that we might use to measure innovation can significantly impede the process itself.

One reason is that the pursuit of innovation necessarily involves a venture into the unknown, and if we try to pin these unknowns down too early in our process we may make it more difficult to recognize and realize good opportunities or solutions. If we try to calculate the value of every idea very early on in the process of its development, we may end up with a meaningless and misleading number that may have disproportionate influence on our thinking at precisely the wrong time.

Another reason is that misapplied metrics may also undermine the spirit of learning, discovery, and intelligent risk-taking that the innovation process requires, by locking us into a particular version of the concept too soon.

A third reason is that the discussion of metrics is sometimes used as a form of intimidation to demean the ambiguity of the innovation process, as compared with other forms of business investment that are more amenable to hard core measurement.

Let's start by looking more specifically at the ubiquitous financial metric ROI, return on investment.

the perils of ROI

Among the many measurement tools available, it's become a reflex among business leaders to apply the marvelously useful concept of ROI to just about everything. This is generally a healthy thing, and as innovation is indeed a form of investment that should absolutely generate a better-than-market-rate return (or why bother?), ROI is a natural part of the innovation discussion. But it does present certain problems that we have to be aware of.

ROI discussions make a lot of sense when we're evaluating incremental ideas that will be applied in existing, well-understood markets, using existing, well understood business processes such as established manufacturing and distribution systems.

But when we're considering ideas that aren't incremental, and when they are in the early stages of development, a huge danger suddenly appears, because ascertaining ROI early on drives us to try to assess what the completed innovation could return to us when we're unlikely to have a realistic idea of what its worth could really be. So we are sometimes forced to guess. If we like the idea then we may be inspired to make wildly optimistic predictions of revenues; or if we don't like it, we may default to drastically pessimistic ones. And if we then make decisions based on our optimistic or pessimistic predictions, although our spreadsheets are still no more than assumptions, we often forget that, and treat them as real. So the entire edifice of our thinking process is built on nothing but air, bits, and bytes.

Innovation thrives in environments of 'what if,' 'how about?' and 'it might…' but it can be very difficult to achieve when there is an insistence on certainties, especially when they don't exist. This reinforces something we already discussed about innovation, which is that it's a process that is suffused with ambiguity. But the ROI conversation is entirely intolerant of ambiguity, and when introduced at the wrong time it is an innovation killer.

The other problem with ROI is that discussing it almost always forces us to try to relate a new idea to an existing market in order to have some basis for comparison. This drives us back to incrementalism even when an idea contains the seeds of a potential breakthrough. Inasmuch as breakthroughs take us to new territory, comparisons to existing models can be self-defeating.

And then there are the chicken-and-egg discussions that go like this:

Question: "What's the value of this idea?"
Answer: "We don't know."
Response: "We can't fund it if we don't know what's going to be worth."
Counter: "We won't know what it will be worth until we get some funding to develop it..."
So around and around you go.

Discerning the intent behind the dialog is an important aspect of figuring out what the conversation actually means. Many executives use the "ROI question" as a zinger or a gotcha, a trick question through which they wish to discredit the idea or the innovator. They know perfectly well that an accurate assessment of ROI is generally impossible at the early stages, so when they play the ROI card in this setting it's an accepted truism in the research and development community that the term 'ROI' really stands for 'restraint on innovation.'

As a result of all these factors, ROI-based assessments tend to favor short term thinking and to disfavor the development of long term, breakthrough, and discontinuous ideas and projects. Premature use of ROI to measure innovation thus endangers the very life of the thing you want to measure, and makes it less likely to achieve the end goal of the process, which is better innovations.

All of this presents difficult problems for R&D and innovation managers who are obliged to look after their portfolios diligently, and to manage their resources effectively, and to provide accurate measurements of their progress. This was evident during a recent meeting at HP Labs when a manager commented that he couldn't even look at a project that didn't have the potential to become at least a $50 million business. The problem, of course, was that he was forced to guess just how big a business every idea that was proposed to him could become. And how could he know?

So what do you include in your research plan, and what do you put aside? Did the researcher whose work led to the creation of HP's multi-billion dollar inkjet printing business know what he was getting the company into when he became curious about the burned coffee he noticed on the bottom of a coffee pot? Could he have said that his idea about superheated ink would be worth $50 dollars, much less $50 million?

Unless he was inspired by an awe-inspiring fit of hubris, certainly not. Yet today HP sells $25 *billion* per year of inkjet printers and inks.

So if someone had asked him to calculate the ROI on his research work, he could either guess, lie, or report that he didn't really have any idea. And if he was nevertheless obliged to assess the ROI at an early stage, chances are he would have abandoned the idea altogether rather than risk his good standing in the organization. (Hence, the importance of the portfolio as a safe context for exploration.)

Yes, there are risks with ROI, and indeed with many other types of measurement. In the end, the root cause is that investment in innovation is necessarily investment in learning, a process that is distinctly open ended and therefore highly resistant to the ways we think about most of the other processes that make a business successful. This one, though, is genuinely different, and if that difference is not respected then its underlying mission to create the future through discovery, creativity, and invention will be frustrated.

And yet having said all that, I know and you know that ROI is an important business concept, and for good reason it's not going to go away. Therefore, use it thoughtfully and not as a reflex. We will revisit it below as part of an inventory of possible metric tools, and discuss the context in which it does make sound business sense.

dr. deming, metrics, and quality

There is no valid measurement without valid statistics, and yet many aspects of the innovation process are intangible and elusive, and they evade our attempts to count them in a meaningful way.

Dr. W. Edwards Deming, the man who is credited with introducing Japanese companies to the principles of manufacturing and business quality during the rebuilding years following World War II, was himself trained as a statistician (that's the field in which he earned his Ph.D.), and as a consultant he learned to focus on what statistics told him about effective management. The numbers, in other words, tell a story that only they can tell, but to understand the story you also have to look behind the numbers.

Dr. Deming was a passionate man with a large, booming voice and deep insights. The quality movement that he contributed so much to, and whose impact on business has been profound and global, originated with a close understanding of the linkage between performance, its measurement, and the methods by which performance was achieved, i.e., the work process itself. Properly gathered and interpreted statistics are essential.

While many of the principles that Dr. Deming ultimately came to espouse at first appear to have nothing to do with statistics, in fact they are all based on and derived from the close linkage he saw between statistical results and the methods that were used to achieve those results, which he studied carefully. He was particularly incensed by counterproductive management behaviors he saw in the workplace, behaviors that prevented work from being done to the standards it ought to have been.

Furthermore, Dr. Deming was dedicated to the principles of innovation, and his writings reflect a profound understanding of how knowledge of statistically-measured performance leads from quantities into innovation, strategy, and business success.

"What business are we in? In the case of carburetors, was it to make carburetors? Yes. The makers of carburetors made good carburetors, better and better. They were in the business of making carburetors. It would have been better had they been in business to put a stoichiometric mixture of fuel and air into the combustion chamber, and to invent something that would do it better than a carburetor. Innovation on the part of somebody else led to the fuel injector and to hard times for the makers of carburetors. A good question for anybody in business to ask is *What business are we in?* To do well what we are doing – i.e., to turn out a good product, or good service, whatever it be? Yes, of course, but this is not enough. We must keep asking *What product or service would help our customers more?* We must think about the future. What will we be making five years from now? Ten years from now?"[75]

Innovation is value delivered, received, and acknowledged, not just value intended.

learning

We've already discussed the necessity that the innovation process must be a learning process, and the theme is relevant again here as we discuss metrics. There will be many 'failures' along the way, and this is normal. In fact, if an innovation process is not reporting frequent failures then it's probably not exploring broadly enough.

This reminds us to consider our underlying attitude about failure. In the innovation process, failure is about learning, and it is absolutely necessary to learn in order to succeed at innovation. The faster you learn, the faster you succeed, which also means that the faster you fail, the faster you succeed.

Measuring the innovation process and its results is a way to assess the value of what has been learned, and also to improve the effectiveness of the learning process.

---

[75] W. Edwards Deming. *The New Economics*. MIT, 1993. P. 10.

measuring in the early stages or at maturity

Measuring the effectiveness of your innovation process is a lot easier to do when the process itself is mature, and you can look back and see tangible evidence of your accomplishments and failures (both intelligent and no so intelligent). At the early stages, which could be anywhere in the first year, or two, or even three, measuring your progress is more difficult because you may not have as much to show for your efforts as you would like to have.

Which is of course ironic, because it's in the first years that most people want reassurance that they're doing it well enough to continue with the effort, and encouragement that the investment they're making will indeed generate that coveted ROI. Convincing proof, however, will usually only come later, when more results are in.

Therefore, please be patient.

twelve particularly useful innovation metrics

In exploring the measurement of innovation we found that across the 7 stages there are at least 92 metrics. About a third of the total are qualitative, or conceptual, and the rest are quantitative. Since 92 is of course a ridiculous number, far too many for any organization to actually use, you'll have to choose the ones that will serve you best, and leave the others aside.

Before we look at the full set, however, I'll highlight the twelve that we've found to be most consistently useful for our clients.

external metrics: impact on brand and image

1.   The outputs of the innovation system significantly enhance the brand. They accelerate the acquisition of new customers, contracts, and/or clients, as measured by the "rate of new customer acquisition." This is evident in new sales to new customers.

2.   The opinion that customers have of our company, as indicated through brand image surveys, customer feedback, and analyst rankings, improves consistently and significantly.

external metrics: impact on ecosystem

3.   The innovation system engages a large and growing set of external partners, customers, suppliers, and others, creating a broad, comprehensive, and thriving open innovation ecosystem. (We will discuss the concept of the ecosystem and the principles of open innovation in Chapter 9.)

internal metrics: impact on growth and revenue

4.   The innovation system results in a significant increase in the number of attractive, new, internally-sourced investment opportunities that are available for consideration by senior managers and the board of directors.

5.   Valuation of the total innovation portfolio increases significantly compared to prior period, year over year. Financial valuation methods would include NPV, asset valuation, and /or option value. Incremental innovation metrics would include percent of products/services revenue attributable to innovation within existing product/services lines.

6.   The net portfolio valuation increase is at least 5x to 10x greater than the capital invested. Financial valuation methods would include NPV, asset valuation, and /or option value.

7.   The number and percentage of projects that are in the innovation pipeline that are judged to be high quality increases steadily.

8.   The proportion of projects in the pipeline that are not

incremental projects (i.e., these are breakthroughs and new business model innovations), increases significantly year over year.

9.   The number of non-incremental projects delivered as innovations to the market increases significantly year over year.

people metrics: impact on culture

10.   Speed of innovation project completion increases year over year.

11.   The number of people who are participating in all aspects of innovation efforts increases significantly year over year.

12.   The quality of the contribution by each person increases steadily, and over time more people are contributing more valuable ideas and efforts in the innovation process.

In summary, successful development of the innovation process will steadily enhance your company's overall capability in many areas of performance including innovation, and the innovation results themselves will also get better and better.

These twelve perspectives are mutually reinforcing, so, for example, as a result of more breakthroughs and new business model innovations being developed and brought to market (#8), the opinion that customers have of the company should improve (#2), etc.

Since at root the innovation process is all about learning, improvement of innovation performance over time is to be expected as you invest effort in developing innovations and at the same time you are investing in improving the process itself.

ninety-two innovation metrics,
qualitative and quantitative

The rather massive list below constitutes our complete set. Granted, 92 are already too many, but it's still possible that there are more, and perhaps some of the ones not included here are the right ones for your organization to use.

So please use this list as a thinking starter, and be open to additional possibilities that may serve your needs better.

The metrics are listed by step in two categories, qualitative and quantitative, followed by transversal and human resources metrics.

- Qualitative metrics often take the form of provocative questions, which are intended to instigate people to think deeply and effectively about the work they're doing and its future consequences. These do not lend themselves to a statistical form, but they can open up new avenues of discussion which may stimulate new ideas and conceptual frameworks. Most of the metrics suggested for steps 1 – 3 are qualitative. They can be used in two ways:
  - o They are very useful as provocative questions in dialog. When a particular aspect of the innovation process is the subject of your discussion, raising these questions can direct the conversation in a fruitful direction.
  - o They can also be used in surveys to gather input from larger numbers of people. To use them this way, you would turn them into statements and then ask people to state their degree of agreement / disagreement, with options such as "strongly agree, agree, neutral, disagree, strongly disagree." This turns a qualitative question into a process that you can use to gather quantitative input, which can be helpful in getting useful feedback from hundreds or even thousands of

people in a very effective format.[76]

- Conversely, the metrics for steps 4 - 7 are mostly quantitative, and they're natural for statistical collection and analysis. ROI, of course, epitomizes this category. And sales itself is of course the subject of many critically important quantitative metrics.

metrics for step 1: strategic thinking

Qualitative Metrics and Provocative Questions

1. Are we targeting the right parts of our business with our existing innovation efforts?
2. Do we change as fast as our markets do?
3. Are we flexible enough?
4. Is our strategic goal clear enough such that we can translate it into innovation initiatives?
5. How well do our strategies match with the way the market is evolving? (For example, if the industry is moving rapidly into a particular technology, does our organization have the requisite expertise?)
6. Do we have an effective innovation dashboard so we know how we're doing? (The dashboard is discussed below.)
7. Are we measuring innovation appropriately and adequately?

Quantitative Metrics

8. How much time do senior managers invest in innovation?
9. What is the average time required from development of a strategic concept to operational implementation as an innovation?

---

[76] The Innovation Audit process that we've developed at InnovationLabs often includes large group surveys to explore many of these topics.

10.   How much capital do we invest in innovation?
11.   How much money do we invest in each type of innovation?
12.   What business growth do we expect from the innovation process, in percent, and in dollars?

metrics for step 2: portfolios & metrics

You probably won't know if you're using the right metrics for this step until the portfolio starts producing results that you can compare to with your initial expectations. So whatever metrics you start with here are assumptions that will be managed, and adapted, over time.

Qualitative Metrics and Provocative Questions
13.   How does our portfolio compare with what we think our competitors may be planning?
14.   Do we have the right balance of incremental and breakthrough projects?
15.   Are we introducing breakthroughs at a sufficient rate to keep up with or ahead of change?
16.   What are our learning brands, the brands that we use for experimentation to push the envelope and track the evolution of the market?
17.   Are we developing new brands at an adequate rate?
18.   Are our metrics evoking the innovation behaviors that we want from the people in our organization?
19.   Are our metrics aligned with our rewards and reward systems? (This topic is discussed in more detail below.)
20.   What did we expect our metrics to tell us compared with the actual performance achieved?

Quantitative Metrics

Metrics related to the performance of Innovation Portfolios

21. What is the ratio of capital invested in the early stages vs. return earned in the sales stage?

22. What is the actual portfolio composition in the sales stage compared with planned/intended portfolio composition in the planning stage?

metrics for step 3: research

The purpose of research is to address the questions that have come up in the process of developing innovation portfolios, as well as to expose new perspectives, evoke new concepts, uncover new possibilities, and create new knowledge.

Qualitative Metrics and Provocative Questions

23. How well have we designed our business to meet the tacit dimensions of our customers' experiences?

24. How good are our models of customer behavior and motivation?

25. How well do we understand the implications and applications of new technologies?

26. How well do we understand the emerging future?

27. How good have our past predictions been at anticipating change?

28. Is our research helping to target the right innovation opportunities?

29. Do we have a broad enough range of models of technology possibilities, tacit knowledge models, and societal trends?

30. Are the ideas that we're developing reaching across a broad enough range of business needs?

31. How good are we at creating an "open sandbox" that accommodates a wide range of possible concepts and

ideas?
32.   Are we encouraging people to share their ideas?

Quantitative
33.   How many customer groups have we explored?
34.   How many instances are there of research results applied in new products, services, and processes?
35.   What is the breadth of participation from throughout our organization in the research process (broader is generally better)?
36.   How much time has our organization invested in research?
37.   How much money has our organization invested in research?
38.   How many ideas have we developed through prototyping?
39.   How many ideas have been contributed by our staff?
40.   What percent of the new ideas that we work on come from outside?
41.   How many people inside the organization are participating in the innovation process?
42.   How many people from outside the organization are participating in the innovation process?
43.   How many ideas were collected in the 'idea gathering' system?
44.   How many collected ideas from the 'idea gathering' were developed further?
45.   How many collected ideas from the 'idea gathering' were brought to market?
46.   What percent of the ideas brought to market came through the strategy-portfolio-research pathway, compared with the percent that originated from the open door idea gathering system?
47.   What is the average length of time it takes to get ideas through research and into development?

metrics for step 4: insight

Qualitative Metrics and Provocative Questions
48.   Are we getting enough solid insights and concepts?
49.   Is our innovation portfolio balanced correctly?
50.   Are we using the right management processes for the different types of innovations that we're working on?

Quantitative
51.   What is the percent of investment in non-core innovation projects?
52.   What is the total amount invested in non-core innovation projects?
53.   How much senior management time is invested in growth innovation as compared with incremental innovation?
54.   What percent of ideas were funded for development?
55.   What percent of the ideas in the research process were killed?

metrics for step 5: innovation development

Qualitative Metrics and Provocative Questions
56.   Are the right people involved in innovation development?
57.   Do we have enough failures to be confident that we're pushing the envelope sufficiently?
58.   Do we have people with sufficiently broad technical competence in all of the relevant explicit and tacit knowledge domains?

Quantitative
59.   How fast do we complete and test new prototypes?
60.   What is the number of prototypes per new product?
61.   How many patents have we applied for in the past year?
62.   How many patents were issued in the last year?

metrics for step 6: market development

Qualitative Metrics and Provocative Questions
63. How well are we balancing our attempts to reach existing customers compared with new ones?
64. How well do we really understand our customers?
65. Are we positioned properly for changes in the attitudes, beliefs, and ideals of our customers?

Quantitative
66. What is the return on our marketing investments?
67. How many new customers did we add in the last year?
68. What is the growth rate of our customer base?

metrics for step 7: selling

Qualitative Metrics and Provocative Questions
69. How well does our sales process match our customers' needs for knowledge?

Quantitative
70. What is the average age of the products / services we are currently selling?
71. What is our gross sales revenue attributable to innovation?
72. What is our gross sales margin attributable to innovation?
73. What is the number of new products / services that we have launched in the past year?
74. How did expected sales results compare with actual results?
75. How many successful results did we achieve per type of innovation?
76. What cost savings were achieved in the organization due to innovation efforts?
77. How many new customers do we have (by number or by

product)?

78.   What is the average time to market from research through to sales?

79.   What is the level of customer satisfaction with new products / services?

innovation system metrics
transversal and human resources

There are also useful transversal metrics that help us to assess the overall performance of the innovation process, and some that assess human resources and training activities involved in teaching people to become more effective at innovation-related activities.

Quantitative metrics across the entire innovation process

80.   Now we can talk meaningfully about ROI. Did our total innovation investment, managed through portfolios, yield appropriate results in terms of sales growth, profit growth, and overall ROI?

81.   What is the performance of our business units as innovators?

82.   What is the percent of revenue in core categories from new products / services?

83.   What is the percent of revenue in new categories from new products / services?

84.   What is the overall percent of profits from new products / services?

85.   What is the percent of new customers from new products / services attributable to innovation?

86.   What is the average time to market from research through to sales?

87.   What is the level of customer satisfaction with new products / services?

88.   What percent of projects were terminated at each stage?

Human Resources and Training Metrics Related to Innovation

89.   How many people participated in innovation training?

90.   How many people used our online innovation tools?

91.   How effective is the linkage between our innovation metrics, the criteria we use to assess performance, and our reward systems?

92.   What is the "contribution to innovation" made by individuals, teams, and departments across the entire organization? And is it improving from year to year?

Gasp. And that's the end of the list.

aligning metrics and rewards

Metric # 19 asks the question, Are our metrics aligned with our rewards and reward systems? The underlying point, of course, is that people in organizations gradually adjust their behaviors to fit the prevailing systems that they're measured on and rewarded for, so if they're not measured for their contribution to innovation then their contribution will probably be less than it could be.

Hence, aligning the innovation system, the metrics, and the rewards is an important piece of work to accomplish.

But it's rarely easy to measure an individual's contribution to innovation unless that person happens to be uniquely creative, or is involved in high-profile projects. Innovation almost always involves the efforts of many people working diligently but perhaps quietly, so setting up an innovation reward structure that recognizes the team element is usually preferable to a process that only acknowledges individuals.

But this remains a controversial topic, as some people believe that the only suitable reward system is one that rewards everyone in the firm. Rewards for individuals can be seen as divisive.

From a broader perspective, the notion of intrinsic vs. extrinsic rewards can be an important element of this conversation as well.

Those who are inspired to probe deeply and find real solutions, and to do so to the highest possible standards, are deeply motivated by what they feel inside. Their interest and commitment is entirely intrinsic; they do this work for the inherent rewards that it brings.

On the other hand, when people are working at tasks because of the need or expectation of external rewards, their commitment is generally not as deep, and the results may not be as good.

This is relevant here because if people are participating in an innovation system because they want to receive some sort of extrinsic reward, a cash prize for example, then over time what we would expect is a general decline in the quality of their participation. In other words, they're doing it for the "wrong reason."

Rewards are a challenging topic in many cultures, including in the USA, because a great deal of society is set up based on the pursuit of extrinsic prizes. For example, the grades that students receive in school are extrinsic rewards, and when you study the problem deeply, you find that grades can be counterproductive and demotivating. Genuine learning is not related to grades, it's about increasing knowledge, skill, and competence, but if we focus on the grades and not the underlying accomplishments then we trivialize the efforts of the student by treating the grade as a bribe; and we all know that bribery is a form of corruption.[77]

The same dynamic applies to innovation rewards. In most situations we recommend against cash awards, and in favor of recognition and appreciation.

Dan Ariely explores these issues in his fascinating study of behavior, *Predictably Irrational*, and among the themes he delves into is an important distinction between market norms, exchanges for money, and social norms, exchanges and relationships based on community and empathy. He notes, "Money, as it turns out, is

---

[77]   If you wish to read more about this topic, I recommend Alfie Kohn, *Punished by Rewards: The Trouble with Gold Stars, Incentive Plans, A's, Praise, and Other Bribes*, Mariner Books, 1999. It's very good advice for parents, also.

very often the most expensive way to motivate people.   Social norms are not only cheaper, but often more effective as well."[78]

We have found this be entirely true in the realm of innovation – people respond well to genuine appreciation honestly earned, as innovation efforts in organizations are social and creative endeavors well before they become financial ones.

dashboards

As you apply the selected metrics and fine tune them to suit the work and culture of your organization, you'll also be developing feedback that can be used to help everyone see how well (or not well) the innovation process is working out.   Information presented on an Innovation Dashboard, accessible via the web, will show what's happening across all the steps of the process project by project and in aggregate.

Some information may naturally be withheld from view to protect corporate secrets or to keep vulnerable projects from unwelcome exposure inside the organization, but the more that is shared the better.   If people feel that the process is open and accessible they will be inspired to participate; if they feel it's secretive and closed they generally won't.

the last word...
choosing

If you tried to implement all the metrics listed here you'd probably die of frustration before you got even half way across the measurement desert, so it's obvious that you've got to choose some, start working with them, and then gradually learn to fit the most useful ones into your own world.   Think selectively, and remember

---

[78]   Dan Ariely. *Predictably Irrational*. Harper Perennial, 2008. P. 94.

that metrics are a critical part of the learning process, so learning when to measure and how to measure is part of the conversation as well. [79]

---

[79] Two resources were particularly helpful in preparing this chapter. The first is chapter 10 of Scott Anthony's *The Innovator's Guide to Growth*. (Harvard, 2008). The other is a study by Boston Consulting Group called *Measuring Innovation*, prepared in 2006. You can download it at: www.bcg.com/publications/files/2006_Innovation_Metrics_Survey.pdf

chapter 7

who innovates

creating the innovation culture with geniuses, leaders, and champions

"I make mistakes. Even though I am a conservative person by nature, I still want to innovate, and when you innovate, you're going to make mistakes. And I want to be able to have that freedom to make mistakes."[80]

Liu Chuanzhi, chairman and co-founder of Lenovo

We've examined why, what, how, and measurement. Now let's consider who, which is to ask, "How can we inspire people to do the things that lead to innovation," and "How should they be organized and managed?"

Organizations that are successful at innovation naturally develop a strong innovation culture. Such a culture is often admired by outsiders, and also experienced among the people inside the organization as a dynamic and innovation-friendly place to be.

But supposing an innovation culture doesn't already exist in your organization. Then how can you nurture it? You might ask,

How do organizations develop the innovation culture?
Who should be involved in the innovation process?

---

[80]   "As China innovates, major challenges await." *San Francisco Chronicle*, February 20, 2011. P D2. A very revealing interview by Marcus Chan.

And what roles should they play?

These are among the questions we explore in this chapter, the fourth sprint in the Agile Innovation Master Plan system.

culture and innovation culture

Every culture, innovative or not, is an expression of the behaviors, attitudes, and actions of the people who are its members. This, of course, is an element of the tacit dimension because culture is mostly a tacit attribute. It does have explicit manifestations – symbols, flags, uniforms, anthems, and codified rules, but behind these lies an entire universe of unspoken understandings. Knowing and conforming to them makes you an insider, a member.

Culture isn't created overnight, but rather it emerges through time, so it also exists as a consequence of history, reflecting what has been done in the past. It gets transmitted from the past to the present with notable continuity, which is often how we recognize its existence. Hence, when we reflect on our own situation today, we can see past trends interacting with new forces during our own times, and the aggregate picture is exactly what constitutes our culture *right now*.

Culture is also a force that influences whatever will be accomplished in our future; culture, that is, is largely self-perpetuating, and indeed its persistence from generation to generation is one of the defining characteristics of "culture" as a concept in and of itself.

The *innovation* culture likewise must develop as a consequence of particular behaviors and attitudes, as well as structures and tools, and most especially actions; the actions that result in innovations of all types - breakthroughs, useful incremental changes, and even radically new ways of doing business.

Organizations that have an innovation culture create innovations, by definition, with some regularity, and actually the concept of regularity is a quick test to see if a company really does have one. How frequently does the company produce interesting new ideas, concepts, products, or services? If cool new stuff seems to be coming out all the time, in different contexts and forums, and if the internal discussion in the organization is also rich with the talk of innovation, then it's indeed likely that an innovation culture exists there.

Since the innovation culture is not all that common among today's organizations we can infer that it's not so easy to create, but we knew that already. We've all worked in companies that felt sluggish and stifling, and most of us yearn to work in organizations that are vibrant and dynamic. A key reason for the rarity is that the characteristics needed to achieve an innovation culture are frequently not viewed as necessary, or even desirable, in successful companies.

It's only a slight parody to say that business leaders love stability and predictability because these are the conditions that make for reliable profits and increasing scale, i.e., growth. The pursuit of innovation, however, is a story of novelty, risk, and the unexpected, of adaptation and change, which is often difficult to live with, and also difficult to profit from. Consequently, many hesitate.

Innovation pursued reluctantly means that we consider changing only when we're absolutely forced to. We generally hate it, because it means we have to give something up that we prefer to keep, which is the old, comfortable way, even though the market may be telling us that the old way isn't good enough any more. Hence the dynamic power of capitalism, a remarkable self-organizing process of introducing novelty into markets through the mechanism of marketplace competition.

Companies die in this process. In the words of Dr. Deming, "Survival is not mandatory;" companies get thrown out entirely when they fail to adapt. So if standardization has triumphed totally over innovation, this is perhaps an indication that the past has overtaken a company. Perhaps it's dead, although various constituents may not have realized it yet.

If no one wants to buy your products, even if they are made to six sigma quality standards, then you have a different sort of problem. What you require are new and better designs, not ever more perfect manufacturing standards; the wrong product, perfectly made, is still the wrong product.

A culture of innovative operations is partly where the genius of firms like Apple, Cisco, and Toyota lies, because their leaders have found a way to standardize or systematize the process of innovation. Perhaps the last sentence seems to express a contradiction – how do you standardize innovation? But that's exactly the point (and that's the same point that I made in the title of my book *Permanent Innovation*). They have created true innovation cultures, which is precisely what it means to make the creation of novelty a consistent output of an organization's behavior, and hence an attribute of its culture.

At Toyota, the fruits of manufacturing innovation led to transformative breakthroughs in simplification, resulting in a company that is universally recognized as the most proficient auto manufacturer. But they didn't stop with quality and efficiency; they also pursued elusive but important goals related to design, engineering, and business innovation, yielding the happy marriage of quality and innovation that led it to become the world's most admired car company.

The means of achieving this, and likewise the commitment to doing it, originated with the very top management of these companies, and then spread throughout. But how did it spread? What did they do? Here is what we've learned.

managing innovation with 3 roles

In the language of systems thinking, a key function of "management" is to eliminate unwanted "variation," which is, broadly, the tendency of things to go off uncontrolled in all directions. Excessive variation is the absolute enemy of profitability; indeed, the entire purpose of practices such as quality control and six sigma is to eliminate unwanted variety.

However, the purpose of innovation is precisely to create a particular form of variation, variety that is valuable novelty. Too often, however, the valued baby, useful variety, is thrown out with the unwanted bathwater, unwelcome variation. So unless variety-creation through innovation is a priority of managers, it may be omitted from management's job description. And it very often is, either because managers fail to achieve innovation, or because they fail to try.

Now, this does not mean that individual people - workers, managers, whomever - are against innovation. In fact, they're probably for it. Most people actually love innovation – new cars, new clothes, new homes, new TVs, new movies, new music, new everything. But the very spirit and process of contemporary organizations, as expressed in how we organize large groups of people to work, often makes innovation extraordinarily difficult, and hence the rarity of the innovation culture.

And yet you'd probably like your own company to be more innovative than it is today. Which means you understand the benefits of innovation and you want your company to be more innovative. You want, that is, to develop the innovation culture.

How?

We've found that the innovation culture comes into being when people throughout the organization actively engage in the three different types of activities that are critical to the creative endeavor:

Some people frame compelling questions, explore hidden factors, conduct rigorous experiments, come up with new ideas, and then explore them to see if they have the potential to become genuine innovations, whether large or small, breakthrough or incremental. They are curious, looking persistently for surprises to develop into ideas, and then into value-adding insights and innovations. **This is what innovation's Creative Geniuses do.**

Some people define the strategic goals and pathways, set the policies and expectations that this strategy-to-idea-to-innovation process is what we're actually going to do, and they set aside the capital to support it. They define a firm's goals and policies to favor innovation. **This is what Innovation Leaders do.**

And some people provide support, guidance, and tools so that the creative process itself can flourish. They support innovators and manage the innovation process by helping creative people overcome the obstacles that otherwise impede their innovation efforts. They also manage the innovation portfolios. **This is what Innovation Champions do.**

In this chapter we'll explore each of these three roles in turn, and then consider some of the factors that bring the work of all three into a cohesive whole.

innovation's creative geniuses

Who comes up with the critical questions that are the beginnings of innovation, and then turns these into ideas and then into insights, and eventually into innovations? They are Creative Geniuses, and they work throughout your company.

They may also work outside, in your extended ecosystem of suppliers, partners, and advisors. And they may be customers; in some industries it is customers who provide the vast majority of innovation ideas. They may even be non-customers; tapping into *their* beliefs and behaviors to create new products and services can create powerful and compelling growth opportunities.

Creative geniuses are often the individuals who bridge the gap between the organization and its customers; we sometimes call them front line workers. They may also be senior managers, who, after all, have plenty of exposure to new trends that may stimulate new ideas. And they may also be middle managers, who are uniquely positioned at the crossroads of many information flows to spot innovation opportunities that others may have missed.   The point is that it doesn't matter so much where these people are located in the organization, or outside of it; what does matter is the mindset that they bring, and the fact of having a productive pathway for that mindset to be channeled into.

If it feels like a stretch to label these people as "geniuses," then let me explain the rationale. Your idea of a creative genius could be Leonardo or Michelangelo, but chances are you don't have many of *them* in your firm.   So you may wonder how, among so many workers in your firm, you'll identify the creative ones.   Who are the creative geniuses?

But this, in our experience, is the wrong approach.

A more useful viewpoint is to assume that given the opportunity and the context, just about *everyone* in the organization can be and is a creative genius.   That's been our experience over many decades of working with thousands of organizations, because we've seen that people everywhere love to come up with great, new questions and new ideas, and often the people you might least expect to have a valuable insight are exactly the ones who do.   So not only is it more useful to consider everyone a potential creative genius, it's more accurate.

Figure 27
Engaging the Creative Genius in Everyone

People love to innovate because it's inherently satisfying, and we can indeed bring forth this spirit throughout our organizations. Starting from this premise means that it's up to the leaders and champions (whose roles we'll discuss shortly) to remove the obstacles that are holding others back. It's also up to them to set the tone and expectations accordingly. Carpet One co-founder Howard Brodsky puts it a bit more bluntly. He says, "If you're not bringing new ideas to our organization, you won't last here very long."

No one can innovate, however, if they simply accept things as they are today. Making innovations requires that we are willing to consider that things might be different, and then to ask the questions that illuminate the roots of current reality, and which lead us to explore alternative future ones, to think about what it means, and to examine why. To engage in this sort of behavior we have to overcome any institutional or bureaucratic inertia that may inhibit our thinking process, and also to challenge ourselves to see beyond conventional viewpoints.

This sort of creative behavior is also a natural and innate human capacity, and indeed it's what people do from the very first moments of life, apparently as an entirely natural function of living. Alison Gopnick explains this beautifully.

"We take it for granted that young children are perpetually 'getting into things.' In fact, a major job for caregivers is to keep this instinct for getting into such things as plugs and electric fans from causing harm. As a do-it-yourself exercise in developmental psychology, find any child between one and two, and simply watch her play with her toys for half an hour. Then count up the number of experiments you see – any child will put the most productive scientist to shame. But when you think about it more closely this is a very odd thing for children to do. They don't get into things in order to satisfy their immediate needs; their immediate needs are taken care of by adults. Why do young children spend so much energy and time, even putting their own safety at risk? It makes perfect sense, though, if you think of toddlers as learning machines. Experimentation is one of the best ways of discovering new causes and their effects and understanding the causes you've already observed.   Although preschool teachers and parents have long felt intuitively that play contributes to learning, these experiments actually show scientifically that this is true.   The drive to experiment seems to be innate, but experimenting provides us with a way of learning things that are not innate. What are built in are techniques for discovering things that are not built in."[81]

All babies are geniuses, and they learn at a phenomenal rate. Our organizational goal is to replicate this entirely natural process as a matter of systematic organizational behavior, and this emphasis on creative thought fits quite nicely with the dictionary's definition of genius, "exceptional natural capacity shown in creative and original work."

I realize that this idea that everyone in the organization is a creative genius is a significant departure from how things used to be.   In the past, people in front line roles were often specifically instructed *not* to be thinkers, not to have ideas, and certainly not to ask questions.   They were supposed to perform pre-defined roles in a repetitive way.

Today, of course, it's the opposite.   We know that front line workers have a unique and invaluable perspective that, with the proper encouragement, can lead to innovation in many dimensions. Hence, the average Toyota worker, including those working on the assembly lines, contributes on average more than one hundred ideas each year.   This is how creative genius gets tapped, and how it contributes to the greatness of a great company.

---

[81]   Alison Gopnik, *The Philosophical Baby*, Farrar Straus Giroux, 2009. p 91. I highly recommend this book.

insider and outsider

It often helps geniuses to succeed when they have a deep insider's knowledge of their industry, but also bring an outsider's perspective to it. That is, because they are not willing to be satisfied merely with what currently exists, they often look for new knowledge outside of their own fields, and this outsider perspective helps them to see things differently, to recognize opportunities that others have missed.

Consequently, a great many of the breakthrough business ideas in recent history reflect this insider-outsider combination. The overwhelming global success of Starbucks, for example, was not driven by the company's original founders, who had in fact a rather narrow view of their business, but by outsider Howard Schultz, who came to Starbucks with a vision of a much broader market than the founders had imagined. It was Schultz who ended up taking over the company and forging it into a global beverage leader.

Another example is Southwest Airlines, which was not created by "airline people," but by a lawyer and an air charter executive who understood a need that their insider competitors had not recognized. Together, they pioneered an entirely new business model in the airline industry, and in the intervening decades their model has triumphed: just about every airline in the world has copied elements of Southwest's business model, while most of the ones that did not do so have disappeared from the market because they were unable to compete effectively.

Likewise, many great companies including Toyota's Scion (RIP), GM's Saturn (also RIP), Home Depot, McDonald's, as well as Amazon and Fedex, were originated by people who combined insider's knowledge with an outsider's willingness to do things differently. They also shared a universal goal, to meet customer needs better than they had previously been met.

Most executives know that outside knowledge is critical to success, and a recent McKinsey study notes that 75% of them report getting new ideas as a result of interaction with outsiders such as suppliers, peers, and partners. You can apply the same underlying principle by ensuring that creative geniuses inside your firm have access to a broad range of experiences beyond the boundaries of their departments or their organization, that they have opportunities to explore into the edges where new experiences and new insights are often found.

But it's probably not enough to expose the people inside your organization to outside viewpoints. In addition, you need to bring the outsiders all the way into the innovation process. Customers, vendors, partners, community members, scholars, and even in some cases competitors can contribute significant insights to your innovation efforts. Further, many aspects of the work can be supported by consultants, either when the in-house staff is simply not large enough to handle the work load, or when they lack specific technical expertise in areas such as research, engineering, and marketing (to name 3).

A broad name for this kind of effort engaging with outsiders is "open innovation," and it is being used successfully in many firms. A more detailed conversation about open innovation is presented in Chapter 9.

A last point about geniuses inside of your firm – the willingness to take risk and overcome obstacles may be a critical part of the genius role as their visionary insights, but what if the budding geniuses are not entrepreneurs? What if they work inside a company, and they don't have the intention or the desire or the political skills to take on the bureaucracy to push their ideas forward? Then it's up to innovation champions to help them, and we will explore their role shortly.

the process of genius

The details of creative work come intuitively to many people, while others need coaching and perhaps training to master it. Champions can support them as well. And even those who approach creativity with ease can still benefit from a bit of structure to help them organize their efforts.   Hence, the purpose of the innovation process described in Chapter 5 is to give the right amount of guidance and structure to both individuals and organizations.

The effort required to master the innovation process takes time, and of course it also takes time to think through innovative ideas. Thus, a critical element that also supports the flowering of creative genius is time to let the process unfold both as a matter of skill development and for the development of specific innovation ideas and projects.   Hence, if the pressure of the day-to-day is so great that there's no time for new ideas, then the flow of innovation will dry up.

But if people do have time to explore, to learn, and to discuss, then they can create great things, which is why companies like Google and 3M have, as a matter of company policy, invited people to spend up to 20% of their time working on projects of their own choosing.   For there is creative genius in each of us, and it may take only the right mix context, curiosity, support and environment for it to come abundantly forth.

innovation leaders

Another central role in the innovation culture is that of the Innovation Leader, someone who significantly influences or even defines the core structures and the basic operations of an organization, all with a clear focus on shaping and assuring its future, which of course includes the necessity of supporting innovation.

Core structures may include the design of the organization itself, as well as its policies and their underlying principles. Metrics and rewards can also be core structures, and we know that people in organizations respond to how their actions are measured, and of course to how their rewards are determined.

All these elements together broadly constitute the internally-defined rules of the game, and leaders are the people who define a lot of them, either by explicit statement of policy, or by the tacit expression of their own behaviors. Since none of these factors are absolute givens from the outset except those that are mandated by law, and indeed most of them can be changed, that's exactly the point: they are subject to *design*, to thoughtful choice about what's best. It's generally within the power of senior managers to change these structures, and when they impede innovation they should be changed to favor it.

Do you think, for example, that the rules at Toyota, both explicit in policy and tacit in culture, are different than the rules at GM or Ford? You bet they are. Toyota's rules have favored innovation for a long time; GM's rules definitely hindered it.

Consequently, figuring out exactly what the obstacles to innovation are is a key management responsibility, and since the creators and champions are probably highly aware of what they are, all you have to do is ask and you'll learn a great deal.

Innovation leaders also set expectations, define priorities, celebrate and reward successes, and encourage disciplined failures, and all of these tasks can be done to make innovation easier. Because each can be arranged to favor the status quo or to favor useful and effective inquiry and change, the nuances do matter.

Leaders also set goals, and they don't need to be modest ones; in fact they can and perhaps should be outright aspirational. By setting ambitious goals that emphasize the linkage between an organization's strategy and the pursuit of innovation, leaders elevate innovation to a strategic concern where it properly belongs. It's their responsibility to also then provide the tools to achieve the aspirations, as goals without the means to achieve them will be rightly seen as a set-up for failure, and this will be demotivating to many people, and therefore self-defeating.

And if innovation isn't expressed as a specific goal of top management then it probably won't be a goal of anyone else, either; policies that are restrictive and make it difficult to test new ideas practically guarantee that there won't be new ideas.

Trust is also critical. Are people suspicious of the motives or behaviors of their leaders or their coworkers? If so, they probably won't be willing to ask the necessary probing questions, or share what they learn if they do ask, because doing so entails organizational risk. In this situation the behaviors that are considered "normal" are the ones that reinforce the status quo.

By their very nature, in fact, behavior in most organizations tends to reinforce the status quo. This, as I noted, is not because of any shortcoming on the part of the people, but because success in the short term is usually enhanced by factors like stability, predictability, and repetition. These are characteristics that managers are trained to manage toward.

The problem, of course, is that getting the job done well often locks innovation out, and executing on the plan can also invoke another meaning of executing on innovation, which is killing it. Hence, the re-definition of execution has to mean the application of principles and policies that enhance innovation efforts as much as it also pertains to the day to day.

When people do feel safe asking the tough questions and they understand the necessity of change, they'll be more likely to explore and develop new ideas themselves. The difference between these two states of being has enormous consequences for the future of the organization, and working to assure a trusting environment is essential to long term success.

Hence, innovation leaders are typically, although not exclusively, senior managers who feel a compelling need to bring innovation to their organizations. They also reduce or even eliminate obstacles that inhibit innovation performance, and it's the overlap between commitment and authority that makes the innovation leader's role unique as well as indispensable.

The actions and attitudes of senior managers are based, ultimately, on their philosophies about management, on their mindsets, which we explored as a key formative factor in the introduction. So if you want to develop the innovation culture in your own organization you must be a willing exemplar for others, in tone and word as well as in your policies and actions.

Let's take a few specific examples. How about budgets? Do your budgets include a line item like "investment in innovation"? If not, are you sure that innovation is getting any investment at all? If there's no budget for innovation, then the likelihood that it will happen declines significantly.

And is there a seed fund for investing in promising new ideas?

Is there a team of people to manage new ideas that do not fit inside of existing business units? If not, then how will such ideas find support?

If tools such as these are not in place, then if innovation does happen it's almost certain to be exclusively incremental, executed only in the regular course of product and service management. What is prevented from happening is anything remotely related to a breakthrough innovation, or the development of a new business model or a new venture.

Another recent survey by McKinsey found that top managers believe breakthroughs will deliver the greatest performance improvements, but without specific budgetary focus they're never going to get there.[82]

So are your business units budgeting for innovation? Are they measured on their innovation performance? Are goals established for the contribution to value growth achieved through innovation?

The same survey exposes a huge disconnect, as only 24% of the responding executives are actually involved in setting innovation budgets. Only 22% of executives say that planning for innovation is part of their annual planning cycle, which means that 78% are not. If it's neither budgeted nor planned for, then is it going to happen? Probably not.

Do you measure the "contribution to innovation" made by individuals, teams, and departments? As a general matter you

---

[82]   McKinsey & Company. "How Companies Approach Innovation," October 2007.

should, as we discussed in the previous chapter.

In summary, the critical function of innovation leadership can be expressed in two words. "Policy" is the first, because innovation leaders have to choose organizational policies to favor innovation. "Tone" is the second, because innovation leaders also set the tone that others follow, either encouraging innovation or inhibiting it through the ways they behave and communicate.

managing a P&L while managing innovation

There are important nuances pertaining to P&L responsibilities, innovation budgets, and performance measurement which also need to be explored.

Two questions frame the issue. First, do you assess and reward P&L managers on the profitability of their operations? Certainly. And second, do you also expect them to lead innovation? Probably.

But if you're requiring them to do both then you're giving them a mixed message, because innovation is not only a short term expense that reduces current profits, but it also carries the risk that there won't be any medium or long term benefit at all. Any investment in innovation therefore reduces the P&L manager's apparent performance, and hence the rewards.

Have you seen companies fail because of lack of innovation? This P&L dynamic is often a key factor, because when a P&L manager also has responsibility for innovation, the decision to innovate must come from a moral, philosophical, or visionary commitment to doing so despite the penalty it will incur. The more short-term the incentive structure is oriented, the greater the threat to innovation. In most companies, the game is rigged against innovation-promoting behavior by this short-term structure of rewards.

A solution is that while P&L managers should definitely have innovation management responsibilities, the capital to fund their non-incremental innovation efforts should be allocated from a corporate budget, not from their own P&Ls. In this way, a manager can generate as much profit as possible and send the funds to corporate, but then corporate returns a portion, to be invested by the manager in the search for breakthroughs.

The manager then has the responsibility to function as a portfolio manager and achieve a solid return on the capital, which, again, is accounted separately from the performance of the P&L. This structure leverages the obvious knowledge and expertise of a key manager, without burdening him or her with an unfair impediment to profitability, and still provides the financial and organizational means for the business unit to evolve and adapt to changing market conditions.

innovation champions

The third role that shapes the innovation culture is the innovation champion, the catalyst who makes every innovation system work. By "innovation champion" I don't mean the ones who competes for their personal glory to win a gold medal, perhaps in the sense of a world champion in sport, but rather as ones who advocate on behalf of others, defending and supporting a greater cause than themselves.

We could also use the terms "guide," "coach," or even "manager" to describe this role.

No matter the name, their responsibility is to create the irresistibly fertile environment for innovation, and provide the necessary tools to support it such that it thrives. Champions are therefore individuals and teams of people who promote, encourage, prod, support, and drive innovation in their organizations.

They do this in spontaneous moments of conversation, coaching, and insight, and through ad-hoc efforts, as well as in highly structured innovation programs and systems. In doing so, innovation champions build the practical means for effective innovation throughout their organizations.

Innovation champions are catalysts, an essential role that's often missing in organizations, and in its absence the spirit of innovation often languishes. There will always be people who want to think innovatively given the opportunity, and there will always be senior managers in leadership roles, whether they favor innovation or not. But there will not be innovation champions unless they are created and supported as an explicit organizational function.

An innovation champion may have a job title in R&D, such as R&D Vice President or Director; the champion's title may also be linked directly with innovation, such as Chief Innovation Officer or Director of Innovation. This person may also have a broader management role, as a Vice President, Director, or Manager of some specific department or division.

Regardless of their title, what they do is take direct responsibility for finding the people who ask really good questions, creative thinkers in other words, and encourage them to explore everything that can be explored, and to seek and hopefully find answers to their probing questions; they help people seek new experiences that may spark new ideas; and they create a regular operations context in which sharing and developing new ideas is the norm.

the bridge from strategy to innovation

While champions may work anywhere in the organization, including in senior management positions, line management roles, staff, or front line operations roles, the specific nature of the Innovation Champion's role is to function in the middle, to provide the bridge between the strategic intents and decisions of senior managers who generally shape policy, and the day to day focus of front line workers who create business results.

In smaller or more compact organizations, and occasionally in larger ones, too, innovation champions are often senior leaders themselves, who have strategic roles as well as operational management responsibilities. The renowned HP practice of management-by-walking-around, MBWA, was a great innovation champion technique for learning about innovation efforts and supporting them. One of the reasons it worked so well is that the founders of the company were the ones doing it. MBWA kept Bill Hewlett and Dave Packard in touch with what was happening throughout their company, and helped them link their strategic roles with the day-to-day thoughts, questions, and opportunities that were being developed by the people working around them. In this role and in recognition of the importance of innovation to their firm, Bill Hewlett himself personally retained the responsibility for managing HP Labs for decades.

But regardless of the size of the firm or where you may sit in the org chart, the key is that champions provide practical support and guidance for innovation. Thus, champions are enablers who work as facilitators and supporters and play a critical, hands-on role in nurturing innovation efforts.

succeeding as a champion

Champions are usually persistent networkers who are in contact with many people and who know what's going in many places. They know who has skills, talents and resources, and they find out who needs them, and then they put them together to accelerate innovation progress. They also want to know about needs, and they spend a lot of time learning about what's not working well for customers, or inside the organization, so that they can point innovators toward likely innovation opportunities.

They spend a lot of their time helping others to develop their skills through coaching and mentoring. They also look for learning opportunities for others to engage in, such as conferences, discussions, external events, and perhaps even trainings. They gather interesting materials - books, web sites, papers, articles - and they distribute them broadly, helping people to discover useful new information.

One R&D director that I knew and admired became the unofficial literature supplier for his executive team. He kept multiple copies of about 100 different books, articles, and magazines in his inventory so he was always ready to respond to questions and conversations with helpful resources. Every time I went to see him I would leave with one or two things to read that were extremely well chosen for the concerns of that moment.

As managers with specific responsibilities in the innovation effort, Innovation Champions are almost certain to be involved in the oversight and review of particular projects. Here they have a critical role to play, because the effective pursuit of innovation must, as we have explored in Chapter 3, necessarily involve a significant degree of failure, and failure is usually a very sensitive issue. Will it be avoided, scorned, tolerated ... or embraced? If it is avoided, scorned, or merely tolerated, then the underlying message is that our organization prefers to remain within its established comfort zone, and we're not willing to accept the challenge of finding new solutions. This path, of course, contains the seeds of self-destruction because it sets the stage for externally-driven change to at some unforeseen point in time overwhelm the inwardly-obsessed organization. Hence, innovation champions embody the enthusiasm for failure, intelligent failure, that is, because disciplined failure is the extraordinary enabler of innovation.

Similarly, innovation champions are always ready to learn about surprises, since surprises may be early indications of market change and innovation opportunity. And further, innovation champions always have a great enthusiasm for new data and information, particularly those data that contradict what we used to know, as they may also be harbingers of change, and the sooner we learn about impending change, the better.

By exemplifying these attitudes in their interactions with a wide variety of people, Innovation Champions carry both a powerful message and they demonstrate an important practical set of attitudes: innovation is important in this company, they proclaim through words and actions, and all the factors that support innovation are carefully aligned to enable the creative geniuses to achieve their maximum potential as innovative contributors to the evolution of the company.

In the language of Malcolm Gladwell's concept of *The Tipping Point*, Innovation Champions function in all three roles that are essential to the spread of new ideas: they are mavens, who have deep knowledge that they are keen to share, salesmen who influence others to take action, and connectors who have strong relationships with many people. In all of these roles, the underlying emphasis is on defining the pursuit of innovation as a normal, expected behavior.[83]

This idea of a norm is central to the concept of innovation culture, and it's a key role of champions to promote these behaviors precisely as "normal." In many organizations, dare I say most, it is the opposite behavior that has been standardized as normal, the behavior that embraces the status quo, and often leads to behaviors that are bureaucratic, anti-change, and sadly of course, ultimately self-defeating.

collaboration and trust

The core of the Champion's role to support and attain innovation thus revolves around three linked activities, building collaboration, and building the trust upon which effective collaboration occurs, and building the skill level of people working on innovation initiatives.

It's not an exaggeration to say that the culture of innovation is built upon the practice of effective collaboration, because innovation is a collaborative endeavor that requires the participation of many different people who may be working inside

---

[83]   Malcolm Gladwell. *The Tipping Point*. Back Bay Books, 2002.

and outside the organization.

This McKinsey study has something to say about the relationship between collaboration and trust.

> "Managers and employees broadly agree about the attitudes, values, and behavior that promote innovation. Topping the list, in our research, were openness to new ideas and a willingness to experiment and take risks. In an innovative culture, employees know that their ideas are valued and believe that it is safe to express and act on those ideas and to learn from failure. Leaders reinforce this state of mind by involving employees in decisions that matter to them. Respondents to our survey of 600 executives and managers indicated that trust and engagement were the mind-sets more closely correlated with a strong performance on innovation. In the same survey, 46 percent said that they were far more likely to seek out a trusted colleague than an expert or manager to get new ideas and feedback on their own ideas."[84]

Innovation doesn't happen easily in environments where trust is absent, because the search for innovation is inherently risky and the lack of trust can stifle even the elemental attempt at innovation because of the fear that will open the would-be innovator to ridicule.

Or stated from the opposite perspective, there is little innovation without collaboration, and there is no collaboration without trust. We will discuss collaboration in more detail in Chapter 9.

Another key role for Champions is building the infrastructure that supports innovation. This infrastructure may involve various tools for collaboration and communication, including online idea repositories and wikis, knowledge management tools, and social networking tools. This is also discussed in detail in Chapter 9.

---

84   Joanna Barsh, Marla M. Capozzi and Jonathan Davidson. "Leadership and Innovation." *McKinsey Quarterly*, 2008.

If we were to choose a single word to describe what Innovation Champions do, that word might be "practice." Innovation Champions implement the essential tools to foster innovation through effective interaction, helpful attitudes, and practical means. They also work to transform abstract concepts and mandates into practical realities.

As I noted above, we might also label them as "guides," those who know the way ahead and help everyone to get there. And they are also coaches, who provide necessary structure and at the same time corrective advice, and abundant encouragement, to carry the creative process through its many difficulties.

complementary roles in the innovation system

To make this approach useful we need to understand how the three roles constitute a whole system, and we especially need to know how this whole is different from the parts that comprise it.

If you're among the many managers who have identified the innovation culture as a goal for your organization to achieve, then getting rid of the obstacles by understanding and applying the three roles defined here should yield a significant improvement in your firm's innovation performance. Latent innovation geniuses, champions, and leaders are already working in your organization, and as you bring specific focus to defining and supporting them in these roles, their work will be validated and their efforts are likely to become much more effective.

Creative geniuses apply know-how that results in new knowledge, insights, ideas, and ultimately in innovation. Creative geniuses *produce* innovation results.

Innovation Champions define the practices that *enable* innovation, eliminate those that impede it, and in so doing enable the entire innovation culture.

Innovation Leaders define the policies that enable innovation, and eliminate those that impede it, thereby taking a lead role in *creating* the innovation culture (but not necessarily the innovations).

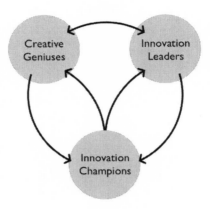

Figure 28
The 3 Roles of the Innovation Culture

Without know-how, without effective practice, and without policy, innovation will be inhibited or stifled outright. Hence, each of these three makes an important contribution to the development of the innovation culture, and all three roles are essential to success.

It doesn't matter which functions originate with which individuals, but it matters a lot that everyone is involved, and that they have a clear understanding of the roles that must be played, and how each contributes to the bigger picture of the emerging innovation culture.

There are many occasions when ideas and idea creators need support; there are times when policies are needed to enhance and enable innovation efforts; there are situations when people need new ways to look at their problems to find new ideas. How well are these three roles understood and applied in your organization?

When your business model is based to any degree on innovation, or requires innovation (and it should), then people in all three roles will be the ones who execute it.

Conversely, the absence of any of the three roles will show up in business operations as painful disconnects. Lacking a systematic innovation culture may cause great ideas to go nowhere due to lack of receptivity, innovative products not to reach customers, innovative services to fail to be delivered, or distribution systems to lack effective products.

Consider a few somewhat oversimplified examples of what happens when the parts don't fit together well. Imagine a company with an amazing breakthrough technology from a team of amazing creative geniuses, but a sales force that is incapable of selling it and a senior management that is largely indifferent to prospective buyers. Actually, that's not so difficult to imagine, nor is it all that oversimplified. I already mentioned that Xerox had that experience; the company practically invented the PC, but was not successful in bringing it to market.

Why not?

Because Xerox management didn't actually understand who would use the product, or what for, so they pushed it through an entirely unsuited distribution channel, to a market that was neither prepared for it nor able to understand it. So it went nowhere for Xerox.

But Apple and Microsoft did make excellent use of Xerox's technology, and in subsequent years they made billions by applying Xerox inventions to their own products and services.

Now imagine a company with a brilliant sales force that learns of important market trends, but the company ignores the warnings? This disconnect happened to IBM, which overlooked the emerging workstation market and allowed Sun to become the market leader because IBM failed to even make an attempt to address the new client-server IT paradigm in the 1980s. The eventual collapse of the mainframe market led to 200,000 IBM layoffs.

Or let's look at cars. GM's vast dealer network is pervasive throughout North America (and indeed the entire world), but the company somehow couldn't manage to produce an Oldsmobile-branded car that people actually wanted to buy. The pipeline was there, but not enough good stuff came through it, and GM was eventually compelled by its persistent lack of innovation to shut down Oldsmobile entirely.   Soon thereafter it also shut down Pontiac, Saturn, and Hummer, an epic failure of brand management.

what's missing?

If Xerox's creative geniuses had been able to convince top management that its personal computer technology constituted the basis of a new and powerful business model then perhaps the results would have been different.   If IBM had understood that workstation computing was a new and important business model perhaps Sun would never have gained a foothold in the market and IBM could have begun to transform itself without the trauma of impending collapse two years later.   If GM had reconsidered Oldsmobile's business model early enough, perhaps Olds would still be viable.

With these examples it's impossible to know the root causes without talking to the actual people involved and understanding how they reasoned through their problems, but the self-destructive failures strongly suggest top managers were probably not asking the right questions about the future and how to adapt to it.

The critical role missing in each case seems to be the innovation champion's, as it constitutes the bridge between strategy and creativity.   It's the champion who facilitates communication between the two vastly different styles of thinking, the operational/strategic and the creative/innovative.

Champions nurture the innovation cultures that achieve a successful style of collaborative innovation, through which leaders define effective strategic positions, creative geniuses develop the ideas, projects, and manifestations of the strategy, and innovation champions themselves facilitate, coordinate, stimulate, coach, and prod both the leaders and the champions as the work progresses.

And when we look at the companies that are successful

innovators we see these three roles working together actively.

For example, Southwest Airlines developed an approach to the airline business unlike any other company, and has sustained its unique business model to become the most financially successful company in what has at times been a highly troubled industry. The leaders of Southwest thought through their business goals in a comprehensive way, and did not simply copy the operating model of the times, but rather re-thought it from top to bottom. The company has not attempted to be a mighty global airline, but has instead focused on understanding its niche and serving it excellently and profitably. The company's culture embraces all the qualities that contribute to innovation, and all three roles are clearly articulated in its design and operations.

Today, as a result, the market value of Southwest is higher than United, American, and Delta Airlines although it's a much smaller company by revenue than any of them. Why is this? Because Southwest is the only airline that's been consistently profitable. The company's business model is entirely suited to its market, and investors reasonably believe that it has great prospects for the future. Tomorrow it's possible that a competitor's innovation or some other change in the market landscape could change that perception, but for today the market has defined its expectations, and they're based on decades of demonstrated, innovative performance.

the organizational paradox

You may have noticed a paradox here, which is that on the one hand the old style of rigid hierarchy usually inhibits innovation, while on the other hand leaders as senior managers, champions as middle managers, and geniuses as everyone fits pretty well into hierarchical boxes we're so familiar with.

However, even among overtly hierarchical companies, the tone of culture and organization can reflect stifling obedience to those "above," or it can have a much different feeling of openness, trust, and learning.

For example, a senior manager at Toyota recently spoke about a project team he was leading, and he mentioned how he went about choosing the people to be on the team. In addition to skill and talent, the primary selection criterion he emphasized was that everyone on the team had to be willing to speak up if they thought an idea was wrong. He refused, in other words, to have anyone on the team who just went along with whatever he, as boss, or anyone else believed. The team was tremendously successful; they created Toyota's Scion brand, as we discussed in Chapter 5.

To draw the contrast starkly, imagine a rigid hierarchy in which senior managers exert dominating control over the entire operation, and the entire structure of the firm is geared around preserving the status quo.

The table on the following page shows this behavior in the left hand column.

The firm that's obsessed with the status quo probably won't last very long, but some managers still seem to believe in this model, and their domineering attitudes and behaviors reinforce it.

We've also seen organizations that are fluid and openly seeking innovation in all its many manifestations, ones that are characterized by an innovation culture, as shown in the right hand column. In these organizations, change is a catalyst for innovation, and innovation is a catalyst for change.

This contrast between the two styles is quite clear. And while this table is certainly overstated and thus a bit of a caricature because it's so unlikely that any organization would describe itself exclusively in the left *or* the right hand columns, it nevertheless does express underlying truths that you're probably familiar with. Somewhere between the extremes of total stagnation and utter abandon is the appropriate target zone.

	Status Quo Culture	**Innovation Culture**
1.	Predictability	Un-predictability
2.	Seek stability	Seek novelty
3.	Focus on core competence	Focus on edge competence
4.	High success rate	High failure rate
5.	Reinforce the organizational hierarchy	Reinforce organizational networks
6.	Fear the hierarchy	Focus on creative tension
7.	Avoid surprises	Embrace surprises
8.	Focus on inside knowledge	Combine inside and outside knowledge
9.	Easy to live with	Hard to live with
10.	Corporate politics	Moving the cheese
11.	Efficiency through standardization	Efficiency through innovation
12.	Extend the status quo	Abandon the status quo
13.	Avoid change	Embrace change
14.	Measure stability	Measure innovation
15.	Look for data to confirm existing management models	Look for data to contradict existing management models
16.	Senior managers have the critical knowledge	Everyone has critical knowledge
17.	Look for certainty	Embrace ambiguity
18.	Accept things as they are	Ask tough questions
19.	Protect the past	Create the future

Table 2
Status Quo Culture and the Innovation Culture

Scan the table and see how many of the attributes shown in the left column reflect your thinking, or the behavior of your organization.   On the right, you'll see the corresponding idea suggesting how things could be different in a setting that favors innovation.

Wherever the attitude described in the Status Quo Culture column is too strong, making the transition to the Innovation Culture is not going to be easy. But each pair of concepts offers an opportunity to think and work differently, and each shift will help to bring the new culture into being.

Perhaps the greatest weakness of the status quo culture is shown on line 16; organizations which tacitly assume that the big bosses already know what's important are learning-disabled. Because of their supposed superior knowledge, senior management's role is to give direction, while unique knowledge and new learning gained by everyone else is discounted, or even ignored. Thus, two of its outcomes are the suppression of learning and the suppression of its application.

In contrast, the innovation culture supports learning in all of its many forms; people in innovative organizations learn voraciously, and readily transform their learning into creative outputs.

> "In the innovation-driven organization, the resource of knowledge is required in the work of nearly everyone. The results of each individual's work are not brought together at the end of a linear process, but are communicated throughout the process. Further, with respect to the product development process itself, growing numbers of people are involved in generating ideas and bringing those ideas together. Innovation is complex and unfolds in many steps, both big and small. Everyone must be up to date with respect to information, and all must coordinate their work – both of which impose on the organizational structure in a variety of ways."[85]

Simply bringing the contrast between these two models to awareness can be a useful step forward, as it begins to foster an organizational climate of openness and exploration, which will in turn support the emergence of the innovation culture.

---

[85]   Thomas J. Allen and Gunter W. Henn. *The Organization and Architecture of Innovation*. Elsevier, 2007. P. 13.

Of course this table simplifies many realities that are considerably more complex. Nevertheless, the intent is to highlight important underlying differences that may help you to think about the organization and culture that you want to foster as you set about to create the dynamic innovation culture in your own organization.

three key attributes: an attitude, a behavior, & a skill

We have spent many hours, days, and weeks working with successful geniuses, champions, and leaders, and we've observed that there is a set of behaviors that they tend to share. Over time, we realized that these attributes are common to the process of and love for innovation, and it doesn't matter so much whether one is working as genius or a leader, as much as one's attitude about exploration and change.

This discovery reinforces our observation that the specific role an individual plays at any given time is much less important than the attitudes, behaviors, and skills that each of us brings.

Here are three key characteristics we've noticed as being exceptionally important:

attitude: curiosity

Innovators are inherently curious. They always want to know more, and they are steadily building their own skills so as to get better at satisfying their own curiosity. As such, their basic motivation comes from within, and they take great satisfaction in achieving understandings and discoveries. This lends their demeanor a certain determination, and the myth of the rebel comes, I think, from this characteristic. They do what they feel is right, and if that requires them to act like rebels, then so be it.

Another consequence of inner-directness and curiosity is persistence, the determination to stay with it all the way. This often requires considerable powers of concentration, the capacity to hold a problem in one's mind for a prolonged period of time. Isaac Newton, for example, was apparently able, "to hold a mathematical problem in his mind for weeks."[86]

behavior: patience for ambiguity

At the behavioral level, innovators are willing to live with ambiguity until they understand the problem and find solutions, even if that takes months or years. This is important in the innovation process, because one of the most common causes of innovation failure (not the good kind of failure, but the bad kind) is that people are unwilling to live with ambiguity long enough to get to a real root cause; instead, they grasp at the first half-baked understanding that comes by, but it ends up wholly unsatisfying.

Tolerance for ambiguity also enables a certain type of risk-taking, which is often very important for innovation results to be achieved. After all, a risk is simply an investment with a highly uncertain outcome. Living with such uncertainty is another way of expressing the willingness to live with ambiguity.

There can also be a down side to the tolerance for ambiguity, though, which is that it persists indefinitely. Hence, those with very high tolerance for ambiguity may need the hearty shove from a leader or champion to get the thing finished. At some point, excessive patience transforms a would-be innovator into an indecisive cogitator.

skill: connection-making

Innovation requires that we make connections between disparate pieces of data and information that others may not have connected, and so the capacity to identify patterns and connections across the boundaries between disciplines and industries is a common characteristic. (This is also sometimes called "lateral

---

[86]   Fritjof Capra. *The Science of Leonardo: Inside the Mind of the Great Genius of the Renaissance*. Anchor Books, 2007. P. 29. This passage from Capra's book also discusses the importance of curiosity and memory to the creative genius.

thinking.")

Interestingly, doing this well requires that we are able to look at reality for what it is, that we make effective assessments of what patterns are actually out there. So we have to respond not only to the pull from inside, but to the voice of reality that is outside.

It also requires that we retain a lot of knowledge in memory from a variety of sources so that we can at some point establish the connections between them. Innovators therefore tend to build their own personal libraries to support their ongoing learning process.

There are of course other attributes that may be important to the success of geniuses, champions, and leaders in any specific situation, so this short list is not meant to be exhaustive, but rather to point out a few characteristics that are sometimes overlooked, and which we have found to be particularly important.

what about rebels and mavericks?

A persistent theme in the innovation literature describes and often glorifies the role played by "rebels" and "mavericks." The myth has it that organizational rebels emerge to fight the bureaucracy and innovate even in the most status quo organizations, often by developing a "skunkworks" where innovation can be done quick and dirty.

Yes, it can be fun to be a rebel, but organizations that endorse that sort of behavior on a consistent basis are really just self-convicting themselves of innovation incompetence. The problem with this, of course, is that it glorifies an elaborate workaround. It makes a lot more sense to develop a culture of innovation and overcome the habits of the status quo on a consistent basis, than to endorse a set of redundant and parallel structures.

taking action:
designing and implementing your master plan for culture

We all know that innovation is difficult for organizations to accomplish, especially on a consistent basis. There are many reasons for this, and we've discussed a lot of them. Structures, processes, and attitudes can encourage innovation, or inhibit it. Other barriers include lack of attention from top management, lack of a precise innovation methodology, and lack of time to pursue new ideas.

Innovation doesn't happen without leaders who embrace it, nor can it happen without people who have ideas and are willing to risk failure to experiment with them. Nor does it happen consistently without champions to bridge between the strategic and operational questions and help the individuals who have ideas and want to explore them.

And of course it happens best, and fastest, when all three roles are consciously implemented and mutually supporting. But this does not mean that each individual can play only one of these roles; many people are geniuses, *and* leaders, *and* champions, and at various times many individuals play all of these roles.

So what's important is not that we classify people into the various categories; in fact, don't do that. But do make sure that all three roles are being played, and played well, so that defining, developing, and implementing ideas and transforming them into innovations becomes the norm.

From an implementation perspective, each role has a few aspects that we've found to be most important.

For leaders, the critical factor is the mindset, which we have discussed at length already. If that mindset exists then all else will follow; and if it does not exist, then the rest will be a huge (and unnecessary) struggle. In addition, they must focus on defining the right innovation goals, setting the right expectations that are high enough to instigate meaningful progress, but not so high as to invite ridicule, setting policies that favor innovation, and communicating always in a tone that makes it clear that innovation is imperative for the future, starting now.

For creative geniuses to work effectively, it's essential for them to have a sound working knowledge of the creative process itself; it's so important that it's the subject of the following chapter.

As for innovation champions, here are four key success factors:

champion's ksf #1: support

A big part of the Innovation Champion role is to let people know that you're available to help them with innovation.

Invite them to talk with you or email no matter what stage their ideas are. It doesn't matter if it's the first glimmer or a fully developed product concept, getting people to talk about ideas gets the momentum moving.

The more conversations you have with people, the more good ideas will eventually come up to the surface.

champion's ksf #2: time

When innovative and creative people rank the value of various innovation tools, their responses show that what's most important to them is not software tools, trainings, case studies, or guides, all of which are considered of low to moderate importance.

Instead what is most important to them? Time! Time to think and work on their ideas.

"Innovating" requires thinking - looking for problems, asking questions, exploring, following curiosities, developing insights, looking for inspirations, looking for unknown and unmet needs, and looking, ultimately, for ideas, all of which take time.

As an innovation champion, helping people find time to work on their ideas, and on the ideas of others (which is almost as much fun), is an essential part of the job. Sometimes that's quite difficult to do, though.

Here's a small innovation champion vignette about finding time: a company's controller had a few ideas she wanted to explore, but the day to day pressures were too demanding to allow even a few hours to get a team together and work on them. The solution: her organization's innovation champion invited her and three others to discuss the ideas over a working lunch at a nice-ish restaurant, and only asked in return that they write up a few paragraphs on the ideas and their conversation about them. The result: ideas exposed and explored, useful potential developed to improve the company's innovation portfolio, some creative tension usefully channeled, and the innovation culture enhanced.

champion's ksf #3: make it visual

Ideas are usually useful only when someone can communicate them clearly, so it's important not only to describe the idea in text, but also to make drawings, photos, maps, diagrams, charts, or visual models of any kind to help people understand what you want to explain to them.

As an Innovation Champion, part of your job is to help people develop their ideas and present them clearly, to help them to make their ideas as visually complete and interesting as possible.

champion's ksf #4: communication and openness

The success of an Innovation Champion depends in large part on how people feel when you communicate with them: building trust is essential.

People most respect a champion who is open and honest with them, even if the feedback is "negative" or critical because their ideas still need work. They will appreciate and respect honesty as long as the message is delivered in a positive way, and as long as they feel you're being sincere and giving enthusiasm and encouragement.

And if you're managing the innovation pipeline or portfolio, it's important to keep people informed about the status of their ideas as they move through the innovation process. Because if ideas are proposed and then just disappear into some organizational black hole, people will lose interest in the process, lose respect for management, and stop participating.

the agile innovation culture sprint

What's the prevailing attitude toward innovation in your organization? Do people embrace it enthusiastically? Or do they avoid it like a head cold?

If they avoid it, it's probably because the deck is stacked against innovation across many tacit as well as explicit dimensions of work and organizational culture. These are the obstacles that must now be overcome.

How to do that? At the beginning of this chapter I posed four questions, and I want to address them specifically now that we've talked through the innovation culture model and I've explained the three roles and how they work together. The questions were:

How can you nurture the innovation culture?
How do organizations develop the innovation culture?
Who should be involved in the innovation process?
And what roles should they play?

I hope it's clear to you now that to nurture the innovation cultures requires a concerted effort from many perspectives. The right tone and communications from senior leaders are essential, and they're complemented by formal processes and procedures including the innovation portfolio and a rigorous innovation process that promotes learning with discipline.

When you engage in the sprint to design your culture, you'll therefore need to *understand* exactly what the current reality is. This may take some digging to expose, as people may not be entirely willing to share their inner concerns and dissatisfactions in fear that being too open will have a detrimental effect on the their careers. Establishing a safe space for candor is essential; if there are any negative repercussions from anything said, it will have a chilling effect on innovation, possibly for years to come.

Expectations, metrics, and rewards also have to be properly designed so that they're aligned with your strategic intents, which by the way have to be explicitly stated and calibrated to what's actually happening in the market, and what's likely to be happening in the future. *Divergent* thinking can expose new and creative options here, and you'll naturally enough *converge* on a set that makes the most sense.

And then comes a step that is often omitted in designing culture, which is *simulation* and *prototyping*. Too often a set of senior leaders goes off on a retreat and "redesigns the culture" only to find that what they came up with does not resonate throughout the organization. Better, then, to test ideas in small scale prototypes and simulations which will then validate or invalidate design hypotheses.

Implementing a rigorous innovation process and defining roles clearly is essential to developing the culture, and of course as we learned in this chapter, the three roles of genius, leader, and champion must be well understood and well executed, even if it's the same person or people who are performing them.

the last word ...

Any organization's culture is the expression of its operations as a system, and so an innovation culture cannot be artificially grafted onto an existing company that is pervaded by anti-innovation rules, regulations, procedures, and attitudes. Instead, the whole approach has to be thought through and implemented systematically, and when you do so the rewards will be abundant.

chapter 8

the creative process

"Creative problem solving is an intentional process of defining success and setting out to achieve it.   Two behaviors are creative necessities: the need for *Curiosity* ... an ever-developing interest in taking things apart to discover what 'makes them tick,' and the need to *Improve Things* ... a concern for being constructive, a drive to make things 'tick' better."[87]

Don Koberg and Jim Bagnall

There are a lot of wonderful books on creativity, and there's no need here to try to repeat or even summarize them here. (A few of the best are included in the Bibliography.) But there is one aspect of creativity that is not often discussed in the vast literature, and I want to highlight it because it's pivotal to evoking creative behaviors from individuals and groups, and to achieving creative results from organizations. This is the creative process itself.[88]

In our work we've found that there are more effective and less effective ways to guide and support the pursuit of creative ideas, and the intent of this discussion is therefore to outline a useful

---

[87]   Don Koberg and Jim Bagnall. *The Universal Traveler*. Crisp Publications, Inc., 1991. P. 23.

[88]   This chapter is adapted from Chapter 7 of my earlier book, *Managing the Evolving Corporation*.

structure for creativity, keeping in mind, of course, that like the innovation process, the creative process model described here shouldn't be followed rigidly.

the creative process model

Although each individual approaches creativity intuitively, and therefore differently, there is nevertheless a universal process, a discipline, which suggests something far different than the common stereotype of the wild-eyed creative (mad?) genius working in a cluttered laboratory on a dark and stormy night. Einstein with a tidy haircut might not inspire the same awe, but with his hair exploding in all directions, surrounded by the apparent chaos of papers piled high, or standing in his frumpish sweater beside rows of unintelligible blackboard formulas, this is the creative genius!

Despite the compelling imagery, however, the real secrets to real creative genius are disciplined hard work and a sound underlying model that tells you how to go about it. Koberg and Bagnall, who I quoted at the start of this chapter, wrote a fabulous guide to the creative process in 1973, and it remains as valid today as it was then. Not everything that follows is in complete alignment with their model, but it's nevertheless a great resource in its funky, 1970s style.

The key to the creative process model is a simple distinction, the principle that creativity doesn't start by looking for solutions, it starts by creating the problem that is to be solved.

start by creating the problem

When Martin Luther King, Jr. proclaimed "I have a dream!" he condemned the realities of segregation and racism, and simultaneously expressed his determination to overcome them. His powerful voice still echoes, transcending time and distance.

President Kennedy proclaimed a commitment to send men to

the moon, and eight years later astronauts Neil Armstrong and Buzz Aldrin stepped from the Eagle and extended the reach of humanity further into the universe.

The protesters of Tiananmen Square were driven by a vision of Chinese society that compelled them to risk their lives attempting to create it.

And on the day that Nelson Mandela was released from 27 years of imprisonment he said, "Today the majority of South Africans, black and white, recognise that apartheid has no future. It has to be ended by our own decisive mass action in order to build peace and security. The mass campaign of defiance and other actions of our organisation [referring to the African National Congress] and people can only culminate in the establishment of democracy. I have fought against white domination and I have fought against black domination. I have cherished the ideal of a democratic and free society in which all persons live together in harmony and with equal opportunities."

Today, individuals throughout the world persist in their own quests to fulfill their own visions, and whether they live in northern Africa in Tunisia and Egypt for example, and the Americas, and across South Asia, the voices of past visionaries, of Dr. King, Tiananmen Square, and President Mandela and many others still echo.

A compelling vision, well expressed, is one of the most powerful of forces in the human experience. It sets up the contrast between what is and what could be, and because of this contrast there emerges a stark and driving force, a compelling motive that we call "creative tension." This is the energy that drives visionaries, whether they are artists or statesmen, scientists or entrepreneurs or educators, missionaries or presidents, revolutionaries, or parents. And it is from this energy that problems worthy of being solved are created.

Great leaders define visions that express the spirit and the potential of their times and by doing so they infect others with a compelling tension that suffuses the atmosphere and begs for action. Such a vision contrasts so strongly with the current condition that the idea of what could be is overwhelmingly powerful, magnificent and motivating, so much so that people may willingly sacrifice a great deal in the quest for its fulfillment.   It becomes the defining element of a professional life or perhaps a personal life, and gives meaning to what might otherwise be a mundane existence.

Vision is the key enabler of creative genius, the ability, or willingness, or indeed the compulsion to see things not only for what they are, but for what they could be.   This difference is the source of creative tension.   In the arts, the sciences, in education and civil service, and in business, people who experience creative tension are intrinsically motivated and often feel compelled to make change, when they want to and even sometimes against their better judgment.   They aspire to bring to reality that which they have imagined or envisioned, and consequently they work with dedication and persistence to overcome the obstacles they may encounter along the way.

World-renowned choreographer Twyla Tharp expresses her experience of creative tension this way.   "I was fifty-eight years old when I finally felt like a 'master choreographer.'   The occasion was my 128th ballet, *The Brahms-Haydn Variations*, created for the American Ballet Theatre.   For the first time in my career I felt in control of all the components that go into making a dance – the music, the steps, the patterns, the deployment of people onstage, the clarity of purpose.   Finally I had closed the skills gap between what I could see in my mind and what I could actually get onto the stage."[89]

That gap between the mind's eye and what it the physical eye beholds is a dynamic, electric place, a powerful source of motivation and momentum.

There are plenty of business examples to draw from as well. Jeff Bezos articulated a vision of a radically different online consumer marketplace that took many years to prove out, but now Amazon is one of the world's leading retail companies, having pioneered what it means to sell goods over the internet.   The

---

[89]   Twyla Tharp. *The Creative Habit*, Simon & Schuster. 2003. p 232.

successful business model closed the gap between the vision and reality.

Fred Smith established Fedex over many years and countless obstacles, his vision driving him forward despite the fact that he ran out of cash on more than one occasion.

And Chester Carlson, the inventor of xerography, labored for years to achieve his vision, and then for many more years to commercialize it, overcoming massive obstacles in both phases of his project.

Entrepreneurs like these exemplify the formative spirit of creative tension, and having understood how a business, a product, a service can be different and better than what currently exists, they have the drive to make it happen, often taking significant risks along the way.

Conversely, if you lack drive and don't take action to fulfill the vision, it will remain in the vague and distant future, inconsequential, a fantasy. But once you start to do something about it, the nebulous future coalesces toward distinct shape and form in the present, and offers possibilities that once were only dreamed of. Hence, the fulfillment of a vision alters the track of time, and because of creative drive a new possibility emerges.

The vision and the way it contrasts with the current condition has, in fact, created a problem. The current condition is suddenly, obviously, and inescapably undesirable or even unacceptable, and the vision offers *the* solution.

But be careful here, because although the act of defining a vision has led directly to the creation of a problem, it's important to make sure that it's a problem that's actually worth solving.

Some of the struggles of General Motors illustrate this point. During the 1970s and '80s, GM's design staff settled on a standardized look for many of its cars across brands, and an entire generation of Chevrolets, Buicks, Oldsmobiles, Pontiacs, and even Cadillacs looked so similar to one another that customers couldn't tell them apart. A lot of people didn't care for that, as the identities of each brand were lost to a single general design style. Sales declined, and GM's market share dropped.

However, the cars that looked similar on the outside were very different on the inside, designed and manufactured differently, and because of this there were no significant economies of scale in their manufacture. What GM should have done, of course, was to make the cars look different on the outside but be the same, or similar, on the inside. This would have enabled the company to offer more variety to the marketplace while still achieving significant economies of scale in design and manufacturing. This approach is now known as the platform concept, and it's applied in many industries, from food to technology, to, yes, cars.

The question in GM's case is, How could the company have gotten it so amazingly, backwardly wrong? What strange vision must have inspired GM's leadership to formulate the problem precisely backwards, opposite of how they should have thought about it?

While GM was losing customers, Toyota, Honda, and Nissan were achieving success by steadily increasing quality, marketplace variety, and manufacturing cost control. They gained market share by introducing new cars that were assembled around a few basic chassis and engine configurations, platforms that kept costs lower, the same on the inside but different on the outside.

Hence, the warning that a mis-directed vision creates the wrong problem, and is the beginning of the wasteful organizational wild goose chase.

advertising and creative tension

Portraying a vision is also fundamental in attracting customers for a company's products and services, which is why marketplace competition is often expressed through differing brand visions. As advertising is designed to influence the process by which customers choose, it's thus the attempt to influence the customers' visions of themselves: drink this beer and you'll be attractive; drive this car and you'll be successful; wear this clothing; smoke this cigarette; eat this food; use this product to become a better you. In this way advertising is intended to induce creative tension inside each of us, and then to persuade us that the solution, the means of resolving the tension, is their product. When someone says, "I've got to have that!" then it's worked.

Failed products, on the other hand, are those that didn't inspire the customers' vision, because if the difference between the way things are now and how they would be after the purchase is not compelling, then there are no customers. No vision means no creative tension means no sale.

So let me repeat the key insight that launches the creative process: the problem to be solved is *not* given, it must be created. That act of creation launches the subsequent creative pursuit, through which solutions may come, eventually.

Peter Drucker addresses this when he points out, "... the ability to connect and thus to raise the yield of existing knowledge (whether for an individual, for a team, or for the entire organization) is learnable. ... It requires a methodology for problem definition - even more urgently perhaps than it requires the currently fashionable methodology for 'problem solving.'"[90] What Drucker refers to as "problem definition" is what I mean by "creating the problem." And yes, it is definitely learnable.

In the innovation process, it is strategic intent that defines a vision, which means it also defines a problem or a set of problems to be solved. The design of an innovation portfolio then refines the vision into a risk-adjusted pursuit strategy, and in so doing it creates its own problems that we then set out to solve.

And then research does it again, pinpointing problems that are real and compelling for customers, many of which have perhaps been hidden. The customers' problems are the problems that we want to solve, but how will we do that? In which directions shall

---

[90] Peter Drucker. *Post-Capitalist Society*. New York, HarperBusiness, 1993. p. 193.

we search for the best solutions? And in which contexts will solutions be found?

create the solution *context*

To solve the problems that have resulted from the expression of a vision requires the application of resources. But what resources are available?

At this stage, the scope of ambition must be tuned to fit the resources that we can find, and when the scope and the resources fit together, then this fit defines the context in which solutions (there may be more than one) can be discovered.

On the other hand, when the solution context is not well defined then the possibility that things will not work out so well is pretty high. History offers countless examples of under-funded visions, projects abandoned before they were completed because the money ran out, or the magic of the vision was lost, or competing needs took precedence.

For example, Leonardo da Vinci's artistic output was limited, and some of his projects met untimely ends. A great equestrian sculpture intended to honor the leader of Milan was reported to be a stunning artistic achievement; alas, the 72 tons of bronze intended for the horse was used instead, during a crisis, to make cannon.

In our times, the Superconducting Super Collider began in 1983 with the promise of advancing fundamental science, and ended ten years and $2 billion dollars later as a 14 mile tunnel under Texas (out of a planned 54 miles total). The US Congress cancelled the project when the projected cost had escalated from the original $4 billion to $12 billion. Later, an entrepreneur suggested, tragically for some, but without a hint of irony, that it might be a good place to grow mushrooms. The site is presently abandoned.

By designing to a meaningful and well-expressed context, this outcome can usually be avoided. But as with anything involving innovation, cost overruns are always a possibility because the innovation endeavor involves uncertainty and learning. Nevertheless, having defined a context where resources and the vision are in alignment, then the focus of the creative process moves forward.

creating solutions

Now is the time to search for and find solutions, when the iconic spirit of the creative genius takes the lead, the hair does fly wildly in all directions, the ideas flow, and the white boards get filled up with every kind of possibility, from the lame to the sublime, and from the inconceivable to the practical.

Questions, mistakes, and surprises; experiments, errors and assumptions; uncertainty, ambiguity, and discovery, this is the right time and the right place for all manner of exploration.

Solutions can be derived from explicit and tacit research findings and models. They may be stimulated by questions about the status quo and how it came to be, and also by examining assumptions.

- Why is it the way that it is?
- What decisions from the past have influenced the way things are now?
- What were the assumptions that led to the existing situation?
- What are the unspoken needs?
- The unknown ones?

Possibilities emerge: We could do it this way, or this, or this!

The solutions that seem best are selected from such options, and studied further. The learning curve model shows that in each cycle through the production process, improvements of 10 to 30 percent are achieved when we're really paying attention to what we're doing, and such improvements are achievable in the iterative creative process as well. As multiple iterations yield results that cannot be achieved in a single linear attempt, the cycle of understanding, diverging, converging, simulation and prototyping, validation, and the innospective is followed repeatedly until it's clear that best possible solutions have been found, and we arrive at insight. A vital moment of clarity and synthesis arrives and enables us to make the future different from the past.

The capacity to achieve insight requires the preparation of the earlier stages of the creative process, and also perhaps a lifetime of preparation. It is here that the deeper benefits of the proclivity to learning are realized, for the habit of learning expresses itself in the creative act of devising genuine solutions.

The power of such an insight will ideally match the power of the initial vision, for if it falls short it will never inspire the level of commitment that is needed to achieve fundamental change.

creativity

Creativity is of course fundamental to this stage of the process, yet many of us wonder why some people seem to be so creative while others aren't. One reason is that some people *like* being creative, and another is a basic quality that they share: they ask questions. In fact, they ask questions incessantly, and they also persistently attempt to answer them.

As I discussed in the previous chapter, most people are born with tremendous curiosity, and as they learn to speak they quickly acquire the habit of asking questions. Why is the sky blue? Why does it rain? Where are you going? What's that? How does it work? What is it good for? All of which leads, of course, to "Can I try?," the need to actually touch it when we see something cool and we know that the experience of doing it ourselves is part of the magic.

As they grow up, some sustain this questioning habit while others do not. Those who continue asking learn to see the world in unique ways, to explore the ideas that hide behind commonplace explanations.

The very act of asking, "Why it is so?" leads some of us to wonder, "Why can't it be better?" Those who ask questions in this way don't immediately accept the status quo. Instead, they use their imaginations to create entire worlds, entire universes, new mousetraps, and new industries (possibly all at the same time).

Figure 29
Awakening the Spirit of Creativity in a Large Group

Although not so many people continue the childhood habit of asking questions, this spirit can be reawakened. Most status quo organizations, however, take the opposite tack. Social pressures tend to filter *out* questioning, and suppress the very creativity upon which every company depends. This tendency is expressed from the top in the reflex to control (which is of course counter-productive), and from everyone else in the form of a desire for predictable and steady employment. Both are debilitating, and also self-defeating.

Leaders, geniuses, and champions each can help to reawaken this vital spirit. Leaders do so by asking questions themselves, in an open and genuinely curious way, and not as a gotcha; openness sets the right tone. I have long believed that the best CEOs are not the ones who have all the answers, but the ones who ask the best questions, and then listen to what people say.

Geniuses do this because they are innately curious and they love to learn.

Champions are systematic supporters of the process, and working as catalysts and facilitators they help guide their organizations toward robust questions and satisfying answers.

details of development

After many questions and answers and iterations, solutions emerge that reflect the best ways to move beyond insight. Now there's a shift in the thinking process, for the concern moves from creating and understanding the problem and solving it, to testing how best to implement the solution.

Precisely how much will it cost? How long will it take? How much will it weigh? What color will it be? How will it be assembled and delivered? These are questions to ask in innovation development and market development, each of which has it's own underlying discipline and it's own operational frameworks. There is still a strong requirement for creativity, but this work is more likely to involve engineering, which is a form of creativity that relies on reasoning from established knowledge rather than the earlier stages of the creative process, where the learning was reaching into new knowledge domains. While the distinction between the two does reflect a gray area rather than a sharp line, in practice most people recognize that creating a new concept is different than engineering to a detailed specification and blueprint.

Engineering completed, materials are obtained and fashioned. Tests are run. Drawings are consulted; progress is assessed; money is spent. And then ... voila! ... something new has emerged.

Although some would suppose that the creative process is now completed, new information is still waiting to be discovered, information that may have a substantial impact on final solutions. New materials with new performance characteristics become available, offering the possibility of unforeseen cost savings or performance enhancements. Sudden shifts in marketplace demand emerge, making features that were once considered as options suddenly mandatory. Sometimes the parts don't fit together correctly, forcing design teams back to the drawing boards.

using and feeding back

And all through this process, learning is occurring that is directly and indirectly related to the project at hand. The assessment of this learning, and the application of its consequences, means that even a finished, built solution is still an active subject of the process.

In addition, sales will put completed innovations into the hands of users who will express their own creativity by finding new ways to use products that their designers may never have imagined.

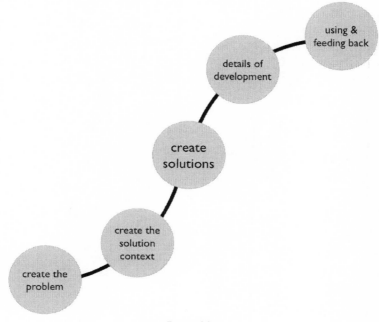

Figure 30
The Creative Process

Thus, from an inspiring vision and its implicit rejection of conditions at the moment of its birth has come an end product which has brought the future into the present. Does this new reality measure up to the expectations that drove the process? Do customers appreciate the benefits that they were expected to favor so strongly? Is the creative tension resolved?

The experience of use is the ultimate assessment of the vision and its implementation, and from this experience a new condition emerges. Life is different. But is it as it should be? Or is there now a gap between the new reality and a newer vision that is dawning, against which today's condition is suddenly inadequate? If a new vision comes into focus, creative tension grows again, and there is a problem, a new problem to be created.

The creative process begins again. How can it be done better? What resources are available ...?

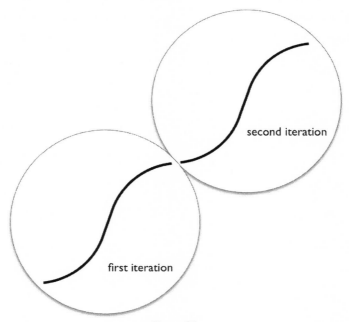

second iteration

first iteration

Figure 31
Using and Feeding Back leads to the creation of new problems and
opportunities, and the innovation cycle begins anew.

taking action:
managing creativity

Creativity is indeed a discipline, one that can be taught and can be learned, providing helpful guidance to individuals and teams that are faced with complex design challenges.

And because there is a generalized model of the process, we know that creativity can be managed, and that it can be facilitated. Yes, there are limits to what management and facilitation can do, but the limits are usually far beyond what an unstructured, unmanaged, and unfacilitated process can achieve.

So does this model of the creative process seem familiar to you? Perhaps it reminds you a bit of the innovation process. It probably should; it's essentially the same thing, simply working at a different scale of focus.

The Innovation Process: Organizations	**The Creative Process:** Individuals and Teams
Why: Strategy	Create the Problem
What: The Innovation Portfolio	Create the Solution Context
How: The Innovation Process: Research	Create Solutions
How: The Innovation Process: Insight	
How: The Innovation Process: Innovation Development and Market Development	Details of Development
How: The Innovation Process: Selling	Using and Feeding Back

Table 3
The Innovation Process and the Creative Process

While the innovation process is something that organizations and even ecosystems of organizations do, creativity is something that's uniquely and entirely human; it's what people do individually and in teams. For the future of your organization both innovation and creativity are powerful tools, and both are fundamentally important.

The creative endeavors pursued throughout the innovation and creative processes can be made easier, or more difficult, by the presence or absence of the infrastructure that supports the entire innovation process, so now we'll turn our attention there.

chapter 9
where we innovate
the innovation infrastructure

"If you maximize the potential that people in an organization can and will communicate, you will vastly increase the likelihood of knowledge transfer, inspiration, and hence innovation. Organizational structure and physical space must be configured to encourage the very communication that spurs innovation. The success of the innovation process today depends on the employment of both tools."[91]

Thomas J. Allen and Gunter Henn

There have been many instances throughout the preceding chapters where I've mentioned that the tools to support the innovation process and the innovating people are critical elements of your infrastructure, and now I'll discuss it in detail.[92]

Traditionally, the term 'infrastructure' is often applied to information technology, telecommunications, road, and rail networks, but here I will extend the concept to include four key

---

[91] Thomas J. Allen and Gunter W. Henn. *The Organization and Architecture of Innovation*. Elsevier, 2008. P. 2.

[92] This chapter is adapted from my paper, "The Innovation Infrastructure," published in the *International Journal of Innovation Science*, Volume 1, Number 1, 2009.

innovation tools: open innovation methodology, effective collaboration, the physical work place, and the virtual work place. Separately and especially together, these four can make a tremendous difference in the performance and the satisfaction of individuals, teams, and your entire organization.

open innovation and the innovation ecosystem

As you know, an ecosystem is an environment in which there are many living organisms interacting in the course of their normal process of living. They compete and cooperate to survive in a complex web of relationships, many of which are difficult to recognize or identify even though they're critical to every creature's and plant's survival.

Similarly, innovation happens in a market ecosystem that has countless influences, as it consists of a firm and its customers, plus competitors, suppliers, and all manner of stakeholders who have something to say about what could be done, what should be done, and why.

As complexity increases in society and in the marketplace, an important determinant of success is the capacity to actively engage that ecosystem, which is largely people and organizations who are outside of our firm, in the innovation process that's going on inside our firm. That's what we mean by "open innovation."

While in the past many organizations kept the innovation process as a closely guarded domain that stayed entirely in house and was shrouded in secrecy, and some, such as Apple, still do, many companies have switched their viewpoint and found that openly seeking new ideas from outside, from customers and non-customers, suppliers, partners, experts, community members, and pretty much everyone else, and opening up the innovation process, can significantly improve the flow and quality of new ideas. "Open innovation" is a name for this new style of working that taps into other people, perspectives, ideas, critical thoughts, and advice.

Hence, P&G's CEO Alan Laffley became famous for insisting in 2002 that 50% of P&G's new product ideas should come from outsiders. This constituted a 180 degree reversal from P&G's prior practice, which had been deeply insular and mistrusting of the outside world.

P&G's web site describes it this way:

"Historically, P&G relied on internal capabilities and those of a network of trusted suppliers to invent, develop and deliver new products and services to the market. We did not actively seek to connect with potential external partners. Similarly, the P&G products, technologies and know-how we developed were used almost solely for the manufacture and sale of P&G's core products. Beyond this, we seldom licensed them to other companies. Times have changed, and the world is more connected. In the areas in which we do business, there are millions of scientists, engineers and other companies globally. Why not collaborate with them? We now embrace open innovation, and we call our approach 'Connect + Develop.'"[93]

P&G put systems in place to make this happen, realizing that without tools that make the intent into reality it would be hollow, a platitude.   Among those systems were the processes of measurement and reward, which are of course central to behavior and performance.

Another example of open innovation is entirely transforming the telecommunications industry. Apple's App Stores for iPhone, iPad, and Mac are also open innovation through which Apple provides an open platform (OK, so it's not totally open, but it's close; and there's that platform idea again), and individuals and organizations then develop applications for those devices using a standardized toolkit. Apps are sold or given away through the platform's storefront.   There were 300,000 applications in the iPhone App Store as of October 2010, and a stunning cumulative

---

[93]   https://secure3.verticali.net/pg-connection-portal/ctx/noauth/PortalHome.do

total of more than 7 billion downloads over the 27 months since it opened in July 2008. The applications themselves range from the most frivolous, such as Crash Bandicoot Nitro Kart 3D, to Google Earth and Facebook, and even serious tools such as a step by step lesson in CPR that has been credited as helping save the life of a young athlete who suffered cardiac arrest during a basketball practice; his coach had downloaded the CPR app only the day before, and put it to good use...[95]

By harnessing the creativity of people around the world in an open development environment, Apple has created tremendous momentum for the iPhone, and a new source of economic growth for the ecosystem that consists of the company, app authors, and app users.

The App Store is just one example of a new creative genre that's become common to internet companies, all utilizing the principle that a company with a sufficiently large customer network can create a business platform that promotes an entire ecosystem that other individuals and companies can then use to create content and transact their own business.

The term "crowdsourcing" describes this new way that many people can participate as contributors of content. The resulting breadth and depth of content is what makes many of the highly successful internet businesses so compelling. Wikipedia, eBay, YouTube, and Google are examples.

Google is now the world's largest advertising agency, but all the web sites that Google searches and indexes are created not by Google, but by others. In 2008 Google's indexing system was sorting more than 1 trillion different URLs, all created not by Google, but by the crowd, namely, us.

In Don Tapscott's recent book *Wikinomics*, he makes a persuasive argument that these companies are examples of an emerging economic model that supports knowledge aggregation

---

[95]   http://rivals.yahoo.com/highschool/blog/prep_rally/post/Coach-uses-iPhone-app-to-help-save-collapsed-pla?urn=highschool-291472

and social networking, which suggests that open innovation is not only a business practice, but a new style of economic activity.[96]

Reflecting these principles and the powerful new capabilities that the internet provides, a broad range of companies in addition to P&G have set up online idea gathering systems. Among them are Dell, BMW, and even Shell Oil, as well as Lego, Electrolux, Kraft, and many others firms that invite people to share their ideas using the internet.[97] By "ideas" I don't mean just customer feedback, which nearly every company does today, but actual product suggestions and business concepts.

The South Korean cosmetics maker Missha has taken this even further by engaging 1.8 million of its customers as members of its innovation team. They play three important roles: as sources for new ideas, as participants in product development and testing, and as evangelists for the brand. The entire process seems to be handled on line.

I've already discussed the problems with random idea generation, including the deficiency that most of the ideas that come through an internet-based open innovation process aren't very good. So why do it? There's always the possibility that a good idea might actually come through every once in a while, enough to make the whole thing pay off. Furthermore, these efforts convey an important message about openness and the commitment to innovation that sets the right tone for both insiders and for outsiders to hear. For insiders it's a reminder that top managers know that their ideas are important, and that leaders are committed to looking for good ones throughout the business ecosystem. For outsiders it reaffirms a brand identity built on innovation.

Another benefit of the open process for innovation is that it can engage a more diverse group of people than a closed model. This is significant because diverse inputs to the innovation process tend to yield much better results.

[96]   Don Tapscott, *Wikinomics*. Portfolio, 2010.
[97]   To get a sense of the vast scope of open innovation examples, try
       http://www.openinnovators.net/list-open-innovation-crowdsourcing-examples/

And it's not just companies that have opened up their innovation thinking to the outside. New York City is looking for great ideas, too. "Have an Idea to Save NYC Money? Deputy Mayor Goldsmith is looking for innovative ways to save New York City money. If you have ideas for finding efficiencies in government, submit them today." You can share yours with Mr. Goldsmith through the city's web site, nyc.gov

Tools to augment and help accelerate the open innovation process include Innocentive, a pioneering open innovation software platform that was originally developed at Eli Lilly, and was subsequently spun out as a separate company. Its competitors include 9 Sigma and Innoget. Their web sites present success stories that explain how creative thinkers worldwide have been successfully engaged through these platforms to help develop solutions to complex business and technical problems.

They're are all defining new ways to collect knowledge and make it more useful, and also create new knowledge through open innovation collaboration.

Should your innovation infrastructure reflect these same open innovation principles to foster effective collaboration that connects insiders and outsiders? One way to address an issue such as this, a complex and open ended one, is through collaborative problem solving, the second major element of the innovation infrastructure.

effective collaboration

To deliver innovation consistently requires that people have the skills to effectively explore, understand, diagnose, analyze, model, create, invent, solve, communicate, and implement concepts, ideas, insights, and projects. These attributes are all facets of "learning," and any organization that thrives in a rapidly changing environment has surely encouraged its members to learn and to apply active learning results to keep up with external changes.

The link between learning and innovation is a strong one that has come up repeatedly in this book, and it's worth noting that speed definitely matters. The faster people learn, the faster they can apply that learning to create the next generation of products, services, business models, and process improvements. By developing a positive and self-reinforcing feedback loop of accelerated learning to create innovation, organizations then obtain more learning, leading to more innovation. The results are manifold: shorter product life cycles, which leads to quicker learning; and then yet shorter product life cycles, better profits, etc., all contributing to competitive advantage. It is that supremely desirable, virtuous cycle that I described in the Introduction.

Involving more people in this process, and doing so very effectively, is one of the best ways to accelerate the pace and improve the quality at the same time. Alan Mulally, formerly a senior manager of Boeing and later CEO of Ford put it this way when he described the development of the company's new 777 aircraft: "We can't make a better airplane unless we can figure how to get everybody's knowledge included in the design."[98]

Innovation is thus a collaborative process, as it's absolutely necessary for people to work together to create and solve the problems that inevitably arise across a wide range of disciplines and areas of expertise. Ideas almost always get better as they are shared, discussed, and reworked, and then combined and recombined with other ideas on the way to becoming innovations. And this will be true regardless of the physical location where people are working, whether they're in the same room or thousands of miles apart.

Most of the organizations that we admire for their innovation prowess are also noted for the quality of collaboration that they carefully and continuously promote. Toyota, for example, has developed a distinct environment where employees are not just welcome to put forth ideas, but expected to do so. Year after year, literally millions of ideas build on one another to add tremendous value for the company and its customers. In contrast, Toyota's

---

98   Karl Sabbagh. *Twenty-First-Century Jet: The Making and Marketing of the Boeing 777*. Scribner, 1996. p. 70.

largest global competitor, GM, is known not for the quality of collaboration that it evokes, but rather for the confrontational nature of its labor relations. Decades of conflict between labor and management resulted in a culture of discord, which made it perhaps inevitable that the company would have to go through the trauma of bankruptcy to restore its viability.

A happier story is that of the 777. Through the early years of its history, Boeing Corporation developed a company culture that was at times very adversarial. Conflict characterized the relationships between the company and its suppliers, and the company and its unions.

With the development of its new 777 aircraft during the late 1980s and early 1990s, Boeing's leaders consciously chose to adopt a more collaborative approach. The goal was to enhance innovation to achieve a better result, and a milestone in commercial aviation. By reducing or eliminating the conflicts and choosing a win-win approach, Boeing achieved and perhaps even exceeded its goals, as the 777 team produced the new airplane in record time.

Developing new insights, testing new ideas, and developing them into innovations of value to the market are inevitably collaborative processes that may involve tens, hundreds, or even thousands of people. The 777 development team consisted of 5000 Boeing engineers, and many thousands more who worked in Boeing's supplier companies.

About their work together, Mulally commented, "The biggest problem with communication is the illusion that it has occurred. We think when we express ourselves that, because we generally understand what we think, the person that we're expressing it to generally understands it in the same way. When you're creating something, you have to recognize that it's the interaction that will allow everybody to come to a fundamental understanding of what it's supposed to do, how it's going to be made. We should always be striving to have an environment that allows those interactions to happen."[99]

One of the methods that supported their success was their office environment. The entire work force was organized into project teams, and each of the 250 teams had its own, dedicated work place to optimize their effectiveness. They also used an electronic drafting system that enhanced collaboration among the thousands of people involved, and to help assure that everyone was sufficiently informed and aligned, there were regular meetings of all 5000 Boeing employees on the project. But since the largest meeting room available could only hold 2500 people, the meeting was held twice, for consecutive half hours, once a week.

All is not rosy at Boeing, however, for success in one product does not assure success in the next. Its latest jet, the 787, was beset by a series of significant design, engineering, and production problems that resulted in airplane deliveries 2 years late, and cost the company billions in lost profits and billions more in the erosion of its market cap. During one difficult stretch, company officers were compelled to announce yet another delay in the 787 while boldly affirming that the problems would be resolved and the course righted, only to go back to the press six months later with the same message, and then again six months after that ....

One of the major differences between the two aircraft is that the 787 utilizes many plastic composite parts to reduce weight, replacing the traditional aluminum, but shifting to the new material proved far more difficult to fabricate than anticipated for Boeing and its suppliers. Ironically, one of the key problems was attributed to a lack of coordination between Boeing and key suppliers, which makes one wonder how much of the success of the 777 was due to Mulally, and what Boeing lost with his departure to Ford. It will be interesting in future years to read the inside story of the 787's troubles to learn where the process really broke down.

While Boeing may have addressed the obvious issues and problems, some non-obvious or hidden assumptions at the tacit

---

99 Karl Sabbagh. *Twenty-First-Century Jet: The Making and Marketing of the Boeing 777*. Scribner, 1996. p. 36.

level of the company's culture could turn out to be the root causes of many of the problems.

tacit knowledge in the collaborative process

In Chapter 5 we explored the differences between tacit and explicit knowledge, and examined why tacit knowledge research is so important as a way to expose the hidden factors that are critical to successful innovations. Now we need to return to this important tool, because identifying instances of tacit knowledge is also important for enhancing communication and collaboration throughout innovation teams.

The discussion in Chapter 5 noted that the difference between how our brains process tacit knowledge and how we process explicit knowledge is significant at both the sensory and conceptual levels, and this pertains not only to the learning we seek through research, but also to the way that people interact. Nuances of tone, inflection, timing, cadence, body language, attention, smell, and facial expression are all richly present in every face to face encounter, and these nuances can be critical to successful communication, design and problem solving activities when we depend on many people to integrate their unique knowledge and diverse vantage points to address complex problems.

The importance of these unspoken elements is one of the reasons that face to face interaction is so important for innovation, as the subtle nuances are captured only partially – if at all – in interactions via phones and computers. From our personal experiences we know that these factors contribute enormously to the completeness of communication, to our ability to dialog effectively with one another, to grasp new and difficult issues, to brainstorm and work through options, to be complete in our reasoning.... This is not to say that phones and computers don't have their uses, but we all know that there's something unique and irreplaceable about working together in the same room. So while we can't always work face to face, it is often preferable. MIT professor Tom Allen and architect Gunter Henn help us understand that complexity is the root cause:

> "Managers communicate by telephone far more than do engineers and scientists, and hence they tend to believe that the telephone (or email) will work as well for the engineers as it does for them. 'Why do they need to travel?' managers often ask about engineers and scientists. Managers must remember that, on average, they deal with less complex information than do the engineers and scientists reporting to them. Compared with technical information, a much greater proportion of management information can be communicated by telephone. Notably, when managers face a complex issue, they too recognize the need to meet with the other parties in the same room."[100]

And what about the very common experience, that interaction leads to new insights? As I've already mentioned, physiology and cognitive science tell us that the brain and the memory work by association,[101] and that interactions between people stimulate new associations and new connections that can lead to breakthroughs. Face to face interactions also enable people to share experiences, through which they connect as they share tacit and explicit knowledge, and in the process create new knowledge. From this process we get the title of James Burke's engaging study of innovation called *Connections*, which we also call "creativity."[102]

We can summarize the tacit dimension of collaboration with a comment from Glaxo Wellcome chemist Dan Sternbach, who noted that, "Nothing replaces two people standing at the board and drawing things, which is the way we communicate a lot. It's an

---

[100] Thomas J. Allen and Gunter W. Henn. *The Organization and Architecture of Innovation*. Elsevier, 2007. P. 63.
[101] William H. Calvin. *The River that Flows Uphill: A Journey from the Big Bang to Big Brain*. New York, MacMillan, 1986.
[102] James Burke. *Connections*. Simon & Schuster, 2007.

interactive situation where, when somebody's drawing something the other guy says, 'Well that reminds me of this thing.' As soon as you try to do that by email it takes more time. You can do some of it that way, but the same conversation would probably happen in a day versus 20 minutes because of the give and take that goes on."[103] Face to face interaction, that is, stimulates the associative powers of the mind, which I discussed in Chapter 4 (see page 116, linear processes and nonlinear thinking).

facilitating collaboration

In many situations, the effectiveness of collaborative efforts can be greatly improved through active facilitation, not only for small teams but also for groups of tens or even hundreds of people.

Figure 32
A Facilitated Collaborative Workshop

Facilitators (who are often innovation champions) guide groups through the stages of the creative process using many tools, including of course a deep understanding of the creative process itself, as well as psychology, which helps them anticipate how various individuals will participate throughout the process, group psychology which helps them understand and support the needs of

---

[103] Langdon Morris. "Social Design: The Link Between Facility Design, Organization Design, and Corporate Strategy." An InnovationLabs White Paper, 1999. Downloadable at www.innovationlabs.com/publications

large groups, and business knowledge, which of course provides the context in which many problems are to be solved.

There are many different collaboration techniques, ranging from tightly scripted and facilitated design sessions that are often used to address complex technical challenges, to more loosely structured or self-organizing processes.

One of these, Appreciative Inquiry, focuses on understanding what's working in organizations and building on success rather than on identifying and solving problems. The underlying rationale is that there are plenty of problems to solve, and we'll certainly find them if we go hunting for them, but focusing a specific effort on understanding what's working well and enhancing it is an affirming and effective way for people to build resonant organizational cultures.

Another technique called Open Space was developed by management consultant Harrison Owen when he noticed that the most interesting conversations at many conferences were those that took place during the coffee breaks. He therefore designed Open Space as a way for groups of people to identify the topics that each member of the group is most interested in, and then organizing a fluid process to work through the topics and seek solutions.[104]

In addition to designing and leading the collaborative process, one of the biggest challenges facing any facilitator is creating an effective work environment for the people and projects. The design of the physical work place has a great deal of influence on the quality of the work not only in a workshop setting, but also in the day to day work, so it, too, is a key element of the infrastructure.

the physical work place

There's probably a conference room in your office, one that you've spent many hours in. And it's probably very similar to

---

[104] http://www.usfoundation.org/openspace.htm

conference rooms you've sat in at other companies.   Is it a rectangular room, with a longish table surrounded by chairs?

The physical environment has tremendous influence on our behavior, yet it's an unspoken assumption that our meeting room has to fit this traditional shape, size, and layout, which reminds us that hidden influences and tacit behavior patterns are prevalent in organizations just as they are in customer groups.[105]

Unfortunately, the architecture profession and office furniture manufacturers have standardized on this utterly drab and uninspiring concept of what "the meeting room" should be.

Figure 33
A Traditional Conference Room. Ug!

The style is derived from the corporate board room, and the single chair for the chairman at the head of the table conveys its primary social purpose, reinforcing hierarchical authority. Need I mention that this isn't a very good environment for innovation or creativity? Yet in most organizations, that's all there is.

Consultant and author Michael J. Gelb has done some work on this topic, and he makes the following observation. "For many

---

105 Dr. Brigitte Jordan. "Ethnographic Workplace Studies and Computer Supported Cooperative Work." Institute for Research on Learning, Report No. IRL94-0026, 1994.

years, psychologists have known that the quality of stimulation provided by the external environment is crucial to brain development in the early years of life. Recently, however, brain scientists have discovered that the quality of environmental stimulation affects the continuing development of the adult brain." Gelb then goes on to lament the sterile office environments where most people work, and describes a project through which a team of people redesigned their own workplace. Among the changes that they made were removing photos of machines and replacing them with reproductions of favorite paintings, replacing fluorescent lights with full spectrum lights, bring in fresh flowers, and changing the coffee room into a "creative break room." They also instituted the practice of a ten minute "brain break" every hour, and over the course of the following year their organization studied the work effectiveness of the people in the new environment. They found that productivity had improved by 90%.[106]

That's an astounding difference, and it certainly affirms our experience that the work place is a pervasive influence, although its importance is often ignored. It's the container for everything that doesn't happen in the virtual world, and actually in a sense it's even the container for that too, because nearly all virtual work involves a person who's sitting at a computer or on a phone, clicking, reading, writing, talking, and thinking, and that person is inevitably in a room somewhere (if they don't happen to be on a beach or an airplane).

Tom Allen and Gunter Henn also address this issue in their lively book: "Most managers will likely acknowledge the critical role played by organizational structure in the innovation process, but few understand that physical space is equally important. It has tremendous influence on how and where communication takes place, on the quality of that communication, and on the movements - and hence, all interactions - of people within an organization. In fact, some of the most prevalent design elements of buildings nearly

---

[106] Michael J. Gelb. *How to Think Like Leonardo da Vinci.* Dell, 1998. P. 138.

shut down the opportunities for the organizations that work within their walls to thrive and innovate. Hence, the implications of physical space for the innovation process are profound."[107]

So what are the learnings? To answer this question we'll consider characteristics of effective R&D laboratories.

what we learned from the best r&d labs

Imagine what it would have been like to work in the coolest labs where amazing stuff was being invented - Thomas Edison's Menlo Park lab where the light bulb was perfected, or Ford's workshop where he created the Model T, or the Wright Brothers' airplane workshop, or Douglas Aircraft when the first DC-3 was built, or at Xerox PARC when the PC was being invented. You'd be surrounded by lots of brilliant, creative people solving difficult problems with astonishing levels of insight and inventiveness. You'd be having rich and provocative conversations, making sketches and designing and making models, arguing, laughing, and building, testing, learning with great enthusiasm and dedication.

And if you're going to provide today's innovators with that sort of work environment to help them succeed in today's challenging world, this is exactly the kind of place you'll create.

To explore the details and features you might include, we conducted a study of some of today's best biotech, high tech, and pharmaceutical R&D labs around the US, to find out how they're being designed and used.[108] In a typical lab you'll find scientists, engineers, and technicians preparing and conducting experiments, the purpose of which are to create useful new knowledge. It may be knowledge of the uncharted physical world of chemistry or biology, or knowledge about the behavior of man-made products, or

---

107 Thomas J. Allen and Gunter W. Henn. *The Organization and Architecture of Innovation: Managing the Flow of Technology.* Elsevier, 2007. p. 14.

108 Langdon Morris. "Social Design: The Link Between Facility Design, Organization Design, and Corporate Strategy." An InnovationLabs White Paper, 1999. It is downloadable at www.innovationlabs.com/publications

knowledge about how people interact with each other and with physical artifacts.

From the architect's perspective, designing a research lab is not a simple problem. Since optimizing interaction is central to R&D success, facilities should maximize person to person interaction, but at the same time private space for thinking, writing, and researching in peace and quiet is also essential. Figuring out the right space layouts to balance interaction and privacy gets tricky, and cost considerations complicate the matter further because separating lab and office functions reduces construction costs but may compromise the goal of enhancing collaboration.

Tom Allen's 1977 book on interaction in the R&D laboratory, *Managing the Flow of Technology*,[109] explores the linkage between lab design and researcher interaction, and offers some unique insights. One of his key findings is that the frequency of interaction between people is a function of the distance between their offices, and when their offices are more than 50 feet apart, the probability of unplanned interaction drops below 15%.

Since it's impossible to have everyone in a large group of people located less than 50 feet apart, and since frequent face-to-face interaction is accepted as a critical design goal for every R&D lab, developing strategies to optimize interactions is a primary architectural goal. We use the term "social design" to describe these strategies.

In the labs we visited, business leaders and architects had used 90 different specific design features, all applications of social design, and all intended to optimize interaction, thinking, and creative outputs. They converged into four major theme areas:

- **Organize for interaction**
  28 different organizational strategies and features intended to promote high quality interactions between people.

---

109 Tom Allen. *Managing the Flow of Technology*, Cambridge, MA, The MIT Press, 1977, 1995.

- Design for interaction
  54 features designed into the facilities to increase the
  frequency of person-to-person interaction, as well as its
  quality.

- Design for flexibility
  8 design strategies intended to enhance the flexibility of a
  building so that over time it would be easier to adapt it to
  changing requirements.

- Design for beauty
  A persistent theme of importance to architects and building
  users alike. Everywhere we looked, we saw examples of
  the continuing quest to make buildings beautiful,
  uncountable in number but pervasive in influence.

Interestingly, even in these very costly facilities, where thought
was given to every detail of the design and execution of the
building, even here we found the same sterile, ineffective conference
rooms that I lamented at the beginning of this section. The
pervasive (and erroneous) belief that a conference room has to be
deadly dull and boring is a strong and dysfunctional assumption
that deprives individuals and organizations of productivity every
day.

How could it be different?

innovation centers (or innovation labs)

There's a new type of work environment that's becoming more
common, a great space designed specifically to support innovative
and creative work, whether for day to day issues or for the
facilitated collaborative activities I discussed above.

It is sometimes called an "innovation center" or an "innovation
lab," and it's a place where people bring their ideas, where they
work to understand complex systems and create innovative

solutions to problems that impact their customers and their companies and their communities. In effect, it's a sand box for grownups, where people work together to create products and services that may become the future of their enterprises.

It contains lots of large vertical work surfaces, giant white boards, that make it easy to collaborate. The furniture is on wheels, making it easy to reconfigure to accommodate many small teams that are working at the same time, or one large one. Light, colors, and décor are relaxing and inspirational rather than sterile and lifeless.

An example of this relationship between innovation, collaboration, and the work place is the "Collaborative Labs" innovation environment operated by St. Petersburg College in Florida, specifically designed and equipped to foster dynamic interaction and spur creativity. The 10,000 square foot facility provides unique spaces for activities such as strategy design, leadership development, issue forums, and creativity and innovation projects with local businesses and the community.

Andrea Henning, Executive Director of the Labs, recently shared some of the keys to success that the Labs staff has learned from their work over the last few years.[110]

> "We've found that getting the right stakeholders in the room to work together face to face is very important. These may include internal as well as external people, representing all levels of an organization, as well as all functions, and all aspects of organizational expertise. [open innovation]
>
> "Asking the right questions through the medium of a well-thought out, facilitated design for the collaborative process is the key to a successful engagement, where we want to take complex, multidimensional issues and organize them into 'manageable information chunks,' helping design teams focus

---

110 Andrea Henning, Executive Director, Collaborative Labs, EpiCenter, St. Petersburg College, Florida 33760.
http://www.spcollege.edu/central/collaborative

for the best results. [effective facilitation]

"Our uniquely designed facility includes furniture that enables groups to work very productively in creative tasks like brainstorming, decision making, and detailed design as well as in information sharing and even traditional meetings. [the work environment]

"We use collaborative tools and technologies to get the most robust, accelerated results from teams. We use collaborative brainstorming software that enables multiple teams to brainstorm hundreds of ideas and prioritize them into meaningful categories quickly. [virtual tools, see below]

"And our staff captures information as it's being created in a detailed real time document that includes every aspect of the collaborative project, which frees the participants from note-taking while providing a complete roadmap of all the ideas discussed.

"Together, all of these elements work together to help groups achieve exceptional productivity and innovation."

Andrea's comments show how these key elements of the infrastructure work together and reinforce one another. The right people drawn from inside and outside, provocative questions delivered through effective facilitation, good virtual tools, a facility specifically designed to support this work, and a complete record of the work that was accomplished constitute a system that leads to and supports high productivity.

At InnovationLabs we've been designing and using facilities like this for many years, and we have found that this approach to the infrastructure is an essential element in the innovation system that compresses weeks or even months of work into a matter of days.

Another recent project that gave us the opportunity to bring these concepts together came about when we helped a client conceive of its new R&D lab. We conducted a collaborative workshop involving 350 people, the entire research department.

We divided the participants into teams of 7 people, and asked each team to identify the key attributes of their ideal lab. Each team then built a model of their ideal lab using craft supplies like you'd find in a typical art supply store. We then studied all 50 models and synthesized the key ideas into a single design, not in the expectation that it would ever be built as we drew it, but to help them think about what would in fact be ideal as they continued to refine their visions of how and where they would work. It will be no surprise to you that what they came up with was definitely not a bunch of traditional and boring lab spaces, offices, or conference rooms.

Figure 34
Designing an Ideal R&D Lab
350 participants worked in teams of about 7 people to design 50 models of their ideal R&D lab. The models were then displayed on a row on tables, in front of flip charts that explained the key design concepts. Each person then voted for the design features they thought most important. The design preferences were then synthesized into a single design, a shared vision of their future lab.

Instead, they developed a visually rich, multi-textured environment for individual, team, and organizational creativity, a place where assuring optimal productivity in each setting was the central organizing theme.

Sometimes, however, you don't need an elaborate facility to help people do their best work together. A simple cup of coffee can also be an effective catalyst.

coffee and collaboration

One day not long ago I met with a retired former employee of HP Labs, the company's R&D department. He lamented the sad decline in the Labs' output, and the lack of esprit de corps he noticed there. This bothered him a great deal, and he had thought deeply about why it happened. He attributed some of the decline to the departure of Bill Hewlett, who had been a very effective leader of R&D, but he also said that the decline was due to the invention of the small coffee maker, and the change in corporate culture that it caused. I was frankly a bit skeptical about the coffee maker part, but I listened as he explained it to me.

During the best days in the Labs, in the 1950s, 60s, and into the '70s, coffee was brewed in big pots in a basement kitchen. Twice a day the kitchen staff would bring up the pots on a cart, and everyone would fill their cups and stand around for ten or fifteen minutes to chat while enjoying their coffee.

What they'd chat about, in addition to the weather, the favorite teams, or the news, was work. People often talked about where they were stuck, and sometimes your naturally-curious colleagues (this was an R&D group, after all) would help you by brainstorming possible solutions to design and engineering problems right then and there.

And if today's ideas didn't work out, tomorrow's coffee breaks were another opportunity to get creative input from some very smart people who were by now aware of what you were doing, and might even be thinking about it for you. A lot of tough problems got unstuck at the coffee break.

This is yet another version of the story we all know, the chance conversation that opens new insights that later proves to be important; HP Labs' twice-a-day coffee break was an organizational tool that promoted this type of collaboration almost invisibly, and thus an elegant example of social design.

But when coffee makers became small and cheap (another industry's innovations), the kitchen staff no longer brought the big pots around on a cart because all over R&D there were personal little pots that simmered all day. No more structured coffee breaks, no more spontaneous brainstorming, and as far as our friend was concerned, the beginning of the end of the great days of HP Labs.

As I mentioned, I was a bit skeptical about this, but a couple years later I happened to read Steve Wozniak's autobiography, *iWoz*, and when I read the following comment about his days working at HP I found that my skepticism had been entirely misplaced:

> "Every day at 10:00 am and 2:00 pm they wheeled in donuts and coffee. That was so nice. And smart, because the reason they did it was so everyone would gather in a common place and be able to talk, socialize and exchange ideas."[111]

So there it was, confirmation that the structured coffee break is indeed a tool to promote effective collaboration, the exchange of ideas, useful at HP and nearly everywhere else.

We subsequently applied this principle in the design of a new workplace for a team of 200 software engineers. In addition to giving them dynamic spaces for collaborative work, we included a café, and insisted that personal coffee makers be banned. This caused everyone to frequent the café, and thereby increased the frequency of the chance encounters that promote innovative thinking.

The new, high performance work place is a flexible and inspiring place, not a boring one. There is a significant productivity

---

[111] Steve Wozniak & Gina Smith. *iWoz: Computer Geek to Cult Icon*. Norton, 2006. p 122.

increase to be gained by supporting the essential activities that constitute effective innovation: thinking, creating, problem-solving, and collaborating.

And we know that the work place which best supports these activities is not a traditional conference room. In fact, conference rooms are proven creativity killers, deadly dull, inflexible, and made really just to support information exchange in a hierarchical setting. Avoid them at all costs if your goals have anything to do with innovation and creativity.

Instead, astute innovation leaders and champions develop labs and innovation centers and idea rooms that offer stimulating and tool-rich settings for the important work of innovation.

Implicit in this approach is the question, Can better buildings make for a better quality of interaction and of innovation? Our answer: Absolutely.

But it's not the entire story, of course. While critical aspects of the work will be done in face to face environments, like all business processes today and tomorrow, a great deal of it will take place online in the virtual work place.

the virtual work place

As we spend more and more time working and collaborating online with our internal colleagues and outside partners, customers, and vendors, the quality of our tools and our skill in using them can make a significant difference in the productivity of our innovation efforts, especially since the we are tending now to address issues via email that are more and more complex.

But since we shouldn't necessarily accept as a given that the IT department has chosen the right tools for us to use, and because the productivity stakes are too high to delegate the choice to someone who may not fully understand our needs, it's often helpful for an innovation champion be actively engaged in the selection and adoption of the right tools to support the innovation process.

There are a lot of tools available that may help you, including these:

1. Social Networking Tools help people connect with people.
2. Knowledge Repositories help assure that we don't waste time and money recreating work we've already done, and we can easily find the past results that we're looking for in an archive.
3. New Idea Repositories help us to gather new ideas and maintain the overview of the process as we develop each one of them.
4. Ecosystem Intelligence systems help us to gather and organize information on external changes, competitors, new technologies, etc.
5. Idea Voting Engines enable us to get quick feedback on ideas.
6. Wikis give us a tool to aggregate and organize knowledge.
7. Blogs provide individuals with creative outlets for their own explorations, and a way to share their interests and discoveries with others.
8. Archives & Directories are useful for giving access to all forms of digital content such as Reading Lists, Videos, Podcasts etc.
9. Innovation Tutorials are helpful for training.
10. Open innovation platforms, as we have discussed, facilitate connections between insiders and outsiders to bring new ideas and talents to solving problems.
11. Online collaboration tools, such as Skype, enable people to connect easily from anywhere, and the ability to chat with video is an improvement over voice-only communications.
12. Project management tools become important when planning and managing complex projects and multiple projects that occur simultaneously, a normal occurrence for innovation portfolio managers.
13. Creativity aids such as mind mapping tools to help organize

our thinking around complex issues and problems.

14. And lastly, the innovation dashboard is an essential tool to help innovation champions, portfolio managers, and senior executives maintain a good overview of the process, the details, and the results.

Software is a rapidly evolving field, and because it changes so fluidly I won't mention specific products or tools because by the time you read this the products available will probably have changed.

Further, choosing the right tools for you is like choosing the right innovation metrics for your organization; start with one or two, and add others. It may also be helpful to put a small task force together to design your ideal tool set, see what's currently available on the market, and decide the priorities for what could add the most value and work best for your organization.

the agile innovation infrastructure sprint

These four elements of the innovation infrastructure constitute a "productivity optimization framework," a system for supporting creative and innovative people through the many phases and iterations of their work in the innovation process. When these methods are combined effectively they can make a tremendous difference by helping individuals and teams achieve much better and much faster results.

Should your organization invest in this infrastructure?

If you have offices, you already have. But are they as good as they can be?

And if you have software tools, you have also invested. So given the enormous productivity gains that can be achieved, it's usually a very fruitful investment to see about how they can be optimized.

Hence, if you frame the question as an alternative between

implementing the right infrastructure or not implementing it, then it's not really much of a choice at all; thoughtful investments in infrastructure are the right thing to do, so the question becomes one of prioritizing and planning.

In doing so you will seek to understand what works and what does not.

Defining the specifics that are right for your organization is the work to be done, and a good first step is to assess the current status of your infrastructure through surveys, interviews, or discussions with people who are and will be the end users. Then you should experiment and learn by doing in small pilot groups, and scale up the elements that add the most value. This is, in effect, applying the research process to your own infrastructure.

Perhaps you will do some ethnographic research focused internally on your own set of tools and techniques that support innovation and innovators.

- What works well?
- What falls short?
- Where are the workarounds and hindrances that prevent us from doing our best?
- If we could fix just one thing, what would it be?
- If we could fix everything, what would the upside results be?

As you have by now fully grasped, the understandings you generate stimulate productive *divergent* thinking, which you then narrow down by *convergence* to arrive at *simulate*-able or *prototype*-able concepts. You build, test, *validate*, and cycle rapidly to optimize.

You then *innospectively* assess your own performance and note how you will do it better, more smoothly, more creatively, the next time this sort of inquiry is called for.

Refining your infrastructure is a process that happens progressively over time, just as improving your total innovation system is also a progressive accomplishment.

Innovation Champions are often the ones who shepherd these tools, methods, and environments into reality, and thereby support the quest for high performance for their own organizations.

conclusion

"Everyone has a plan 'till they get punched in the mouth."

Mike Tyson

The innovation system described here is intended to provide a comprehensive approach to a difficult, challenging, and significant problem for organizations, the problem of how to manage innovation in the face of excruciating change. My goal has been to help you attain a higher level of mastery, and to guide you through the preparation of your own master plan so that when the punches start to fly, your plan has prepared you to succeed.

mastery

In most fields, mastery occurs through stages. It proceeds from ignorance to awareness that the topic itself is one of value and perhaps even importance (and I have certainly argued that innovation is very important). This launches a quest to understand what it means. As you search, gather more information, and test your initial ideas, you develop greater expertise, gaining confidence while at the same time discovering that additional layers of nuance and depth await you. While the journey may never reach a definitive end point, your capabilities will increase and your results will reflect this progress.

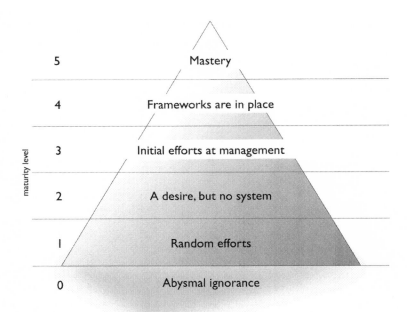

Figure 35
The Pyramid of Mastery

And it has only been through our own pursuit of mastery that we've been able to formulate this innovation framework, through the projects and initiatives and programs for which we've discovered, developed, and tested the concepts and tools described here. We know that we're not finished, but along the way we remain deeply grateful to our clients for having trusted in us and enabled this learning to occur.

Overall, what we've learned is that it seems to work well to frame the issues and challenges this way:

You know **why** innovation matters; it is a core element of your **strategy**, and it leads to results every organization must achieve on the way to its ultimate success in the market.

You know that innovation is a risky domain in which to invest, but also that those investments are mandatory. So **what** do you do? You manage the innovation **portfolio**, which enables you to effectively balance risk and reward.

It's obvious that the quality of your approach to innovation matters a great deal. The difference between knowing **how** and a broken **process** is so huge that it cannot be overlooked.

It's also entirely clear that the innovation capacities of your people are essential to achieving your innovation goals. For **who** will do it if you do not? Your organizational **culture** must therefore define norms that encourage and enhance innovation as long term creators of value.

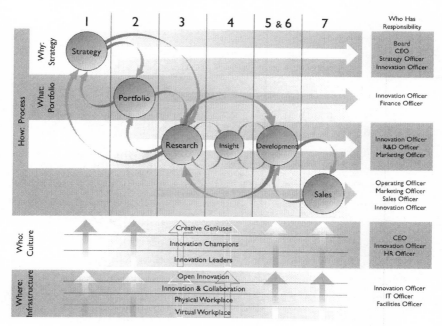

Figure 36
The Agile Innovation Master Plan
5 questions across a process of seven stages
Responsibilities are shown in the column at the right.

And it's clear that the right infrastructure can support a

tremendous improvement in the quality of the process, as well as the satisfaction of the participants, and the value of the results.   **Where** you innovate is defined by the essential **infrastructure**.

These five themes, organized and managed in harmony, constitute an innovation system.   And while there will certainly be improvements to make in the coming years, we've been at this long enough to feel confident that this is an effective platform, and it's working well for many organizations.

By way of conclusion, there are a few key points that I think are worth highlighting.

First and foremost is the idea I mentioned in the introduction, and then returned to at various times throughout the book: success at innovation begins with the right mindset.   Meaningful progress will be made only when leaders adopt the mindset that their organizations must and will innovate, when their words and actions genuinely reflect that mindset, and when they also understand how to go about leading it in action.

But a framework and strong leadership are not enough.   My friend Léopold Demiddeleer of Solvay made this comment, highlighting what else is needed: "Langdon, please put somewhere in the book the idea that no matter how perfect the master plan is, it is the craftsmen and craftswomen of innovation who will make it happen, who will actually build the cathedral. Their team spirit and long term commitment are necessary to realize the potential and the vision. I've seen so many smart plans destroyed by incompetence … just too many."

So please do follow Léopold's advice, and focus on both, on designing the plan, and on enabling the craft of building it out in the full glory of the vision.

I also want to remind you that the framework described here is intended to define a concrete and specific pathway, a methodology

for going about the pursuit of innovation. But that certainly doesn't
mean that every organization will follow exactly the same path. It's
our experience that each of the main themes discussed here needs to
be accounted for in some way as you adapt this framework to your
own needs, so what you will then achieve is actually the
development of your own methodology.

In this regard, it's useful to note the important difference
between methodology and luck when it comes to innovation.

"Methodology" means applying a systematic approach to
address a fundamental business issue or problem (and
innovation is certainly fundamental).

"Luck," on the other hand, is relying on the hope that people
will come up with good ideas to drive the innovation process
forward.

If you frame your alternatives as methodology vs. luck as I do,
then as with infrastructure and all the other elements of the master
plan, the choice becomes no choice at all. Once this context is
accepted then no manager could possibly rely on luck, and certainly
no board member would consider "waiting for luck" to be a
satisfactory approach to fulfilling their fiduciary duties.

A sound innovation methodology, then, is not an option, but a
requirement.

the agile innovation sprint and the meta-sprint

The basic diagram that you're now fully familiar with shows the
agile innovation sprint consisting of 5 elements in a core circle and
the sixth innospective step a bit outside of that core.

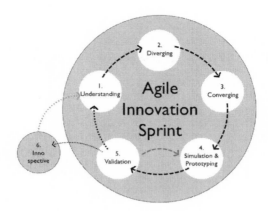

Figure 37
The Agile Innovation Sprint
You have seen this image already.

Having described the entire process through which a sequence of agile sprints defines your agile innovation master plan, we can now add two additional concepts that you may find useful.

The first is a process model showing how the five elements of the master plan have been created using successive sprints.

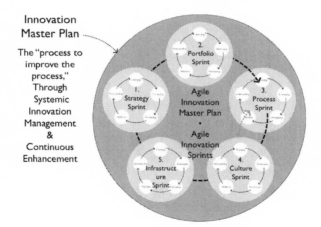

Figure 38
The Agile Innovation Master Plan
5 successive sprints can be used as the process through which a complete Master Plan is prepared. Each of the five sprints can vary in duration from

as short as a few hours or a day to a week, depending on the level of detail that is appropriate to attain. While a large, multi-national corporation would typically take longer and require more detail, a start-up or small firm is probably best served by a quicker and more concise output. The point is to create the right level of detail that provides the necessary guidance.

The second elaborates on the distinction between the core agile innovation sprint and the location of the *innospective* outside of that core process, because its purpose is to improve the core process. Getting really good at the core is of course the intent and the requirement – that's where value gets created.

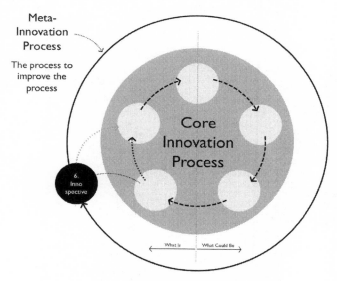

Figure 39
Meta-Innovation Process
While the 5 stages of the Agile Innovation Sprint that constitute the inner circle compose the Core Innovation Process, the Innospective is in fact a "meta-process," a higher level process that is intended to improve the core process.

The agile sprints focused on defining strategy, portfolio, process, culture, and infrastructure are also part of the process about the process, or if you will, the meta-process.

The core is the "doing" of innovation; the outer ring is how we optimize the doingness. As I mentioned in the Introduction, sports teams often practice for many hours to prepare for each single hour of actual competition; their practice is the process to improve the process, corresponding to the outer loop. It is a necessary element of performance in business and government as it is in sports and games and the arts as well, and in this book our intent has been to show you how optimizing the process can and should result in optimal results.

Conversely, neglecting the process is surely a predictor of disappointing and even self-destructive results.

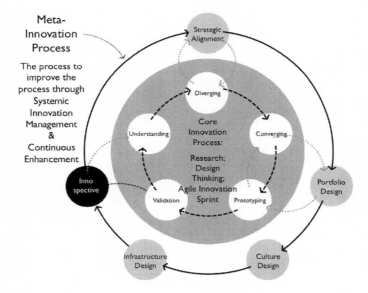

Figure 40
Meta-Innovation Process
The purpose of all of this effort is to achieve the desired outputs from the Core Innovation Process, that is, to innovate. The meta processes surrounding the core are enablers and facilitators — strategy, portfolio, culture, and infrastructure are topics of design and consideration *only* because they are important to enabling the essential outcome that we wish to achieve from the core activity.

the very last word ...
on innovation, change, and luck

The pursuit of innovation broadly defines an important response to the competitive nature of business, and articulates how companies can apply processes and technologies to build and sustain effective relationships with customers, while at the same time searching for enduring competitive advantages.   The experiences that customers have, and the relationships that companies build with their customers, are the critical factors that innovation must serve.   Understanding the essence of positive experiences and relationships, creating them, preserving them, enriching them, and extending them into the future are critical attributes of success.   So everything that's done to pursue innovation must be in their service; relationships and experiences are the point, and innovation is a means to these ends.

Successful innovators earn some sort of competitive advantage to the extent that their results create or enhance successful relationships.   But the useful life span of every innovation is inherently limited by the specific conditions and the technologies available at the time, and due to the unpredictability of change its useful and viable time frame is often unknown.   Hence, advantages may disappear overnight should a competitor devise a superior offer, thereby displacing your company in the mind of the customer.

Just as innovations have a limited but unknown lifespan in the market, companies do also.   The mortality of companies is a real and significant phenomenon, and the mortality rate is increasing as a result of the acceleration of change throughout the economy.

Managers who have the good fortune to preside over a period of calm success should never lose sight of the ephemeral nature of their advantages, and must focus not just on administering the (illusory) stability of today, but on preparing for, or even inducing the inevitable changes that will shape tomorrow.   Another way to say this is that the management which remains unrepentantly focused on stability and continuity, instead of on disruption and change, is looking in the wrong direction, and is possibly courting disaster as the eventual result.

Relentlessly changing conditions mean that the business world evolves rapidly, and innovation is therefore not optional. New products and services coming into the market affect the fate of all participants in the market ecosystem, and while any innovations applied throughout your organization may be important, innovations linked with your strategic intent will likely be life-sustaining.

Further, because the market is so transparent and the performance of every public company is subject to such detailed scrutiny by investors and analysts, changes in an organization's innovation performance can lead to broad swings in stock price, as Nokia's experience makes utterly clear.

Improving innovation performance may lead to increasing stock price, a virtuous and self-sustaining cycle that creates more favorable conditions for companies to then develop and implement future innovations by improving brand image, improving stock currency for making acquisitions, and also by lowering the overall cost of capital. In this way, the results of innovation can be even more far-reaching than their utility for the customers who buy them.

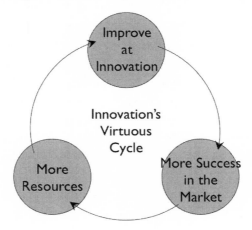

Figure 41
Innovation's Virtuous Cycle

Conversely, declining innovation performance and a falling stock price can lead to a dangerous downward spiral that makes it progressively more difficult to compete for attractive acquisition targets, and which can also increase the cost of capital, and divert capital that could be invested in innovation-related activities such as R&D and product development. Get ahead and push farther ahead; get behind and fall farther behind.

The need for sound thinking about innovation is as important for new businesses as it is for old ones, and among the many examples consider the spectacular start-up and equally spectacular collapse of Webvan. Webvan's business concept, in case you don't remember, was simply to replace the grocery store with a delivery service. Orders would be placed online, prepared in giant, automated warehouses, and brought to your house in a van. The value proposition: no more trips to the grocery store, so time saved, and convenience achieved. Webvan's business model achieved cost savings by eliminating the expensive stores, which more than covered the cost of the fancy warehouses and delivery fleet. So once the company achieved significant scale it would net a handsome profit.

Its management team included a renowned CEO who had formerly been the head of Andersen Consulting, and everyone involved was so confident in what they were doing that the company invested hundreds of millions of dollars in a huge distribution infrastructure even though market demand that would generate a return was completely unproven. That is, they *believed* that they could make the business work, and fooled themselves into thinking that their own belief was sufficient basis for betting their capital on a business model that had never actually been fully tested. In the end, hundred-million-dollar warehouses were built but never used, never generating even a cent of return. The business folded when it turned out that customers just weren't that interested, and more than a billion dollars of capital was invested, spent, and lost.

Why did Webvan fail? Well, there's always the temptation to

build a business according to a preconceived idea, and one key reason is that the company's leaders apparently didn't take into account some of the important tacit factors related to shopping.

Yes, they would have been wise to ask, "Why do people shop at all?"

And in response, they might have realized that for many people grocery shopping is perhaps like hunting or gathering for food, an activity that more than any other is probably hard coded into human DNA, and one not so easy to let go of.

So Webvan offered a brilliant engineering solution to a problem that really has little to do with engineering excellence, but rather has everything to do with our instinctive – and tacit – sensibilities concerning what it means to be human.

For these reasons it's necessary to explore the tacit factors underlying your innovation concept, not mention your entire business model. Managing the tacit dimension is as essential as managing for change: it is an absolute requirement. But many (should we say most?) managers still aren't very good at dealing with change or with tacit knowledge acquisition and modeling. And managing that innovation thing is tough, too.

Nevertheless, recognizing that change in the marketplace is real and inescapable, and that adapting to its tacitly-driven, turbulent evolution through innovation is a necessity, this is an issue that confronts all executives. For although we may remember periods that seemed stable, they are in fact long gone and never to return.

As markets continue to evolve and competition becomes ever more demanding, engaging in the search for innovation therefore becomes not just an interesting possibility, but a requirement. To survive, all business leaders must develop a comprehensive approach to innovation, and I hope that the framework offered through this concept of the Master Plan can help them and their organizations to be more effective; that it can help *you* and *your* organization to be more effective.

In the end, when we look at the business world it's clear that the story of change is still the important story to tell, and the process of leading an organization in the face of change remains the critical skill. Innovation will inevitably play a leading role in the unfolding marketplace drama, and the capacity of your firm to innovate will eventually go a long way toward deciding its fate.

The Greeks thought that each individual's fate was given, predetermined at birth, and that it could not be avoided. Achilles, they told us, was inescapably and tragically destined to die from the inevitable wound to his heel.

But we know differently. There is no predestiny when it comes to innovation; what matters is what *you* can accomplish, not the gifts that the gods gave to you, nor the ones they took away.

Yes, your firm can become a brilliant innovator, and alter the course of the market. To do so will require skill, as well as luck, but mostly skill. So when chemist Louis Pasteur said that "luck favors the prepared mind," he was giving us guidance. So was golfer Gary Player when he said, "the more I practice, the luckier I get."

Will you wait for luck to arrive, or will you prepare your mind and your organization, practice diligently, and create your own future? I know, it's really not a choice when I frame the alternatives that way. Preparation or luck? No, if innovation is in your future, and I believe it has to be, then it's up to you and your colleagues to make it so. And I hope that your own version of the agile innovation master plan will significantly help you to attain your goals.

•••

bibliography

Note: I have found all of these books very useful in my studies of innovation, and they're all insightful and well written. Those books marked with a double asterisk ** are highly recommended.

Aaker, David. *Brand Leadership*. Free Press, 2000.

Ackoff, Russell, Jason Magidson and Herbert Addison. *Idealized Design*. Wharton School Publishing, 2006.

Allen, Thomas. *Managing the Flow of Technology*, Cambridge, MA, The MIT Press, 1977, 1995.

** Allen, Thomas J. and Gunter W. Henn. *The Organization and Architecture of Innovation*. Elsevier, 2007.

Anthony, Scott and Mark Johnson, Joseph Sinfield, and Elizabeth Altman, *The Innovator's Guide to Growth*. Harvard Business Press, 2008.

Apple Human Interface Guidelines: The Apple Desktop Interface. Addison-Wesley, 1987.

Ariely, Dan. *Predictably Irrational*. Harper, 2010.

Barsh, Joanna, and Marla Capozzi and Jonathan Davidson. "Leadership and Innovation." *McKinsey Quarterly*, 2008, no 1.

Beckwith, Harry. *Selling the Invisible*. Warner Business Books, 1997.

Bernstein, Peter. *Against the Gods: The Remarkable Story of Risk*. Wiley, 1998.

Bhidé, Amar. *The Origin and Evolution of New Businesses*. Oxford, 2000.

Burke, James. *Connections*. Little Brown and Company, 1978.

Calvin, William H. *The River that Flows Uphill: A Journey from the Big Bang to Big Brain*. New York, MacMillan, 1986.

Campbell, Joseph. *The Hero with a Thousand Faces*. Princeton, 1968.

Capra, Fritjof. *The Science of Leonardo: Inside the Mind of the Great Genius of the Renaissance*. Anchor Books, 2007.

Chabris, Christopher and Daniel Simons. *The Invisible Gorilla*. Crown, 2010.

Colvin, Geoff. *Talent is Overrated.* Portfolio, 2008.

Crouhy, Michel and Dan Galai and Robert Mark. *The Essentials of Risk Management.* McGraw Hill, 2005.

Csikszentmihalyi, Mihaly. *Creativity.* Harper Perennial, 1996.

De Geus, Arie. *The Living Company.* Harvard, 1997.

Deming, W. Edwards. *The New Economics.* MIT, 1993.

Dorner, Dietrich. *The Logic of Failure.* Perseus Books, 1996.

Drucker, Peter. *The Age of Discontinuity,* Harper & Row, 1968.

** Drucker, Peter. *Innovation and Entrepreneurship.* Harper & Row, 1985.

Drucker, Peter. *Post-Capitalist Society.* HarperBusiness, 1993.

Fetterman, David. *Ethnography: Step by Step.* Sage Publications, 1998.

Friedman, George. *The Next 100 Years.* Anchor Books, 2009.

Gelb, Michael J. *How to Think Like Leonardo da Vinci.* Dell, 1998.

** Gerstner, Louis V. *Who Says Elephants Can't Dance.* HarperBusiness, 2002.

** Gopnik, Alison. *The Philosophical Baby,* Farrar Straus Giroux, 2009.

** Hall, Peter. *Cities in Civilization.* Fromm International, 1998.

** Hirshberg, Jerry. *The Creative Priority: Driving Innovative Business in the Real World.* HarperBusiness, 1998.

Holland, John. *Emergence: From Chaos to Order.* Perseus Books, 1998.

Janis, Irving. *Groupthink.* Houghton Mifflin, 1982.

Johnson, Steven. *Emergence: The Connected Lives of Ants, Brains, Cities, and Software.* Touchstone, 2001.

Jordan, Dr. Brigitte. "Ethnographic Workplace Studies and Computer Supported Cooperative Work." Institute for Research on Learning, Report No. IRL94-0026, 1994.

** Kahney, Leander. *Inside Steve's Brain.* Portfolio, 2008.

Keegan, John. *Intelligence in War.* Alfred Knopf, 2003.

Koberg, Don and Jim Bagnall. *The Universal Traveler.* Crisp Publications, Inc., 1991.

Kodama, Fumio. *Emerging Patterns of Innovation.* Harvard Business Press, 1991.

Kohn, Alfie. *Punished by Rewards: The Trouble with Gold Stars, Incentive Plans, A's, Praise, and Other Bribes,* Mariner Books, 1999.

Kuhn, Thomas S. *The Structure of Scientific Revolutions.* University of Chicago Press, 1996.

Kurzweil, Ray. *The Age of Spiritual Machines: When Computers Exceed Human Intelligence.* Penguin Books, 1999.

Lakoff, George, *Moral Politics: What Conservatives Know that Liberals Don't.* Chicago, The University of Chicago Press, 1996.

** Mark, Margaret and Carol S. Pearson. *The Hero and the Outlaw*. McGraw Hill, 2001.

Markowitz, Harry. *Portfolio Selection. Efficient Diversification of Investments*. Wiley, 1959.

McCraw, Thomas. *American Business Since 1920: How It Worked*. Harlan Davidson, 2000.

McCraw, Thomas. *Prophet of Innovation: Joseph Schumpeter and Creative Destruction*. Belknap Harvard, 2007.

Meyer, Marc and Al Lehnerd. *The Power of Product Platforms*. Free Press, 1997.

Miller, William L. and Langdon Morris. *Fourth Generation R&D: Managing Knowledge, Technology, and Innovation*. Wiley, 1999.

Moore, Geoffrey. *Crossing the Chasm*. Harper Perennial, 1991, 1999.

** Morris, Langdon, Moses Ma, and Po Chi Wu. *Agile Innovation*. John Wiley & Sons, 2014.

** Morris, Langdon. *Foresight and Extreme Creativity: Strategy for the 21st Century*. FutureLab Press, 2016.

Morris, Langdon. *Managing the Evolving Corporation*. John Wiley & Sons, 1995.

** Morris, Langdon. *Permanent Innovation*. Innovation Academy, 2006, 2011.

Morris, Langdon. "Social Design: The Link Between Facility Design, Organization Design, and Corporate Strategy." An InnovationLabs White Paper, 1999. Download at www.innovationlabs.com/publications

Piel, Gerald. *The Acceleration of History*. Knopf, 1972.

Polanyi, Michael. *The Tacit Dimension*. Peter Smith, 1983.

Ramo, Joshua Cooper. *The Age of the Unthinkable*. Little, Brown, 2009.

Ratey, John. *A User's Guide to the Brain*. Vintage, 2001.

Ries, Al, and Laura Ries. *The 22 Immutable Laws of Branding*. Harper Business, 1998.

** Rogers, Everett. *Diffusion of Innovations*. Free Press, 1983.

Roussel, Philip, Kamal Saad, and Tamara Erickson *Third Generation R&D*, Harvard Business Press, 1991.

Sabbagh, Karl. *Twenty-First-Century Jet: The Making and Marketing of the Boeing 777*. Scribner, 1996.

Scenarios: An Explorer's Guide. Shell International BV, 2008. www.shell.com/scenarios

Schumpeter, Joseph, *Capitalism, Socialism, and Democracy*, Harper & Brothers, 1942, 1947, 1950

Schwartz, Peter. *The Art of the Long View*. Doubleday Currency, 1991.

Smith, Charles. *Navigating from the Future*. 2009.

Smith, Dougles and Robert Alexander. *Fumbling the Future: How Xerox Invented, and the Ignored, the First Personal Computer*. Quill, 1988.

Smith, General Rupert. *The Utility of Force: The Art of War in the Modern World*. Knopf, 2005.

Suchman, Lucy. *Plans and Situated Actions: The Problem of Human-Machine Communication*. Cambridge, 1987.

Surowiecki, James. *The Wisdom of Crowds*. Abacus, 2004.

Taleb, Nassim Nicholas. *The Black Swan*. Random House, 2007.

Taleb, Nassim Nicholas. *Fooled by Randomness*. Random House, 2004.

Tapscott, Don, *Wikinomics*. Portfolio, 2010.

** Tharp, Twyla. *The Creative Habit*, Simon & Schuster. 2003.

Tharp, Twyla. *The Collaborative Habit*, Simon & Schuster. 2009.

Tichy, Noel M. and Stratford Sherman, *Control Your Destiny or Someone Else Will*. New York, Currency Doubleday, 1993.

** Tuchman, Barbara. *The Guns of August*. Ballantine Books, 1962

Underhill, Paco. *Why We Buy: The Science of Shopping*. Simon & Schuster, 1999.

** Watson, Peter. *The Modern Mind: An Intellectual History of the 20th Century*. Harper Collins, 2001.

Wiener, Norbert. *Invention: The Care and Feeding of Ideas*. The MIT Press, 1993.

Wilkinson, Paul. *International Relations*. Sterling, 2007.

Wozniak, Steve and Gina Smith. *iWoz: Computer Geek to Cult Icon*. Norton, 2006.

Zimmermann, Manfred. "Neurophysiology of Sensory Systems." *Fundamentals of Sensory Physiology*, Robert F. Schmidt, ed. Berlin, Springer-Verlag, 1986.

Index

F

Facebook, 63, 65, 66, 127, 158,
    294
failure, 13, 33, 41, 45, 54, 55, 87,
    91, 95, 97, 98, 100, 101, 102,
    105, 106, 107, 146, 147, 154,
    189, 190, 192, 221, 249, 256,
    258, 265, 268, 270
Faraday, Michael, 185
Farley, Jim, 173
fast-follower, 125
Fedex, 246, 279
Finkelstein, Edward, 62
Ford Motor Company, 91, 92, 93,
    249, 297, 299, 306
Foster, Richard, 7
framework, 11, 12, 23, 43, 51, 54,
    55, 108, 109, 181, 316, 320,
    322, 330
Frito-Lay, 40

G

Galileo, 215
Gatorade, 40
Gelb, Michael J., 304
Genentech, 100
General Electric (GE), 37, 90, 100
General Motors (GM), 40, 62, 63,
    92, 112, 121, 246, 249, 261,
    262, 279, 280, 298
Germany, 199
Gerstner, Louis, 1, 2, 9, 38, 39, 54,
    55, 62, 149, 334
Gladwell, Malcolm, 257
Glaxo Wellcome, 301
globalization, 1, 65, 66, 67, 68, 77
Goldstein, David, 31
Goodyear, 62
Google, 4, 30, 32, 63, 126, 127,
    128, 147, 158, 248, 294
Greenspan, Alan, 107, 108, 110,
    121

H

Haloid Company, 90
Hargeysa, Somalia, 67

health care, 73, 76
Henn, Gunter W. , 266, 291, 301,
    333
Henning, Andrea, 309
Hewlett, Bill, 255, 312
Home Depot, 63, 246
Honda, 49, 66, 92, 105, 280
Honeywell, 7
*How to Think Like Leonardo da
    Vinci*, 305
Hewlett Packard (HP), 218, 219,
    255, 312, 313
HP Labs, 255
Holland, John, 185
Hummer, 262

I

IAC/InterActiveCorp, 32
IBM, 9, 26, 36, 38, 39, 40, 41, 48,
    53, 54, 55, 62, 69, 70, 90, 124,
    158, 208, 261, 262
idea voting engines, 315
ideation, 13, 168, 181, 183, 184,
    185, 186, 196, 200, 203, 210,
    284
ideation methods, 182
Ikea, 69
India, 64, 65, 69, 75, 79, 146
Indonesia, 79
Industrial Revolution, 71
Innocentive, 296
innospective (phase of Agile
    Innovation Sprint), 18, 19, 145,
    168, 193, 323, 325
innovation - definition of, 14, 20
nnovation centers, 308, 314
innovation champion, 13, 142,
    214, 242, 253, 256, 257, 259,
    271, 318
innovation culture, v, 11, 13, 33,
    100, 124, 212, 214, 237, 238,
    239, 241, 248, 250, 253, 257,
    259, 260, 261, 264, 266, 267,
    272, 273, 274
innovation dashboard, 235
innovation development, 146,
    202, 204, 207, 213, 230, 286

acknowledgments

As with nearly everything I've ever written about business, it is the interactions with our clients and colleagues that have provided the foundational questions, discoveries, and insights underlying this book, and I am grateful to all of them for the opportunities they've given us to work with them.

More specifically, building upon the concepts of the original edition of this book, Moses Ma was kind enough to share his insights on how to significantly improve the master plan framework by "agilizing" it, and his thoughts are reflected throughout this revised edition. And we continue to benefit enormously from our work with Agile pioneer Jeff Sutherland.

In addition, many people were kind enough to review various versions of this book, and I deeply appreciate their many contributions. I would like to thank Sara Beckman, Bryan Coffman, Griff Coleman, Réne van der Hulst, John Holmes, and Justin Lin for their detailed critiques, as well as Michael Barry, Jacqueline Byrd, Léopold Demiddeleer, Kim Dempsey, Signe Gammeltoft, Michael Kaufman, Kate Lee, John Purcell-O'Dwyer, Martin Schwab, Avnindra Sharma, and Jay Smethurst for their thoughtful and very helpful comments.

Made in the USA
Columbia, SC
04 November 2018